D1458372

RSA

Library

THE ROLE OF BUSINESS ETHICS IN ECONOMIC PERFORMANCE

Library

WITHDRAWN

The Role of Business Ethics in Economic Performance

Edited by

Ian Jones

and

Michael Pollitt

174.4 Jon

 First published in Great Britain 1998 by
MACMILLAN PRESS LTD
Houndmills, Basingstoke, Hampshire RG21 6XS and London
Companies and representatives throughout the world

A catalogue record for this book is available from the British Library.

ISBN 0-333-71741-4

 First published in the United States of America 1998 by
ST. MARTIN'S PRESS, INC.,
Scholarly and Reference Division,
175 Fifth Avenue, New York, N.Y. 10010

ISBN 0-312-21313-1

Library of Congress Cataloging-in-Publication Data
The role of business ethics in economic performance / edited by Ian
Jones and Michael Pollitt.
p. cm.
"This volume is based on the proceedings of a workshop on 'The
role of business ethics in economic performance' held on 28 October
1996 at Robinson College Cambridge"—Pref.
Includes bibliographical references and index.
ISBN 0-312-21313-1 (cloth)
1. Business ethics. 2. Capitalism—Moral and ethical aspects.
I. Jones, Ian, 1943– . II. Pollitt, Michael G.
HF5387.R65 1998
174'.4—dc21   97–42641
                                                           CIP

This book is printed on paper suitable for recycling and made from fully managed and
sustained forest sources.

10   9   8   7   6   5   4   3   2
07 06 05 04 03 02 01 00 99

Printed and bound in Great Britain by
Antony Rowe Ltd, Chippenham, Wiltshire

Contents

List of Tables

List of Figures

Preface and Acknowledgements

This volume is based on the proceedings of a workshop on 'The Role of Business Ethics in Economic Performance' held on 28 October 1996 at Robinson College, Cambridge. The workshop was organised under the auspices of the ESRC Centre for Business Research (CBR) based in the Department of Applied Economics at Cambridge.

The idea for the workshop emerged out of work done by the editors, sponsored by the CBR on the relationship between biblical ethics, management practice and economics. The context for the workshop (and the volume) was the heightening sense that Anglo-American firms are under increasing pressure to justify their behaviour to a sceptical public. Although no serious economic challenger to the capitalist system has yet emerged, there has been a growing sense of public unease with some of the unethical practices of individuals and firms in the economic sphere. The volume brings together a number of experts in the fields of economics, management and business ethics to debate the links between ethics and economic performance.

The editors would like to acknowledge the support of the CBR for supporting their original research which led to the workshop and for organising a very successful day. They especially thank Alan Hughes, the Director, and Sue Moore, the administrative secretary, for the efficient organisation of the arrangements for the workshop. They also gratefully acknowledge co-sponsorship for the workshop from the Foundation for Business Responsibilities, represented by Simon Webley and John Treasure. Sara Jones carefully and patiently edited the final draft. Katherine and Nicholas were supportive and distractive in the last days before submission. Above all, however, the editors acknowledge the effort of the authors of the chapters for their sustained commitment to the project.

IAN JONES
MICHAEL POLLITT

List of Contributors

Professor Norman Barry, Professor of Politics, University of Buckingham.

Sir Adrian Cadbury, former Chairman of Cadbury Schweppes plc and Chairman of the 'Cadbury Committee'.

Professor Mark Casson, Professor of Economics, University of Reading.

Dr Maurie Cohen, Ove Arup Research Fellow, Oxford Centre for Environment, Ethics and Society.

Dr Simon Deakin, University Lecturer in Law and Assistant Director of the Centre for Business Research, University of Cambridge.

Lord (Dr John) Eatwell, President of Queens College and University Lecturer in Economics, University of Cambridge.

Professor Neil Hood, Professor of Business Policy and Director of the International Business Unit, University of Strathclyde.

Professor Ian Jones, Visiting Professor of International Management, University of Exeter, and Research Associate, Centre for Business Research, University of Cambridge.

Dr Michael Pollitt, University Lecturer in Economics, University of Cambridge, and Research Associate, Centre for Business Research, University of Cambridge.

Russell Sparkes, Fund Manager, Central Board of Finance of the Methodist Church.

Dr Frank Wilkinson, Senior Research Officer and Assistant Director of the Centre for Business Research, University of Cambridge.

Clive Wright, Consultant and formerly Director of Public Relations, ARCO UK.

xi

1 Introduction

Ian Jones and Michael Pollitt

RECENT INTEREST IN BUSINESS ETHICS

This volume has developed within the context of widespread concern about the ethical environment in which modern economic activity in advanced capitalist economies occurs. Firms, trade associations, individual consumers and investors and the politicians and regulators who oversee them have been increasingly required to justify their actions and decision-making processes not just on the conventional grounds of profitability within the law but on higher standards of business ethics, voluntary codes of conduct and the difficult-to-define concept of social responsibility.

The reasons for this upsurge in concern for the *way* economic activity is conducted rather than merely its *results* are complex. On the one hand, long-run underlying economic forces such as the increasing use of depersonalised information technologies, globalisation of trade and the decline of national sovereignty, the emergence of new products with capacities for both benefit and harm, and the realisation of the global and national environmental consequences of modern production have brought new ethical questions to the fore. On the other hand, long-run social forces such as widespread family breakdown and a persistent underclass in otherwise rich countries, rising crime rates and prison populations, declining religious observance and increasing moral confusion, and growing disillusionment with materialism in many advanced Western countries have led to a renewed interest in all aspects of morality in the public and political debate. While it may well be the case that many of these reasons are hyped by the media rather than real, there is little doubt that the concern generated by repeated reference to them is real. There is also little doubt that even if the moral basis of capitalism is an issue that has been around for several hundred years it is one which is little closer to being settled.

Much of the recent interest in business ethics has been a response to well-publicised problems in the economic arena which have raised moral questions or highlighted ethical lapses. We can identify four major areas, by responsibility, where the debate has been focused:[1] consumers, investors, business practice, and politicians and the law.

1

Consumers

Ultimately it is as consumers that we are responsible for the choices which shape the conduct of economic activity. Questions about which products we should buy and what lifestyle we adopt give rise to answers which in aggregate have global effects. Consumers can make choices to pay premiums for environmentally friendly products and fair trade imported goods, and to boycott the products of certain companies or even countries on moral grounds. Increasingly consumers have been recognising that many environmental issues such as local congestion or global warming are not the responsibility of 'others' but of their own transport choices and purchases.

Investors

Investors may be viewed as a powerful subgroup of consumers who are wealthy enough to make choices which affect the actions of producers via their ownership of stocks and other financial assets. Investors have the power to marginalise certain forms of economic activity and to support others. Investors have increasingly been challenged to justify their support for certain activities such as defence procurement, tobacco and gambling and to provide finance for companies committed to improving the environment, worker conditions and good business practice. Institutional investors, such as pension funds, have been challenged to use their voting power to discipline managers who underperform financially and also ethically.

Business Practice

Consumers and investors are largely external to the productive units of the capitalist economy (though the same individual may act in different capacities). Modern production is characterised by a separation of owners and managers. As such, senior executives have a large degree of power and autonomy to make economic decisions affecting their firms. Recently, there have been well-publicised cases of ethical lapses on the part of managers and employees. Such lapses have ranged from individual cases of dishonesty and fraud (for example, at BCCI, Barings, Maxwell Communications, Sumitomo Corporation), to corporate decisions to invest in countries with doubtful human rights records (for example, oil companies in Nigeria) and the actions of firms with respect to their suppliers (for example, UK clothing retailers), customers (for example, mis-selling of personal pensions) and competitors (for example, British Airways–Virgin Dirty Tricks campaign). In addition there has been public concern over the continuing high rate of growth of executive pay which is apparently only weakly related to corporate performance.[2] In response to these sorts of concerns two major industry committees have been looking into corporate behaviour and have produced reports (1992 and 1995): the Committee on the Financial Aspects of Corporate Governance (Cadbury Committee) and the Study Group on Directors' Remuneration (Greenbury Committee).

Politicians and the Law

Market economies need to be regulated and to be supported by public investments. As such there is a need for political interference and oversight of market activity. The law which governs business practice is continually being strengthened but there have been notable problems with its implementation (for example, several Serious Fraud Office cases have failed on the grounds of the complexity of the charges, while competition law still does not allow for financial penalties in cases of predatory pricing). Direct political involvement in the economy leads to a capacity for corruption of the political process and civil servants by business as companies seek unfair advantage over others. In the USA, corporations and other bodies support an $8000m-a-year lobby industry employing 67 000 people in Washington to influence just 550 elected representatives.[3] While much of this may be justified on the grounds of providing informed advice to the legislatures it does invite investigation and comment. In the UK some MPs have recently admitted taking undeclared money to ask parliamentary questions and to lobby for businessmen of questionable reputations. Even within the British civil service, there have been cases of fraud, such as the prolonged mishandling of public money by officials of the Welsh Development Agency.[4] In response to public disquiet the UK government has launched an ongoing enquiry into standards in public life (headed by Lord Nolan).

It is only natural in democratic societies that public attention should focus on the negative and on ethical problems. However in parallel with the areas of concern raised under the four headings above there have been significant movements in a more positive direction.

Consumers are now much more aware of the local and global effects of their economic choices. This has been manifest not just in micro consumption decisions to buy more fair trade and green products (10 per cent of all new products in the USA are labelled as 'green' or 'environmentally friendly' (Davis, 1992)) but also in the rise of the environment as an issue on the national and international stage (for example, the Royal Commission on Road Transport Report, 1994, which highlighted the need to limit road traffic growth in the UK, and the Montreal Protocol, 1987, which reflected agreement on global reduction of CFC emissions).

Investors are now beginning to become more active with the rise of ethical investment products and the growth in the use of ethical screening by investment funds. Institutional investors are taking a more active interest in the decisions of corporate executives with some funds notably outperforming on the basis of such active fund management (for example, CalPERs, the large Californian public employees' pension fund).

Business practice is beginning to recognise the external pressure to raise standards of conduct and the internal advantages of having well-developed corporate ethics. Many companies have codes of ethics or standards of employee conduct and since mid-1993 it has been a condition of listing on the London Stock Exchange that company annual reports must detail the extent to which they have implemented the recommendations of the Cadbury Report (see Wright and Cadbury in this volume). Many companies and individual businessleaders are actively supporting efforts to promote business ethics, and industry-funded societies such as the Institute for Business Ethics have been formed.

Political and legal reform is ongoing but already there has been a significant increase in the disclosure requirements of members' interests for UK MPs. Increasingly open government and a possible Freedom of Information Act will continue to ensure close ethical monitoring of government activity. In addition the law is being strengthened to limit the legal but unethical activities of companies: a draft UK Competition Bill already exists awaiting debate (DTI, 1996) and developing European Union (EU) law is further limiting companies' ability to exploit unfairly their economic power (for example, the EU Unfair Terms Directive; see OFT (1996)).

Research interest in the whole area of business ethics has undergone something of a revival in the past few years since the early 1970s in the USA and more widely in the 1990s. Several highly respectable journals on the subject are flourishing and several international societies for its promotion exist.[5] Business ethics is rapidly becoming a separate academic discipline. It is benefiting from increased interaction between businesspeople and academics. Even within the more traditional disciplines of economics and management, significant work is being done on the theoretical and empirical role of ethics in the economy in general and in organisations in particular. Academic work has also sought to investigate empirically some of the links between law/ethics and differential economic performance between nations, notably brought to popular attention in Francis Fukuyama's well-publicised book entitled *Trust: The Social Virtues and the Creation of Prosperity* (1995). Policy-orientated research has also highlighted the role of spreading best practice reporting standards in order to promote better economic performance (see Commission on Public Policy and British Business, 1997).

All the above sets the scene for the present volume. The authors pick up and elaborate on all of the major areas highlighted above. In what follows in this introduction we discuss the definitions of business ethics and economic performance, describe the rationale behind the structure of the volume and give a brief description of the organisation of the book.

DEFINITIONS

This book is entitled The Role of Business Ethics in Economic Performance. The terms 'business ethics' and 'economic performance' are ones with which many are familiar and happy in general usage. However it is useful to be clear about what they mean at the outset in order to contextualise the work in the book.

Business ethics refers to the rules of conduct according to which business decisions are made.[6] It clearly implies that such ethics are merely a special class of behavioural rules to be applied in a particular context. As modern economic activity is all-pervasive both in time, scale and scope, questions of the appropriate ethics to be adopted by business cannot be separated from wider questions of ethics, morality, personal beliefs, values, religion and culture.[7] There are three important things to note about ethics in this context. First, ethics are closely related to and reflect the objectives and values of the persons or organisations. If businesses value profit to the exclusion of all else, this will be reflected in their rules of conduct. Second, ethics may be formal or informal (or written or unwritten). We use the terms formal or informal in the sense of North (1990, p. 4). Thus by implication ethics may or may not be associated with a penalty for their violation or their application. Therefore, ethics can go beyond the written law. Third, ethics may be localised in scope, thus different nations, institutions and individuals may have their own ethics. However, the higher-order groups must to some extent reflect the ethics of their constituent parts.

Ethics is a morally neutral term. Thus the rules of conduct according to which business decisions are made can be 'good' or 'bad'. A company ethic could be 'to do business in such a way as to win at all costs'. Such a rule may be carefully articulated and communicated throughout the company and the senior management may motivate their employees accordingly. However this rule may clearly lead to morally undesirable outcomes – for example, theft, murder and so on. Thus a statement like 'business ethics is a good thing' is technically incorrect. One should rather say 'good business ethics is a good thing'. The approach of this book is to examine both how 'good business ethics' impact positively on economic performance and how 'bad' business ethics impact negatively on economic performance. We note however that all of the authors drop the adjective 'good' and use (business) ethics in the conventional sense of being something which is morally desirable.

Business ethics are 'defined' in a number of ways. First, via the law: criminal, contract and competition law govern the activities of individuals in the economic sphere and the actions of companies. Such laws have the effect of defining the boundaries of socially acceptable behaviour and of prescribing socially acceptable penalties for their violation and also procedures for enforcing contracts. Although some have argued strongly (see Barry, this volume) that 'good' business ethics should be defined solely as obedience to the law, we suggest that 'good' business ethics is something to be encouraged by the law rather than completely legislated for. Exemplary behaviour usually involves obeying not just the letter of the law but its spirit and follows standards higher than the statutory minimum.

Second, via regulatory bodies and trade associations: many firms adhere to quasi-legal rules imposed by external organisations which further refine and define acceptable behaviour within particular industries. Such organisations have the advantage of being able to impose tougher standards and penalties than the law and to adapt more easily to new information and changing circumstances. Examples of the regulatory bodies include the Advertising Standards Authority, to which advertisers must subject themselves, while examples of the trade associations include industry trade associations such as the Confederation of British Industry (CBI) which represents the whole of British industry and the Association of British Travel Agents (ABTA) which regulates just the UK travel industry.

Third, via company codes which are specific to individual firms: many leading companies, such as Hewlett Packard and Shell, publish their code of ethics laying out the corporate standards of conduct in doing business and making specific mention of how employees should and should not behave in dealings with customers, suppliers, competitors and so on.

Finally, in addition to all the written or formal definitions of business ethics, both internal and external, to which firms choose to or may be forced to adhere, ethics are defined by the personal morals of individual managers and employees. The unwritten ethics to which individuals adhere themselves reflect the informal decision-making environment within the firm and the informal ethics of the society within which the company is doing business and from which its employees are drawn.

The above discussion of the ways in which rules of business conduct are defined suggests two major ways in which business ethics may be 'bad'. First, because of weaknesses in the structure of the written rules: it may be that such rules are difficult to enforce because of the problem of identifying violations, proving wrongdoing and the inadequacy of penalties, and the incentives of those agreeing to them. 'Good' conduct is rather more difficult to measure than good financial results. However the weaknesses in written rules of behaviour, revealed by experience, are constantly being addressed in law, quasi-legal external codes and in internal standards of conduct. Second, following on from the difficulty of writing enforceable standards, ethics must ultimately operate through the actions of individual managers and employees: there will always be individuals or even whole companies who behave badly by violating either the letter of the written rules or just their spirit. No free society can expect to eliminate unethical business practice no matter how good its written rules of behaviour.

The book investigates the links between business ethics and economic performance. *Economic performance* is conventionally measured in terms of material well-being using such indicators as the gross national product (GNP) per head. However economic performance has become increasingly difficult to define because of dissatisfaction with such measures as GNP and because of economists' relentless advance of economics into the wider implications of self-interest and their measurement of such things as income distribution and environmental damage which older measures take no account of.[8] In this book the authors do not spend time on the important measurement issues which economists are now investigating. We abstract from these issues and discuss the utilitarian effects of business ethics,[9] recognising the wide range of utilitarian effects which economic activity has on the environment and other quality-of-life variables, such as job satisfaction, which individuals are prepared to pay for. Thus economic performance may be defined as a measure of the utilitarian output of productive activity. So defined, we assume that higher levels of such output are a 'good' thing. Thus we are interested in the links between 'good' business ethics and better/higher economic performance. Such an exercise is designed to illuminate the enlightened self-interest in behaving ethically, where enlightened self-interest may be defined as what is to a decision-making unit's *well-informed* unit-specific advantage (where a decision-making unit may be an individual or an organisation), taking into account *all* the factors affecting the satisfaction of the unit's objectives.

Although our approach essentially analyses the enlightened self-interest in the economic consequences of actions, in line with most popular debate, business practice and economic analysis, we note two important points. First, we recognise that not all actions are or should be taken on the basis of self-interest. There has been a tendency in economic analysis to 'explain' all human behaviour by reference to an appropriately defined utility maximisation problem. Thus analysis has been provided of the decision to marry, have children, charitable giving and even church-going on the basis of pure self-interest.[10] While there is a deal of truth and logical rigour in such analysis it is not clear that it is healthy or wholly accurate to reduce all human behaviour to this level. Sen (1977) has distinguished carefully between the concepts of 'sympathy' and 'commitment' in his work on the philosophy of economic behaviour. Some actions to help others may occur because we value the other person's happiness (sympathy), that is, it is in our self-interest to be 'good'. Other actions are taken because of 'commitment' to a set of principles regardless of personal utility and cannot be rationalised (for example, death in war, voting in general elections) except by non-falsifiable all-inclusive explanations such as fear of eternal damnation. Thus if ideal behaviour involves commitment rather than sympathy, appeals to enlightened self-interest are not going to encourage it. Nowhere do any of the authors suggest that ideal behaviour will never involve accepting a reduction in a utilitarian measure of economic performance. Thus they suggest that all ethics cannot or should not be defined solely on their consequences for economic performance, and by implication that rationality and self-interest should not be the sole motives for human behaviour.

Second, we note that while we are interested in the economic welfare effects of business ethics, our primary focus is on efficiency rather than on distribution. Economists traditionally distinguish between two welfare effects of economic actions: the effect on the allocation of resources to the activity in which they add the highest value (efficiency) and the effect of allocation of wealth and income and publicly provided goods, such as education and health care, to those who most 'deserve' them (distribution). Questions of efficiency are seen as being of primary importance for economists, while questions of distribution are seen either as matters for private choice (for example, via charitable giving) or for the political process (for example, the extent of redistributive taxes). While simple microeconomic analysis fully separates these questions, economists recognise that extremely unequal distributions of economic wealth have undesirable efficiency consequences (via political unrest, low productivity, crime and so on) and that economic analysis can be extended to encompass questions of distribution by introducing the concept of social welfare and mechanisms for adding up the effects of economic actions on individuals within society.[11] Clearly the distribution of income, wealth and publicly provided goods are ethical questions but they are matters for political debate rather than (relatively) disinterested economic analysis. Thus we concentrate on how business ethics improves the economic performance at the level at which decisions are made rather than at some higher level. We abstract from questions of distribution which lie clearly in the political realm (for example, tax rates). We note that between advanced capitalist economies there is a narrowing range of political disagreement about distributional issues (as evidenced by the rates of taxation as a percentage of GNP) and that within countries the variation between the tax and expenditure policies advocated by major political parties is even narrower (for example, the three main parties contesting the 1997 UK general election, where the range of variation between the proposed budgets was less than 0.5 per cent of GNP). Our 'efficiency' approach moves our focus away from the recent political debate in the UK about stakeholders (groups with a 'stake' in society) which itself raises many distributional questions.[12]

Thus this book looks at how business ethics impacts on economic performance, that is, the *transmission mechanism* from rules of behaviour to economic variables which we are interested in improving. It is recognised that such a transmission mechanism can have a feedback loop from economic performance to business ethics by which good or bad economic performance based on a particular ethic can lead that ethic to be encouraged, codified or legislated on. This is not a book about ethics but about how economic performance can be improved by good ethics.

STRUCTURE

The book is structured in such a way as to highlight several of the major ways in which business ethics is impacting on economic performance. We apply a four-part structure, familiar to economists, to organise the analysis of the problem: we begin by looking at conceptual and empirical issues and then go on to analyse institutional, demand- and supply-side factors in turn.

While the authors address various aspects of each of these four subjects it is important to consider why each is important. First, the importance of economic analysis needs to be highlighted. One of the major problems with a lot of work done on business ethics is that it can be naive in one of three areas: displaying little understanding of ethics, business practice or economic processes. Economic analysis can contribute to an understanding of the transmission mechanism we are interested in via its understanding of economic processes, its theoretical analysis of business behaviour and by empirical work on the behaviour of companies. The history of economic theory is a history of the understanding of economic processes from Adam Smith through to the present day. What is particularly interesting from a study of this intellectual history is that many of the earliest modern economists were acutely concerned with the links between economics and ethics (see Waterman, 1991). What is regrettable is that this is somewhat obscured by much of modern economic analysis and by many modern economists. However, modern analysis can be usefully applied to demonstrate the importance of the links and recently there has been a lot of new work done using game theory and conventional marginal analysis to show how ethical behaviour can lead to superior economic results.[13] Empirical work has also begun on attempting to measure some of the linkages between ethical principles and economic performance (for example, corruption and degree of competition, returns to ethical investment and the effects of corporate governance on executive pay).[14]

Second, it needs to be recognised that all market-based economic activity takes place within an institutional framework of regulation, law, government and culture. For a considerable period economic analysis neglected the study of the institutions which regulated the market, simply taking them as given for the purposes of economic analysis.[15] However such institutions are not fixed but themselves are subject to 'economic forces' and pressures to change. These institutions set a very significant part of the environment within which buyers and sellers transact. Such external institutions, whether statutory or voluntary, have important roles in defining the rules by which firms behave (for example the law of contract and the Office of Fair Trading (OFT)). In this volume we focus on three formal institutions: contract law, the government and the voluntary association. Others, such as Fukuyama (1995), have highlighted the importance of informal institutions such as 'culture' which gives rise to social capital – 'the ability of people to work together for common purposes in groups or associations, (Fukuyama, 1995, p.10) – and creates the environment within which economic self-help or commitment to public ('good') works flourishes.

Third, we examine the immediately relevant demand- and supply-side factors encouraging the firm to behave according to certain rules. Demand-side pressures come from two groups: consumers and investors. Firms are in the business of satisfying the expressed desires of their customers. As consumers are members of society by another name the ethical concerns of customers about the behaviour of companies are something that firms cannot ignore and need to be taken into account in firms' marketing and production decisions (see Cohen, this volume). Not only can companies seen to behave 'badly' be the subject of widespread consumer boycotts, but negative advertising about the companies' ethics can be very damaging. Ethical concerns about company behaviour can be unrelated to the quality of the final product but may centre around the treatment of suppliers, the working and production conditions, the actions towards competitors or even the behaviour of board members. Thus companies increasingly need to be able to justify their decisions to a wider public than just the employees concerned with implementing them. In addition, such selective discrimination against companies seen to be behaving unethically means that companies need to anticipate the longer-run changes in consumer attitudes which will shape demand for their current and future products. Rising concern about the environment, human rights in developing countries, worker rights, health and safety and so on requires firms to anticipate changes in the regulatory environment and consumer purchasing decisions rather than simply wait for them to manifest themselves.

Closely related to consumer pressure on firms to be ethical is investor pressure. At one level investors behave just like consumers: they 'buy' investments and hence can 'boycott' certain investments in certain companies. The effect of such a boycott can be to make external finance more expensive for the firm and reduce its share price. This disciplines the firm into a change of behaviour directly or by making it more vulnerable to takeover by a 'better' firm. There is some evidence (Sparkes, 1995) that such capital market pressure has been a helpful factor in the end of apartheid in South Africa (US banks, under domestic consumer pressure, refused to refinance short-term South African government debt prior to negotiations between the government and the ANC) and that adverse court rulings against particular firms led to disproportionately large falls in share prices in the USA (Karpoff and Lott, 1995). However, large investors have additional power – they have direct access to senior managers via informal meetings and formal rights to attend and propose resolutions at shareholder meetings. This allows them to embarrass managers face to face with difficult questions about decisions and in extreme cases to carry motions removing executives. The latest figures suggest that at least £13bn of stock in the UK stock markets is actively managed by funds applying ethical criteria to their investments, while in the USA the figure is much higher (see Sparkes, this

volume). The high era of the separation of ownership and control is over (see Markides, 1995).
Finally, we turn to the supply-side forces on firms to be ethical. While it is always the case that institutional and demand-side factors cannot be entirely separated from supply-side factors and that the three interact, it is useful to consider how productive units or firms are themselves taking more of an interest in 'good' business ethics. Firms are dynamic organisations which are constantly seeking new profit opportunities either by process improvements (producing existing products better) or product improvements (producing new products). Firms need constantly to develop better methods of internal decision-making and to update their core capabilities which are the rationale for their existence (Chandler, 1992). Firms with well-developed decision-making processes are likely to be successful, while those that lag behind best practice are likely to do relatively poorly, get taken over or fail. In addition, larger firms suffer from the fundamental problem of coordinating, motivating and monitoring staff at lower levels of the hierarchy. The most successful firms have found that adopting codes of ethics, setting standards of conduct, joining trade associations, being good corporate citizens and so on, have kept them from falling behind. One might suggest that the technology of modern production with its emphasis on smaller numbers of skilled staff and flat management structures means that a higher percentage of company employees are taking decisions which affect corporate performance in a competitive environment where small differences in performance are significant for corporate success. If this is true then there is a need for the company to communicate clearly to all its employees not just decisions but the basis on which they should take decisions. Having good ethics is simply best practice management (see Wright, this volume).

An important part of the general supply-side pressure to be ethical is the increasingly important class of ethical dilemmas confronting transnational corporations. In a global economy these institutions are primary agents for economic development, technology transfer and the spread of best practice management. As such they are arguably having major cultural effects. As ethics is an important part of both national and corporate culture, understanding the ethics of the company and of the society in which it is doing business is crucial for corporate success. Part of the comparative advantage of the multinationals is their superior management procedures (Buckley and Casson, 1985), including their decision-making processes. Thus how to translate these best practice management techniques, including corporate business ethics, across cultures is an important question for this influential subgroup of firms.

THE ORGANISATION OF THE BOOK

The previous section discussed the various forces linking business ethics to economic performance. We now introduce the chapters in the book; we will draw conclusions in the final chapter.

The authors come from a wide variety of disciplines and backgrounds and bring different ethical perspectives and approaches. An interesting feature of the book is that three of the chapters (by Sparkes, Cadbury and Wright) are written by businessleaders who discuss their personal experience of applying 'good' business ethics to achieve conventional economic measures of success.

We begin with three chapters by economists which investigate the links between business ethics and economic performance. Lord Eatwell (Chapter 2) examines the role of ethics in the economics of Adam Smith. He points out that Smith wrote two important books: *An Inquiry into the Nature and Causes of the Wealth of Nations (WN)* and *The Theory of Moral Sentiments (TMS)*. *WN* is more famous in business and economic circles and outlines how 'self-interest' is the motivating force behind economic activity and leads via 'the invisible hand' to the greatest social well-being by encouraging efficiency in production and achieving a reasonable distribution of income. In outlining his theory of the workings of the market economy, Smith was challenging romantic notions which viewed the market as evil and corrupting, and building on the importance of rationality and the benefits of self-interest advocated by earlier social scientists (such as Machiavelli and Mandeville). Smith however recognised that the market did bring ethical problems such as collusion between businessmen to raise prices and deskilling of factory workers. However *TMS* provides the background which suggests that the ethical problems posed by the market are not serious; in this book Smith presents a theory of society driven by self-interest which is not self-centred. This presents man as a moral being who is *self-*interested in the well-being of others (has 'sympathy') because he values the approval of others, and this encourages him to submit his behaviour to the test of public opinion. Eatwell concludes that this morality may fail, thus requiring two things: *openness* so that actions are subject to external monitoring and disapproval and *education* so that the public is educated to know what is 'good' behaviour and has the capacity to judge the actions of others.

Mark Casson (Chapter 3) analyses the positive role of 'good' ethical leaders for economic performance. He presents an economic analysis of 'ethical man', a person who prefers more 'good' things rather than just more pleasurable things. Ethical man can commit himself to a system of values external to himself, that is, he can trade off moral legitimacy against material pleasure to a point where their marginal utilities are equalised. Leaders (alive or dead) can have influence over 'ethical' people by providing moral authority. The exercise of moral authority affects the utility of reflective followers. Casson lists characteristics of effective leaders with moral authority and goes on to argue that such leaders are in short supply in today's world. In addition moral pluralism reduces the authority of individual leaders and hence their capacity to improve the performance of the economy by encouraging their followers to act ethically (via self-monitoring relative to the moral messages of the leader). Casson discusses some of the objections to his model and its implications. He concludes that there is no quick way to reestablish the necessary ethical leadership and hence functionally useful moral values. Casson suggests that changes to the school curriculum, the conduct of the media and public debate are required.

Simon Deakin and Frank Wilkinson (Chapter 4) provide some empirical evidence on how ethics works and highlight the role of the 'institution' of contract law. They begin by observing that cooperation between firms rather than competition is an important element in the relative success of German and Italian industry in the postwar period. This is due to the fact that efficiency in production requires long-term cooperation between firms within an industry and along a supply chain. The efficiency of the economic system depends on the generation and transmission of technical and market information. The key question they examine is how such cooperation can be achieved. One way is through informal ethics, while another is through self-enforcing private contracts; however German and Italian contract law (in contrast to UK law) give legal force to broad ethical values incorporated in 'good faith' clauses, thus allowing reasonable renegotiation of contracts. One of the effects is that German firms operate in a very stable normative legal framework within which inter-firm relations are conducted. Deakin and Wilkinson report on their empirical work comparing the legal environment and economic performance of firms in two manufacturing industries in the UK, Germany and Italy. The results demonstrate a more unstable legal environment with low-trust practices in the UK, a stable legal environment in Germany and a reliance on high-trust cultural norms in Italy. These contractual environments were correlated with lower output and employment growth in the UK firms. They observe that while the best UK firms outperform their foreign competitors, a long tail of underperforming firms gives the UK industries lower average performance. Deakin and Wilkinson conclude that changing the UK law of contract to support 'good faith' clauses would raise economic performance by encouraging high-trust behaviour in the context of a favourable legal climate. Such law would encourage long-term cooperative relations and widespread use of best practice relationships. The next two chapters look further at the institutional environment and its role in encouraging business ethics which improve economic performance. Sir Adrian Cadbury (Chapter 5), Chairman of the Cadbury Committee, provides an insider's view of the role of the Cadbury Report in shaping corporate behaviour in the UK. The Cadbury Committee was an industry response to the perceived lack of public confidence in company reports, accounts and audit statements. The Code of Best Practice contained in the report, specified certain best-practice principles for corporate reporting and it is now a requirement for membership of the London Stock Exchange that companies report the degree to which they are complying with the code in their annual report. Cadbury argues that such a voluntary approach has been effective in raising standards and avoids the need for legislation which would be difficult to frame and more difficult and expensive to enforce. In his chapter Cadbury also discusses his own experience of shaping an ethical corporate culture while he was chairman of the food and drinks giant, Cadbury Schweppes plc.

Norman Barry continues the institutional theme, examining the role of government in shaping business ethics (Chapter 6). Barry begins by contrasting the Anglo-American model of capitalism with its 'social market' (German) and East Asian variants. He points out that shareholder value maximisation is the rationale for the existence of the corporation in Anglo-American economies. His question is whether the corporation can be expected to take on duties which are rightly those of government and beyond acceptance of the generic (basic) moral code. With this in view Barry goes on to examine critically the current calls for increased corporate social responsibility and stakeholder capitalism. He then provocatively argues that the recent criminalisation of insider dealing is a case where it is impractical to legislate for economic behaviour. He further questions whether competition law should be changed to make takeovers more difficult, suggesting that such a change would increase rather than reduce politicisation of the takeover process. His conclusion is that the morality of Anglo-American business reflects its surrounding culture and thus makes it difficult to import ideas of socially responsible corporate decision-making from other cultures; the primary role of government should remain in the enforcement of the generic moral code rather than the encouragement to fulfil supererogatory moral duties.

We then move to demand-side forces facing firms. Maurie Cohen (Chapter 7) paints a big picture of the global environment within which firms operate and which shapes the consumer demands facing them. He begins by outlining the rise in a new class of ecological dilemmas which are latent, global and to which there is a certain amount of resignation (for example, global warming). He suggests however that substantial segments of the populations of advanced economies are now demanding that central components of the business community conform to an enhanced standard of behaviour. Investors and consumers are causing changes in the operational milieu in which firms make their decisions. Cohen discusses the nature of rising investor and consumer pressure manifesting itself in purchase selections, boycotts and even reduced materialism among certain sections of society (voluntary simplicity). He then presents the work of Ingelhart who suggests that better care for the environment occurs along two paths: the rational and the romantic. The rational involves the functional analysis of environmentalism and has led to major environmental improvements in Norway and Japan, while most other advanced countries continue to exhibit romantic notions which only translate into action as higher percentages of the population have their material needs satisfied and emphasise personal freedom, education and self-expression in their choices. Cohen concludes that both development paths will lead to increasing public demand for higher standards of business behaviour and require higher standards of corporate accountability.

Russell Sparkes, a practising fund manager at the Central Board of Finance of the Methodist Church, continues the demand-side theme by discussing the role of the ethical investor for corporate behaviour (Chapter 8). Ethical investment is socially responsible investment and refers to funds where the fund managers apply 'good' ethical criteria to decisions to invest in individual companies as well as conventional financial analysis. Sparkes carefully distinguishes between ethical investment and shareholder activism (where shareholders may ask embarrassing questions at annual general meetings). He argues that businesses need to be socially responsible because they operate in society and argues that the companies which will survive and prosper into the future are those that apply best practice business ethics today. Sparkes suggests reasons why ethical investment criteria will lead to better financial performance for ethical funds. He further presents evidence of the superior performance of ethically managed funds, suggesting that the extra layer of analysis which they employ is the key to fund outperformance. He concludes by suggesting that ethical investors are playing the unexpected role of pioneers who look at business in new ways and that such a movement can be expected to grow.

The final two chapters look at the supply-side forces behind increasing emphasis on business ethics within firms. Clive Wright draws on extensive business experience to discuss the role of ethics within the culture of the firm

(Chapter 9). Wright begins by pointing out the gap between academic and practical interest in business ethics. Corporate culture is defined as that common understanding, purpose and way of doing things that characterises one company and makes it distinct from another. Like Barry, he stresses that culture is conditioned by underlying value systems and that Anglo-American business values differ from continental European and East Asian values. Wright argues strongly that ethics must be part of the 'bloodstream' of a corporation. He goes on to review the survey evidence on managerial attitudes to business ethics, concluding that there are still significant percentages of managers not able to reconcile the reality of decision-making with corporate or personal values. Wright then details the elements behind implementing an effective code of ethics and building it into the organisation's bloodstream, noting that business ethics has to be a management discipline. He gives two examples of ethical dilemmas he has experienced in the petrochemical industry and suggests a method for resolving such dilemmas. He concludes by emphasising that business ethics needs to brought into the decision-making process of the firm and that simple utilitarianism is not enough.

Neil Hood rounds off the main chapters with an analysis of the particular role of ethics in the internal workings of the transnational corporation or TNC (Chapter 10). The foreign affiliates of TNCs account for 6 per cent of world gross domestic product in 1991 and their share is rising. TNCs face a number of distinct ethical challenges: operating across cultures, lax ethical practices in some countries, dealing with joint ventures and dealing with and shaping their regulatory environment. Hood argues that TNCs need to allow their values to be filtered by the behaviour and perceptions of national managers. They must take into account the different legal regimes and climates of public opinion they face. This will involve recognising the particular stakeholders in each of their subsidiaries. In particular this means that US-style codes of ethics where they incorporate universal rules may need to be adapted across cultures. Hood concludes by suggesting that TNCs will have an increasing role as agents of change across the world and as such they need to exercise leadership in business ethics in response to consumer pressure, but that increased external regulation of their activity may not be feasible or desirable.

All of the above chapters contain a great deal of the latest thinking on the role of business ethics in economic performance. Each is written by an acknowledged expert in the field and comes with an extensive bibliography. The final chapter provides a summary of the lessons from the book and a discussion of some of the questions raised by the authors' work, together with a short postscript.

Notes

1. For further elaboration see Cohen (this volume) on consumers, Sparkes (1995) on investors and Jones and Pollitt (1996, 1997) on business practice and the institutional environment.
2. See Conyon *et al.* (1995) for a review.
3. Cited by Robert Monks in a speech in Cambridge in 1996 (reported in 'Investing in niceness', *The Economist*, 31 August 1996, p. 69).
4. For details see Beckett, A. (1994) 'How clean was my valley?', *Independent on Sunday*, 28 August 1994, *The Sunday Review*, p. 4.
5. The journals include: *Business Ethics Quarterly, Journal of Business Ethics* and *Business Ethics: A European Review*. The international societies include: *European Business Ethics Network* and the *International Society for Business, Economics and Ethics*.
6. Our definition of ethics is taken from the Oxford English Dictionary which defines ethics as 'the rules of conduct recognised in certain limited departments of human life' ('ethic', B.4). This definition suggests that ethics can be localised, even to the point of being particular to one individual. Business ethics is taken to be singular where it refers to the subject area of business ethics but plural where it refers to more than one individual rule of business conduct.
7. The terms 'morals' and 'ethics' may be used interchangeably. Values are ultimate objectives which may require certain morals. Religious beliefs may be a source of such values or of associated ethics. Culture refers to a 'common understanding, purpose and way of doing things' (Wright, this volume, p. 174) and reflects the common values and ethics of the institution, group or society in question. All of these terms are closely related and difficult to differentiate between in common usage.
8. For an example of an attempt to adjust conventional UK GNP to account for income distribution and environmental damage see Jackson and Marks (1994).
9. Utilitarian in the sense 'of or pertaining to utility or material benefit': 'utilitarian' B2, *Oxford English Dictionary.*
10. See Becker (1976), Muellbauer (1977), Stark (1995) and Sawkins *et al.* (1997) for examples of papers on each of the subjects listed; also look at the special issues of American Journal of Sociology, 94 Supplement (1988) and the *Quarterly Journal of Economics*, 61 (2) (1996) for collections of papers which analyse social behaviour using mainstream economic methodology.
11. Such adding-up mechanisms are referred to as social welfare functions: the most common being the Benthamite (maximisation of the unweighted sum of individual utilities) and the Rawlsian (maximisation of the utility of the least utility-rich individual); see Varian (1996, pp. 547–549) for more details.
12. See Hutton (1996), chapter 12, for details of 'stakeholder' capitalism and the distributional assumptions which it embodies.
13. See Hausman and McPherson (1993) for a review and Casson (1995) for an example.
14. On these examples in turn, see Ades and Di Tella (1995), Sparkes (1995), and Main (1994).

15. A recent revival of the analysis of the economics of institutions has been led by Oliver Williamson (1975) and is further discussed by Deakin and Wilkinson (this volume).

References

Ades, A. and Di Tella, R. (1995) 'Competition and Corruption', Oxford Institute of Economics and Statistics Working Paper No. 169.
Becker, G.S. (1976) 'A Theory of Marriage', in G.S. Becker, *The Economic Approach to Human Behavior*, (Chicago, Ill: University of Chicago Press).
Buckley, P.J. and Casson, M.C. (1985) *The Economic Theory of the Multinational Enterprise* (London: Macmillan).
Casson, M.C. (1995) *Entrepreneurship and Business Culture* (Aldershot: Edward Elgar).
Chandler, A. (1992) 'Organisational Capabilities and the Economic History of the Industrial Enterprise', *Journal of Economic Perspectives*, 6 (3), pp. 79–100.
Commission on Public Policy and British Business (1997) *Promoting Prosperity: A Business Agenda for Britain* (London: Vintage).
Committee on the Financial Aspects of Corporate Governance [The Cadbury Report](1992) *Report of the Committee on the Financial Aspects of Corporate Governance: The Code of Best Practice* (London: Gee Publishing).
Conyon, M., Gregg, P. and Machin, S. (1995) 'Taking Care of Business Executive Compensation in the United Kingdom', *Economic Journal*, 105 (May), pp. 704–14.
Davis, J.J. (1992) 'Ethics and Environmental Marketing', *Journal of Business Ethics*, 11 (1), pp. 81–7.
DTI (1996) *Tackling Cartels and the Abuse of Market Power: A Draft Bill* (London: Department of Trade and Industry).
Fukuyama, F. (1995) *Trust: The Social Virtues and the Creation of Prosperity* (London: Hamish Hamilton).
Hausman, D.M. and McPherson, M.S. (1993) 'Taking Ethics Seriously: Economics and Contemporary Moral Philosophy', *Journal of Economic Literature*, 31 (June), pp. 671–731.
Hutton, W. (1996) *The State We're In* (London: Vintage).
Jackson, T. and Marks, N. (1994) *Measuring Sustainable Economic Welfare – A Pilot Index: 1950–1990* (Stockholm: Stockholm Environment Institute).
Jones, I.W. and Pollitt, M.G. (1996) 'Economics, Ethics and Integrity in Business', *Journal of General Management*, 21 (3), pp. 30–47.
Jones, I.W. and Pollitt, M.G. (1997) 'Economics, Ethics and Unfair Competition' (University of Cambridge: mimeo).
Karpoff, J.M. and Lott, J.R. (1995) 'The Reputational Penalty Firms Bear from Committing Criminal Fraud' in G. Fiorentini, and S. Peltzman, (eds), *The Economics of Organised Crime* (Cambridge: Cambridge University Press).
Main, B.G.M. (1994) 'The Economics of Organisation, Top Executive Pay and Corporate Governance', *British Review of Economic Issues*, 16 (June), pp. 85–106.
Markides, C.C. (1995) *Diversification, Refocusing and Economic Performance* (London: MIT Press).
Muellbauer, J. (1977) 'Testing the Barten Model of Household Consumption Effects and the Cost of Children', *Economic Journal*, 87 (September), pp. 460–87.

North, D.C. (1990) *Institutions, Institutional Change and Economic Performance* (Cambridge: Cambridge University Press).

Office of Fair Trading (1996) *Unfair Contract Terms, A bulletin issued by the Office of Fair Trading. Issue No.1 May 1996* (London: Office of Fair Trading).

Sawkins, J.W., Seaman, P.J. and Williams, H.C.S. (1997) 'Church Attendance in Great Britain: An Ordered Logit Approach', *Applied Economics*, 29, pp. 125–34.

Sen, A.K. (1977) 'Rational Fools: A Critique of the Behavioural Foundations of Economic Theory', *Philosophy and Public Affairs*, 6 (4), pp. 317–44.

Sparkes, R. (1995) *The Ethical Investor* (London: HarperCollins).

Stark, O. (1995) *Altruism and Beyond: An Economic Analysis of Transfers and Exchanges with Families and Groups* (Cambridge: Cambridge University Press).

Study Group on Directors' Remuneration [The Greenbury Report] (1995) *Directors' Remuneration: Report of a Study Group Chaired by Sir Richard Greenbury: 17 July 1995* (London: Gee Publishing).

Varian, H.R. (1996) *Intermediate Microeconomics – A Modern Approach*, 4th edn (New York: W.W. Norton).

Waterman, A.M.C. (1991) *Revolution, Economics and Religion: Christian Political Economy 1778–1833* (Cambridge: Cambridge University Press).

Williamson, O.E. (1975) *Markets and Hierarchies: Analysis and Antitrust Implications* (New York: Free Press).

2 Ethics and Self-Interest

John Eatwell

INTRODUCTION

It was Adam Smith who first confronted the interrelationship between ethics and self-interest in economic behaviour.

Concern over what is 'ethical' in economic affairs is to be found in the very earliest discussions of economic matters. To the extent that Aristotle confronts economic questions at all, it is as a problem of ethics. In the *Politics* he defines 'natural' and 'unnatural' modes of acquiring wealth (the notion of interest was particularly abhorrent) and in the *Nicomachean Ethics* he considers the problem of the relationship between justice and exchange values. However, as Moses Finley (1987) makes clear, Aristotle 'never pretended to examine the price mechanism or any other aspect of market exchange *as it was practised* (my emphasis). He was offering a normative ethical analysis.' Aristotle's approach was cited (rightly) as the authority for the critique of usury by the medieval church and (wrongly) as the inspiration of Thomas Aquinas's development of the notion of the 'just price' (Baldwin, 1959).

But the link between ethics and self-interest in economic analysis is of more modern provenance. The key development is the introduction of two of the interdependent pillars of economic thinking: self-interest and rationality. The question of ethical behaviour is seen as inextricably linked with the notion of self-interest, and self-interest is itself inextricably linked with the concept of rationality.

Of course the use of self-interest as the foundation of a rational social science had long preceded the development of economics (Hirschman, 1987). One of the earliest examples is to be found in Machiavelli's *The Prince* (1513). For Machiavelli behaviour is driven not by some sort of conventional heroic morality but by self-interest. And it is exactly because the prince is driven by self-interest that his actions are logical, not random, and are restrained by a calculation that often dictates that actions be prudent and moderate. This is in sharp contrast to the notion of wild and destructive passions and the foolish search for disastrous glory which informed the heroic medieval ideal.[1]

21

In economics one of the earliest analyses of the role of self-interest appears in Bernard de Mandeville's scandalous *Fable of the Bees* (1705). Mandeville argued that the pursuit of self-interest by the rich, in the form of luxurious consumption, sustains the prosperity of society. In his fable, once the bees become virtuous and abandon luxurious consumption, then the hive is swiftly impoverished. Public benefits are the product of private vices and not of private virtues. Mandeville defined behaviour motivated by even the slightest degree of self-interest as a vice. He expressed his argument in colourful language:

> I flatter myself to have demonstrated that, neither the Friendly Qualities and kind Affections that are natural to Man, nor the real Virtues he is capable of acquiring by Reason and Self-Denial, are the Foundations of Society; what we call Evil in this World, Moral as well as Natural, is the grand Principle that makes us sociable Creatures, the solid Basis, the Life and Support of all Trades and Employments without Exception: That there we must look for the true Origin of all Arts and Sciences, and that the Moment Evil ceases, the Society must be spoiled, if not totally dissolved. (1705, vol. I, p. 369)

Thus the pursuit of self-interest (vice) is the foundation of prosperity.[2]

SMITH ON SELF-INTEREST

The role of self-interest lies at the very heart of Adam Smith's analysis of society and of economics. Yet Smith's use of self-interest in economic analysis is often misunderstood. It is, therefore, particularly important to identify precisely the roles which Smith assigned to self-interest and to the social expression of self-interest. In particular it is important to distinguish Smith's analysis from the neoclassical conception of the market as the competitive resolution of utility-maximising choices.

Adam Smith developed his theory of the economic value of rational self-interest by combining self-interest with the idea of the 'invisible hand'. Smith only uses the famous expression 'invisible hand' in two instances. It first appears in his *Theory of Moral Sentiments* of 1759, a work in which, as the title suggests, Smith laid out his analysis of human behaviour, of society and of ethics. The idea of the invisible hand is described in the activities of the landlord, who employs and accumulates. The landlord is not described in flattering terms:

[Landlords], in spite of their natural selfishness and rapacity, though they mean only their own conveniency, though the sole end which they propose from the labours of all the thousands whom they employ be the gratification of their own vain and insatiable desires, they divide with the poor the produce of all their improvements. They are led by an invisible hand to make nearly the same distribution of the necessaries of life which would have been made had the earth been divided into equal portions among all its inhabitants; and thus, without intending it, without making it, advance the interest of the society. (1759, IV.I.10, pp. 184–185)

Smith's argument derives not just from the fact that the landlords employ thousands, but also from the fact that 'the proud and unfeeling landlord's stomach ... bears no proportion to the immensity of his desires', thus he cannot consume all his produce, but must either sell it to others or invest it in the future.

The example of the 'invisible hand' which appears in the *Wealth of Nations* seventeen years later is couched in terms of the individual who:

endeavours as much as he can both to employ his capital in the support of domestick industry, and so to direct that industry that its produce may be of the greatest value ... he intends only his own gain, and he is in this, as in other cases, led by an invisible hand to promote an end which was no part of his intention ... By pursuing his own interest he frequently promotes that of the society more effectually than when he really intends to promote it. I have never known much good done by those who affected to trade for the publick good. (1776, IV.ii.9, p. 456)

Smith is here advancing the proposition not only that actions have unintended consequences, but also that it is actions which are the outcome of the pursuit of self-interest which are likely to lead to the greatest social well-being. It is self-interest which dominates his other famous argument:

man has an almost constant occasion for the help of his brethren, and it is vain for him to expect it from their benevolence only. He will be more likely to prevail if he can interest their self-love in his favour, and show them that it is for their own advantage to do for him what he requires of them ... It is not from the benevolence of the butcher, the brewer, or the baker, that we expect our dinner, but from their regard to their own interests. (1776, I.ii.2, pp. 26–7)

Smith has proffered a solution to the fundamental problem of economic analysis in the rational pursuit of self-interest. That problem is how it can be that the actions of a myriad of individuals, operating with no communication other than exchange in the market-place, and motivated only by the selfish calculation of profit and loss, can be consistent with one another, and indeed form a relatively stable means of solving the eternal economic questions of what is produced, by whom, and to whom the fruits of production are distributed. To put the matter bluntly: how does capitalism actually work? Why don't the millions of actions collapse in chaos? Why is the 'market system' a 'system'?

The rational pursuit of self-interest does not by itself provide answers to these questions. To the theory of rational and systematic behaviour must be added a further ingredient: a theory of markets. Smith is asserting that markets achieve the goal of coordinating individual actions through the generalised process of exchange, and, in doing so, achieve an outcome which is socially desirable.

Adam Smith offered no proof of this proposition.[3] He simply identified socially desirable outcomes with the process of accumulation and argued that the market would encourage accumulation. In particular the market would overwhelm the feudal barriers which inhibited the constructive pursuit of self-interest: the powers of the medieval guilds, the restrictions of the mercantile system, the barriers to free trade – all of which limited the pursuit of self-interest. The market would release this powerful force in the best interest of society as a whole.

SELF-INTEREST AND SYMPATHY

The market carried an ethic of its own. Its operations were as François Quesnay had argued in 1756; 'independent of men's will . . . [Market price] is far from being an arbitrary value or a value which is established by agreement between the contracting parties' (Quesnay, 1756, p. 90). The market creates a framework of exchange which is in nobody's control. It is the independent and disinterested arbiter of economic worth. Yet it is the market which embodies the generalisation of the pursuit of self-interest. It is the force of the market which disciplines self-interest, ensuring that self-interest is not manifest in the exploitation of monopoly advantage. Where feudal and mercantilist barriers to competition exist, creating an environment in which the pursuit of self-interest might be socially undesirable, they should be eliminated. The anti-social and the unethical would be driven out by the cleansing force of competition.

Yet in fact, the new industrial economy which was being created in the late eighteenth century did not have the appearance of an ethical society, in which the unbridled pursuit of self-interest was promoting the good of all. Quite the contrary. The new market economy was clearly imposing significant privation on large numbers of people. The old order of society was being broken up, and with it went the certainty of what were believed to be traditional values. Soon conservative writers were looking back to a golden age of higher values. For example Edmund Burke famously argued in his *Reflections on the Revolution in France* (1790) that:

the age of chivalry is gone; that of sophisters, economists and calculators has succeeded; and the glory of Europe is extinguished forever. (p. 111)

Here was an extraordinary transformation. The Middle Ages, seen for so long as rude and barbarous, were now seen to nurture honour, respect and friendship – ethical values which were destroyed by the market. Indeed, Burke argued that the creation of a civilised society must precede the successful development of commerce, not vice versa.

But Adam Smith had not suggested that the pursuit of self-interest was the end of the problem of ethics. Contrary to what is supposed by so many of those who today portray Smith as an uncritical enthusiast for free markets and minimal government, there is a clear recognition in *The Wealth of Nations* that the idealised link between self-interest and social benefit was, in fact, flawed in practice. In particular Smith recognised that the pursuit of self-interest, particularly by the merchants and capitalists, would damage the interests of other classes. Not only are the Masters 'always and every where in a sort of tacit, but constant and uniform combination, not to raise wages' (1776, I.viii.13, p. 84) but these are

an order of men, whose interest is never exactly the same with that of the publick, who have generally an interest to deceive and even to oppress the publick, and who accordingly have, upon many occasions, both deceived and oppressed it. (1776, I.xi. p.10, p. 267)

If this is so, if there are groups in society which by the pursuit of their self-interest can 'deceive and oppress' then there would seem to be no ethical foundation to the market economy. Even in a competitive environment the pursuit of self-interest could produce significant social harm. It was not ethical. Burke's criticism would seem to be well-founded.

But Smith had already produced an answer to Burkean romanticism, thirty years earlier in the *Theory of Moral Sentiments*. There he presented an ethical theory of society which was driven by self-interest, but which was not self-centred.[4] The key to Smith's notion of ethics lay in his concept of 'sympathy'. We have sympathy for others in that we enter into and share their concerns. But this is not mere philanthropy. Smith's idea is that in society we pursue our self-interest by securing the regard of others. And the regard of others is secured by having a proper sympathy for the concerns of others. Having then a proper sympathy, we behave towards one another in the market-place in an ethical manner.

But even so, even if our self-interest leads us to have a proper sympathy for others, will not the pursuit of wealth harm the interest of others? In other words, will not self-interest overwhelm the social expression of sympathy? As Smith himself put it:

> the eagerness of passion will seldom allow us to consider what we are doing with the candour of an indifferent person. (1759, III.4.3, p. 115)

He solves this problem of the defective personal estimation of the needs of others by proposing that ethics be derived from the values of the impartial spectator:

> That precise and distinct measure can be found nowhere but in the sympathetic feelings of the impartial and well-informed spectator. (1759, VII.ii.I.49, p. 294)

The impartial spectator was not a *deus ex machina*. For Smith he or she was the product of the development of society and the evolution of *social* norms of proper behaviour. The way in which sympathy acts to create social duties and institutions is through its social reflection in public opinion. The impartial spectator is the rational embodiment of sympathy, establishing a proper code of social behaviour:

> It is thus that the general rules of morality are formed. They are ultimately founded upon experience of what, in particular circumstances, our moral faculties, our natural sense of merit and propriety, approve or disapprove of . . . The general rule . . . is formed, by finding from experience, that all actions of a certain kind, or circumstanced in a certain manner, are approved or disapproved of. (1759, III.4.8, p. 159)

Our self-interest leads us to seek approval, and accordingly creates the glue of common sympathy which binds society together and defines the rules which are the foundations of ethics and of justice. Most famously Smith argued that:

> [Nature has not] abandoned us entirely to the delusions of Self-Love. Our continual observations upon the conduct of others, insensibly lead us to form to ourselves certain general rules concerning what is fit and proper either to be done or to be avoided. (Smith, 1759, III.4.7, p. 159)

In this way social customs influence us through the impartial spectator. The deceit of self-love which might lead mankind into an inaccurate estimation of the propriety of their own conduct is overcome. The impartial spectator develops rules which self-interest then obeys. This is the social manifestation of self-interest, the social application of reason:

> If we saw ourselves in the light in which others see us, or in which they would see us if they knew all, a reformation would generally be unavoidable. (Smith, 1759, II.4.6, pp. 158–9)

It was that final prosaic sentence which was rephrased by Robert Burns (*c.* 1784, p. 157, my emphasis):

> O wad some Pow'r the giftie gie us
> *To see oursels as others see us!*
> It wad frae monie a blunder free us
> An' foolish notion.

This is the moral basis of Smith's economics.

CONCLUSION

But Smith knew that his was a morality which might fail. The self-interested desire for the regard of others which is the origin of the role of the impartial spectator is clearly manifest most powerfully in small, close-knit communities. The mechanism might break down in the context of a modern economy, due in part to the size of modern factories and of the new growing cities. This was particularly true of the poor:

> the man of low condition [w]hile he remains in a country village his conduct may be attended to [b]ut as soon as he comes in to a great city, he is sunk in obscurity and darkness. His conduct is observed and attended to by nobody, and he is therefore very likely to neglect himself, and to abandon himself to every sort of low profligacy and vice. (1776, V.i.g.12, p. 795)

This might be worsened by the division of labour, the dynamic driving forward the accumulation of wealth. For the sheer repetition of menial tasks would produce a 'drowsy stupidity, which, in a civilised society, seems to benumb the understanding of almost all the inferior ranks of people' (1776, V.i.f.51, p. 783).

So for Adam Smith the desired harmony between self-interest and an ethical society requires two components, neither of which will be provided by the market, and both of which must accordingly be a matter of concern for the public authorities.

First, it is important that there should be full information. The impartial spectator can only play his or her vital ethical role '[i]f we saw ourselves in the light in which others see us, or in which they would see us if they knew all'. So the self-interested search for social approbation is not just 'do as you would be done by', but an exposure of all actions to the approbation or censure of others. The more open a society and the more open the access to information in business and indeed in all corners of economic life, then the more likely is the pursuit of self-interest to result in ethically desirable outcomes. It is the barriers to information which weaken the link between self-interest and respect for the impartial spectator.

Second, a society can only use information effectively if its members are well-educated. If all citizens are both to express their self-interest in the development of social ethics and to be aware of the mirror which society holds up to their actions, then they must not be condemned to 'drowsy stupidity' by lack of education. Smith argued that it was necessary for the state to take responsibility for the education of children not just for economic gain, but to ensure that they could successfully exercise their self-interest in pursuing and securing ethical outcomes.

The apparent contradiction in economic affairs between ethical behaviour and self-interest is resolved by the requirement of open access to information, and by ensuring that all citizens have the ability to use effectively the information which is made available to them. The role of the state is to ensure that these conditions are fulfilled. Yet despite the importance given to the role of the state, this is still a portrayal of the individual in society. There is no consideration of the role which the state might play in circumstances in which the acquisition of open information is nonetheless likely to be costly, at least in terms of effort, or of circumstances in which the interpretation of information requires high levels of very specific expertise. In these circumstances the impartial spectator might assume the more concrete form of the law and the regulator. Then the impartial spectator is not just the name for a social morality grown out of self-interested desire for approbation. Instead, society sustains ethical positions which are more than the sum of individual parts.

Since Adam Smith there have been a variety of attempts to determine the position of the impartial spectator by something other than the social expression of self-interest and the desire of the approbation of others. The best-known is Jeremy Bentham's proposition (1776, p. 393) that 'it is the greatest happiness of the greatest number that is the measure of right and wrong'.

Today writers such as Peter Hammond (1975, 1987), Edmund Phelps (1975) and Amartya Sen (1977) have presented a variety of arguments for the rejection of the proposition that human behaviour can be analysed purely in terms of self-interest. They have attempted to develop the role of altruism and concern for the group and the public interest in ways which do not simply characterise them as the product of self-interest. For example, millions of people regard it as their social and moral duty to vote in British general elections, even though, given the British electoral system, they will be voting in what are in most cases safe seats. They know their vote will make no difference to the outcome, yet they often go to great lengths to cast it. Their civic action does not derive from the exercise of self-interest, or even from a concept of social duty expressed through the impartial spectator.

But these arguments take us beyond the central theme of this chapter and some way from Smith's central message: that ethics are the social expression of self-interest in a society in which we can indeed 'see oursels as others see us!'

Notes

1. The importance of the principle of self-interest in the efficient operation of the state is found in the works of the American Founding Fathers. Alexander Hamilton argued that: 'The safest reliance of every government is on man's interests. This is a principle of human nature, on which all political speculation, to be just, must be founded' (see Hirschman, 1987, p. 884).
2. An echo of Mandeville's ideas is found in Malthus's analysis of 'gluts', that is, of general slumps. Malthus argues that spending on 'unproductive consumption' by the landlords is necessary to maintain demand and prevent slumps: 'if I recommend a certain proportion of unproductive consumption, it is obviously and expressly with the sole view of furnishing the necessary motive to the greatest continued production' (Malthus to Ricardo, 16 July 1821) (Ricardo, 1821–23, p. 19).
3. Smith did not identify well-being with what would (a hundred years later) be formulated in terms of the precise utility-maximising calculus of modern neoclassical economics. But it is there that is found an attempt to provide a proof of the link between the operation of the market and the attainment of social well-being. Unfortunately, the notion of well-being is contained only in the rather

weak notion of Pareto optimality, and the theorems which links the operation of
a competitive market to Pareto optimal outcomes, the two Fundamental Theorems of Welfare Economics, require such extreme assumptions to generate their
conclusions that they are for all practical purposes, irrelevant (see Graaff, 1957).
4. The following paragraphs draw heavily on Macfie, 1967. See also Campbell,
1971, and Skinner, 1987.

References

Baldwin, J.W. (1959) *The Medieval Theories of the Just Price* (Philadelphia
Pennsylvannia: American Philosophical Society).
Bentham, J. (1776) *A Fragment on Government*, revised and edited by J.H. Burns,
and H.L.A. Hart (London: Athlone Press, 1977).
Burke, Edmund (1790) *Reflections on the Revolution in France*, (Chicago, Ill:
Regnery, 1955).
Burns, Robert (c. 1784) 'To a Mouse, On Seeing One on a Lady's Bonnet at Church', in
Kinsley, J. (ed.), *Burns: Poems and Songs* (London: Oxford University Press, 1969).
Campbell, T.D. (1971) *Adam Smith's Science of Morals* (London: George Allen &
Unwin).
Finley, M.I. (1987) 'Aristotle', in J. Eatwell, M. Milgate and P. Newman (eds), *The
New Palgrave, A Dictionary of Economics* (London: Macmillan).
Graaff, J. de V. (1957) *Theoretical Welfare Economics* (Cambridge: Cambridge
University Press).
Hammond, P. (1975) 'Charity: Altruism or Cooperative Egoism?', in Phelps (1975).
Hammond, P. (1987) 'Altruism', in J. Eatwell, M. Milgate and P. Newman (eds),
The New Palgrave, A Dictionary of Economics (London: Macmillan).
Hirschman, A.O. (1987) 'Interests', in J. Eatwell, M. Milgate and P. Newman (eds),
The New Palgrave, A Dictionary of Economics (London: Macmillan).
Macfie, A.L. (1967) *The Individual in Society: Papers on Adam Smith*, University of
Glasgow Social and Economic Studies (London: George Allen & Unwin).
Machiavelli, N. (1513) *The Prince* (London: Penguin, 1981).
Mandeville, Bernard de (1705) The Fable of the Bees: or, Private Vices, Publick
Benefits, 2 vols, ed. F.B. Kaye (Oxford: Oxford University Press, 1924).
Phelps, E. (ed.) (1975)*Altruism, Morality and Economic Theory*(New York: Russell
Sage Foundation).
Quesnay, F. (1756) Extracts from 'Men', in R. Meek (ed.), *The Economics of
Physiocracy* (London: George Allen & Unwin).
Ricardo, David (1821–23) *Letters, 1821–1823*, being Volume IX of *The Works and
Correspondence of David Ricardo*, ed. P. Sraffa with the collaboration of M.H.
Dobb (Cambridge: Cambridge University Press, 1962).
Sen, A.K. (1977) 'Rational Fools: A Critique of the Behavioral Foundations of Eco-
nomic Theory', *Philosophy and Public Affairs*, 6 (4), pp. 317–44.
Skinner, A. (1987) 'Adam Smith', in J. Eatwell, M. Milgate and P. Newman (eds),
The New Palgrave, A Dictionary of Economics (London: Macmillan).
Smith, Adam (1759) *The Theory of Moral Sentiments*, ed. D.D. Raphael and A.L.
Macfie (Oxford: Clarendon Press, 1976).
Smith, Adam (1776) *An Inquiry into the Nature and Causes of the Wealth of Nations*,
ed. R.H. Campbell, A.S. Skinner and W.B. Todd (Oxford: Clarendon Press, 1976).

3 The Economics of Ethical Leadership

Mark Casson*

INTRODUCTION

In this chapter it is argued that culture has an important intermediating role in the relationship between business ethics and economic performance. Cultural intermediation is personified by the social or political leader, who promotes ethical values and is one of the principal beneficiaries of the improved economic performance that results from them.

Not all ethical systems improve economic performance, of course. An ethical system must have instrumental value in order to achieve this. This instrumental value is the prerogative of functionally useful moral values which reduce transaction costs within the economic system. The clearest example of this instrumental value is the way that an ethic of honesty engineers a climate of trust and so reduces the cost of trade.

This chapter is not primarily concerned with the difference between business ethics on the one hand, and ethics in general on the other. Its concern is not so much the problem of how to apply ethical principles to business as the problem of engineering ethical commitments and supporting ethical discourse in the first place. It is possible to attend numerous conferences and training seminars on business ethics, in order to learn how a business and its brands may *appear* ethical, without having any real commitment to confronting an ethical challenge which requires self-interest to be overridden.

THE DIVISION OF LABOUR IN THE SOCIAL SCIENCES

The main problem confronting any study of the relation of culture to economic behaviour is the unsatisfactory nature of the intellectual division of labour in the social sciences. Specialisation in academic research has cre-

* I am grateful to Peter Koslowski for providing the original stimulus to write the paper on which this chapter was initially based. I also thank Ian Jones and Michael Pollitt for detailed and constructive comments on the penultimate draft.

31

ated different disciplines. The performance of an economy in meeting material needs is studied by economics. Culture, on the other hand, is studied preeminently by anthropology. But any attempt to synthesise insights from these two disciplines runs into the problem that their dominant research methodologies are different. Economics tends to be quantitative and positivist, whilst anthropology tends to be qualitative and anti-positivist. Thus there is no unified methodology of social science in which the two disciplines are embedded.

Similar problems have been encountered before – for example, in synthesising economics with political science and with law. The response by economists in these cases has been to extend the domain of their methods of analysis by creating the new subject fields of public choice and the economics of law respectively. A similar form of 'economic imperialism' is adopted here (Buckley and Casson, 1993).

Previous attempts of this kind have achieved only limited success because many of the simplifying assumptions of economics have been transferred to the new subject area without proper critical scrutiny. Assumptions that are plausible in the context of markets are carried over to non-market environments where they may create unnecessary difficulties. It is particularly important to adapt assumptions when applying economic analysis to anthropology because of the very great differences in the relative weights that the two disciplines attach to the study of market and non-market institutions.

The principal change advocated here is to replace the concept of 'economic man' (or homo economicus of economic tradition), as commonly understood, with 'ethical man' (Casson, 1995, 1996). The main effect is that the instrumental rationality of economic man, which links ends and means, is supplemented by another rationality – value rationality – which explains the formation of ends. This concept of value rationality is inspired by the work of Weber (1947) and Knight (1935), although it is not claimed that the particular interpretation of value rationality offered here is directly implied by their work.

Ethical man, like economic man, still prefers more to less, but he or she prefers more 'good things' rather than just more pleasurable things. Thus ethical man may wish to increase his consumption of 'good things' and decrease his consumption of 'bad things', even though the bad things are more pleasurable than the good ones. A calculus of maximising a combination of moral legitimacy and material pleasure therefore replaces the conventional calculus of maximising pleasure alone.

The moral values that are introduced in this way are not mere opinion and prejudice; they have a logic of their own. Ethical man is not necessarily an ethical individualist, whose values are expressed purely in terms of what is 'good for me'. Ethical man can commit himself to a system of values external to himself. This system of values has its own arguments by which it is justified – its own 'value rationality', in other words. This value rationality is used in various ways: to argue in favour of a particular source of traditional religious authority, for example, or to support the view that people cannot claim for themselves rights that they are not prepared to recognise in others. Value rationality consists of more than the purely deductive logic of instrumental rationality. It is a disciplined system of thought which supplements deductive logic with other criteria which are used to determine whether certain principles are plausible and reasonable, or not. Deductions made from these principles establish an objective moral system of universal absolutes rather than just a subjective collection of local moral conventions. The universal system possesses the authority of a natural law; it places everyone who is convinced by its argument under an obligation to comply with its injunctions – in contrast to the local convention, which merely places people under an obligation to conform so long as they are in the locality.

Because the instrumental rationality of economic man is supplemented by another rationality, rather than replaced by it, the concept of ethical man allows the conventional techniques of economic analysis to be retained. People trade off moral legitimacy against material pleasure to the point where their marginal utilities are equalised. This trade-off is effected by adjusting the composition of the goods consumed. Each good is consumed up to the margin where its benefit, in terms of the moral legitimacy and material pleasure it confers, is equal to its cost, in terms of the price that must be paid, or the work that must be done to produce it. The approach is therefore quite conservative in terms of modelling technique. However, the policy implications of economic models are radically changed when the concept of utility is altered in this way. This is because the welfare analysis which is conventionally applied to economic models assumes given individual ends, and its results are subverted once the influence of value rationality upon these ends is recognised. A new system of values can make people better off even though their new pattern of consumption may reduce the amount of pleasure they receive. The innovator of such a value change is not necessarily rewarded under a competitive market process. He certainly cannot be rewarded through the conventional mechanism of earning profit on ordinary goods and services that he supplies. Economic models cease to function as apologies for *laissez-faire*. It is possible that they could become instead a vehicle for articulating rigorously the benefits of communitarian policies. They certainly demonstrate the improved economic performance that can result when government fosters a high-trust culture. This culture inculcates a special form of social solidarity which is compatible with flexibility in resource allocation. This is not a justification for protectionism, nor for a proactive industrial policy. Rather it is an argument for integrating economic policy, social policy and the cultural life of the nation more coherently than has been usual in the West (Fukuyama, 1995).

ECONOMIC MODELLING OF CULTURAL CHANGE

It must be emphasised that the proposed approach is not itself a purely speculative and utopian one. Models of ethical man already exist (see, for example, Casson, 1991), as do models of social man (Frank, 1987). Indeed, there is a long tradition of ethical modelling in economics, going right back to the founding father of the discipline, Adam Smith. According to Smith (1759), everyone desires the approval of the 'impartial spectator', and it is this desire for his approval that constitutes the moral basis of a civil society. Without the foundations of a civil society, the commercial society described in the *Wealth of Nations* (1776) could not exist (see Eatwell, this volume).

The main problem confronting the modeller who wishes to modify the utility function is one of complexity. Economic modelling is guided by the principle of parsimony (that is, no more causes or forces should be assumed than are necessary), and it is vital to apply this principle in the present context. The recommended strategy is as follows.

1 Introduce Legitimacy into the Utility Function

(a) The utility function is a formal mathematical representation of preferences. In economic theory the utility function implies a consistent ranking of alternatives – no more. The Benthamite view of people as mechanisms driven by the pursuit of pleasure and the avoidance of pain is quite misleading in respect of modern utility theory.

(b) The utility function contains some observable variables – for example, consumption and the supply of work, which describe the behaviour of the individual. If ethics matter, they must change the levels at which these variables are set. Thus ethical variables are introduced in such a way that they affect the marginal utilities of the other variables (see, for example, Akerlof, 1982). The ethical variables do not need to be directly observable themselves, for reasons explained below, although the theory is easier to apply if they are.

(c) One of the simplest ways to introduce the ethical dimension is to postulate a need for legitimacy. The perceived legitimacy of an act increases the utility that can be derived from it. Conversely an act that is perceived as illegitimate incurs a utility penalty. A neutral act confers no utility besides the normal material satisfaction involved. If all legitimate acts confer the same moral utility gain, all illegitimate acts incur the same moral utility loss, and all acts are either legitimate or illegitimate, then the ethical variables impact on utility simply by defining the boundary of the set of legitimate actions.

(d) The situation can be explained intuitively as follows. Each act by an individual is followed by a period of reflection. At this time of reflection the action is evaluated. A good feeling is engendered by having performed a legitimate (good) act and a bad feeling by having performed an illegitimate (bad) act. It is the anticipation of these feelings that influences decision-making. If the emotional gain from performing a good act instead of a bad act exceeds the material loss involved then the good act will be performed.

(e) In purely formal terms, a set of additional variables has been introduced into the utility function, but so far no explanation has been given of the way these variables are set. If the variables remain free then almost any kind of behaviour can be rationalised by choosing appropriate values for these variables. What is needed is a theory which explains how the values of the ethical variables are set.

2 Legitimacy is Determined by a Moral Authority

(a) It is important to explain why different individuals from the same social group conform in their view of what is legitimate, whilst members of different social groups often disagree on this. The simplest explanation is that each group has a single source of moral authority, which disseminates information about legitimacy as a 'public good' within the group. It may be spread either by broadcasting or by word of mouth.

(b) The person who acts as a moral authority may be called the leader. Most groups exhibit an internal division of labour between leaders and followers. This allows leaders to specialise in the difficult task of forming moral judgements. In some cases a leader may claim to be simply a representative of another (sometimes impersonal) moral authority – the ultimate moral authority (see Table 3.1).

(c) What exactly is the nature of the moral message? From the standpoint of an economic model, the formalism does not require that this be specified. What matters is simply the cost of sending the message and the effect that it has on the recipients' utility function. Given the utilitarian formulation, though, it is fairly clear that the nub of the message is: 'Your leader approves/disapproves of this action and so if you

Table 3.1   Examples of group organisation

Type of group	Leader	Ultimate authority
Nuclear family	Parent	–
Extended family/tribe/clan	Head of tribe	Ancestors, spirits
Church	Priest	God
Nation	Political leader	National spirit or will

perform it you will obtain, on reflection, an emotional reward/ penalty.'

The leader may back this up with reasons for his or her disapproval. This could merely amplify the utilitarian content: 'God approves/ disapproves of this action and so if you perform it you are likely to go to heaven/hell and enjoy eternal bliss/damnation.'

Alternatively the leader may construct a philosophical argument, for example, 'If everyone performed this action then the result would be harmony/chaos and that is why it is legitimate/illegitimate.'

(d)   A crucial point about the moral message is that it is directed towards individuals who engage in reflective activity. It is meaningless or irrelevant to those engaged entirely in the short-run pursuit of pleasure and the avoidance of pain. The message implies that individuals can distinguish between their reflective nature and their unreflective one. The message is addressed to the reflective faculty and refers to the need for control to be exercised over unreflective behaviour. The subject matter is self-control. The reflective faculty must inhibit some of the purely pleasure-seeking activities that the person's unreflective nature would be inclined to pursue. The message indicates which pleasure-seeking actions can be condoned, and which cannot. Where particular thoughts incite an immoral action, the reflective nature may even want to censor the thoughts of the unreflective one. A moral message normally makes sense only to those who accept this distinction between their reflective and their unreflective nature, and are willing to accept the relevance of injunctions for the former to control or censor the latter in a rational way.

(e)   Not everyone can be a moral authority. There are a number of qualifications for doing the job successfully. Consistency and clarity are the two main requirements. Consistency manifests itself in three possible ways:

- *Charisma*: if the leader is in touch with an ultimate authority he or she should behave in a manner which suggests this.
- *Cogency*: if the leader advances a philosophical argument it should be plausible even though it may not be immune to sceptical criticism.

- *Commitment:* if legitimacy is related to realising a vision or furthering a social goal then the leader should be willing to make a personal commitment of his or her own to the goal in which he or she claims to believe.

Taken together, therefore, this shows that the message, the supporting evidence and the actions of the leader must all cohere with each other. In addition to consistency, clarity is also required. It must be easy for the followers to understand what is being said. Clarity is facilitated by

- simple attention-grabbing rhetoric,
- ritual acts that symbolise the message, and
- conspicuous behaviour that is easy for followers to imitate.

3   The Supply of Leaders

(a)   Leadership generates economic rents from improved coordination (see below). Not all of these rents may be readily appropriable though. If the moral leader also has political power, or works for those who have it, then the rents can be appropriated through taxation. Otherwise the leader may have to rely on voluntary contributions.

(b)   The costs of leadership include the expenses of communication and the opportunity costs of the leader's time. Since it is important that the leader is a talented person, preferably the person best-equipped to meet the qualifications described above, his opportunity earnings may be quite high. The payment must equal or exceed these earnings to attract the right person to the job.

(c)   If the leader enunciates principles of social justice, however, then his own payments may have to be constrained in the interests of consistency, as described above. In this case the leader may be 'paid' indirectly, by an expense account, or by being accorded social deference on account of his high status. History provides many examples of leaders who have chosen to ignore this constraint on the 'perks' of leadership, and have consequently lost legitimacy. Individual leaders may well be able to continue abusing their power throughout their lifetime, but sooner or later their dynasty, and the system which maintains leaders like them in power, will collapse. The high percentage of rents extracted by the leadership undermined the legitimacy of government and led to its collapse in pre-Civil War England, in Tsarist Russia, and most recently in the USSR.

(d) The supply of potential leaders is also a function of demography (the number of people of suitable age), genetics (the intelligence of the population) and training. In the context of education and training it is, of course, the moral dimension as well as the technical dimension that is important (see below). The more abundant the supply of trained and talented people, the lower the scarcity premium that a leader can command.

(e) Generally, it can be said that there is a market for leaders, but that this market is bedevilled by substantial problems of quality control. It would be nice to imagine that a leader could win support for a system of values only if she were totally committed to them herself. By keeping at a distance from his supporters, however, and shrouding her activities in secrecy to maintain their mystique, she may be able to live privately according to values very different from those she professes in public. In so far as such hypocrisy cannot be exposed, leadership tends to attract people who are least desirable in that role – those who desire the job for the lavish material consumption that it can afford.

(f) It is, of course, possible for people to come forward who believe that they can profit from exposing hypocrisy of this kind. The problem is that they may seek to depose the leader only to take power for themselves in her place. A cycle of corruption may develop in which successive leaders discredit one another without performing any better than their predecessors.

(g) In Western democracies the quality of leadership is supposed to be assured by the discipline of forcing leaders to seek periodic reelection. A free press is maintained to ensure fair play during this electoral process. Unfortunately these mechanisms are becoming corrupted too. One of the most dramatic changes in the environment within which leaders operate in the twentieth century has been the emergence of investigative journalism. When it surfaced, around the turn of the century, it was known as 'muckraking', but growing popular disillusionment with professional party politicians has turned muckraking into a respectable, and indeed glamorous, occupation. It is clearly relevant for the public to know when a politician has adopted a moral posture that they do not believe in themselves. The mere threat of exposure may help to maintain standards in political life. In this sense muckraking performs a valuable service. Problems arise, however, when muckraking becomes so indiscriminate that it simply engineers a climate of moral despair. This is part of a still wider problem relating to the abuse of the modern mass media. Leading journalists and news editors, through their ability to censor some items of news and give prominence to others, can influence public opinion in favour of some politicians and against others. They can also pursue a hidden moral agenda of their own. In particular, the visual impact of television journalism allows images to convey implicit moral messages – as, for example, when images of warfare are used to convey the message that there is nothing to believe in that is worth anyone dying for. Through their skill in framing selected factual information to convey an implicit moral message, key media personnel have thereby taken over much of the leadership function from the politicians. Although, unlike the politicians, they do not seek power for themselves, some media personnel seem to have ambitions to become power-brokers. Politicians submitting to reelection now find their position less secure than that of the journalists. If the media exists to discipline the politicians, it may be asked, who or what exists to discipline the media?

FUNCTIONAL VALUES

(a) To maximise the rents that the leader generates, it is important that the leader chooses functionally useful values. The simplest way to analyse the functional value of an ethic is to postulate an economy populated by pairs of transactors, or teams of workers, each of whom has a material incentive to cheat. The transactors, for example, may bluff in negotiations over price, causing the negotiations to fail. If the negotiations succeed, they may then attempt to cheat by not paying for the goods they receive. In the context of team production, workers may shirk in the hope that they will not be discovered doing so.

These classic problems are associated with the Prisoner's Dilemma in game theory, and with asymmetric information in the theory of the firm. According to the Prisoner's Dilemma, cheating dominates honesty from a short-term perspective. Cheating is not only the best defence against another cheat, but an easy way of taking advantage of an honest person too. So everyone cheats on everyone else, even though everyone would be better off if everyone were honest instead. Private rationality leads to collective stupidity when short-term maximisation of material rewards governs behaviour.

Asymmetric information is exemplified by the case where a seller knows about some defect in a good that the buyer does not, and withholds this information. If the buyer anticipates that this is how the seller will behave then she may refuse to buy the good. But if the buyer cannot discriminate between an honest seller and a dishonest one then she may refuse to trade with honest sellers too, and so the potential gains from honest trade will be lost as a result.

In an economy bedevilled by incentive problems of this kind, the role of an ethic is simply to prevent cheating. Individuals who know they will feel guilty if they cheat decide to be honest instead, and this allows the gains from coordination to be generated to the full.

(b) While honesty is the preeminent value that is endorsed in this way, there are many other values that are important in various circumstances. These include

- *loyalty* – important in creating a high-trust culture to support partner-specific investments;
- *persistence* – important in realising long-term goals such as economic development;
- *solidarity* – important in a primitive society with limited opportunities for division of labour and trade and vulnerable to external aggression; and
- *self-sacrifice* – important under war conditions.

(c) The role of the leader is to examine the environment of the group and then optimise the ethic by choosing the set of followers' actions on which she confers legitimacy. In this respect the leader remains autonomous in the traditional way; the model does not therefore dispense with autonomy altogether, but focuses autonomy on the leader. Everyone is rational – both leaders and followers – but only the leader is autonomously so.

SOME EXTENSIONS OF THE BASIC MODEL

The basic model is very simple, but because of its transparent logical structure it is readily extended in various ways. There are three developments of the model which are particularly relevant to the main theme of this chapter.

1 Moral Pluralism and Competition between Groups

(a) So far the analysis has focused on a single social group. Many people (particularly Western liberals) may feel uneasy about the prominent role of the leader within this group. From the standpoint of personal freedom, however, the crucial thing is not whether groups have leaders, but whether people are free to join whatever group they want to.

Indeed, extreme individualism can be accommodated within this theory by allowing every individual to form her own group to which she alone belongs. In this case every individual behaves as a leader and not as a follower. All individuals are thus morally autonomous, but have no one they can trust because everyone else is autonomous too.

(b)   An individual could, indeed, belong to no group at all. This would mean that she had no moral system. All her actions would be neutral in terms of legitimacy. In terms of reflection, all of her acts would be meaningless. Such an individual is likely to have a low level of utility relative to others, unless there are a lot of really enjoyable material outcomes which are ruled out by all moral codes. The morally committed person can ensure that she only gets emotional benefits from her morality by the simple strategy of always doing what is right and never doing anything that is wrong. Provided that the material costs are not too great, this is likely to be better than living in an emotional vacuum.

(c)   The advantages of belonging to a group are likely to be even greater when people can choose to which group they belong. There is, however, a problem of inter-group relations where moralities are very different. This is particularly so if the moralities are conspicuously different – affecting public behaviour, for example, as in the case of dress – and if the groups share public space together. In this case mutual affiliation to some higher-order group will normally be necessary to avoid physical conflict between the members of different groups. Mutual respect and tolerance are likely to be important functional values in the ethos of the higher-level group.

(d)   To say that tolerance is a virtue in inter-group relations does not mean that any kind of new group can be tolerated, however. For example, the leader of the higher-level group cannot tolerate groups which are themselves totally intolerant of others. Any attempt to tolerate such groups will cause the higher-level group to degenerate into a collection of warring factions. Neither can the leader of the higher-level group allow criticism of her moral values by constituent groups to pass without rebuttal. In particular, criticism of the core functional values described above must be decisively rebutted. This does not mean that such criticism should be censored – on the contrary, publicly confronting such criticism provides an opportunity for the leader to restate her core values in a new and even more compelling way.

(e)   It is, however, important that such debate is carried on in a reflective manner, and that sensationalism is ruled out. As noted earlier, in modern societies media professionals have specific skills in manipulating images to promote a covert moral agenda of their own. They also have the means to regulate a leader's access to her followers through the medium they control, so that a considered response to their sensational views may be suppressed. Media professionals therefore constitute a group which has the power to make and to break the rules of moral debate – a group that is more powerful than all other groups, and potentially more powerful than the leader herself. To discharge her responsibility properly, the leader of the higher-level group needs to establish a proper code of practice governing moral debate. Until now, it would seem, no Western political leader has made a serious attempt to set out workable rules for the conduct of moral debate in an era of global mass communication.

2   Comparison with a Legal System

(a)   But what of the role of law? Ethics and law are both normally universal. They both legitimate *classes of actions* for *all* individuals. The law is normally given an ethical justification. But there is a crucial difference. The legal system relies on external monitoring, both by fellow citizens and by specialists such as the police. It also relies on formal methods of adjudication in which witnesses present evidence against the accused. The ethical mechanism dispenses with external monitoring; it is based on people being *self-monitoring*, through the *power of reflection*. If this system works it effects a major economy in information costs, since no other party is involved in the process.

(b)   Another difference between ethics and law is that the law relies on material penalties whilst the ethical mechanism relies on emotional ones. Emotional penalties are usually much cheaper in material terms. There is no destruction or confiscation of the offender's property, and no cost of administering this either. It is, however, sometimes difficult to fine-tune ethical penalties. Some individuals who are insensitive to moral argument may experience little guilt from a given crime, whilst very sensitive individuals may suffer guilt for the rest of their lives. Societies relying on emotional penalties need to have not only an effective way of sensitising people to moral values, but also a mechanism for forgiving people after they have made a suitable admission of their guilt.

(c)   Ethics and the law are, in fact, at two extremes of a broader spectrum. While ethics associates self-monitoring with emotional penalties, the two do have to be linked in this way. In some primitive societies, for example, guilty individuals punish themselves materially – for example, by making sacrifices to the gods. Conversely, it is possible to have emotional penalties based on external monitoring, such as the penalties of shame or 'loss of face' when an offence is discovered by other people. This latter mechanism of 'peer group pressure' works reasonably well in small compact and stable groups where everyone knows each other well, but is less suitable in larger groups whose membership is more mobile and dispersed. Ethical mechanisms have the power to extend the scope of the emotional mechanism by encouraging the individual to adopt the group point of view when making judgements on herself. A strong ethical mechanism may, however, require fairly frequent communication between the leader and her members. The ethical system may therefore have a comparative advantage in groups of medium size, leaving the relatively impersonal legal system as the system most appropriate to large, dispersed and highly mobile groups.

3 Language, Communication and Leadership

Note how the moral mechanism economises on information. Making difficult moral judgements of functional value is specialised with the leader. The leader broadcasts a simple message expressed vividly. It covers classes of actions and applies to everyone. Individuals then apply this information to themselves. They do not, for example, report their actions to the leader for individual approval/disapproval. Not only does the leader not have to monitor individuals, but individuals do not have to refer their proposed actions to the leader for advice or judgement.

One way of looking at this is to say that the leader coordinates the society by taking an intermediating role. Other examples of intermediation involve entrepreneurs creating markets in new goods and services. All intermediation, of whatever kind, depends on communication, and communication in turn requires language. But language is costly – it requires a considerable investment for individuals to learn a vocabulary and acquire the rules of grammar.

There is a significant difference between moral leadership and entrepreneurial market-making in the amount of such investment that is required. Markets economise on language because they rely on highly quantified communication. In its limiting case a market simply requires three numbers to be communicated: a code number to identify the product, the quantity demanded or supplied, and the price. But moral rhetoric requires much more than this. It requires a language capable of describing emotions such as guilt and shame, social concepts such as peace and harmony and their opposites, war and conflict, and so on. It requires a grasp of grammar sufficient to understand a complicated argument explaining why it is plausible to require people to enter into certain obligations to one another. Thus if a society is to benefit fully from the reduction in monitoring costs afforded by a system of moral obligation it must invest in educating its citizens in the language necessary to communicate and assimilate moral reasoning.

An effective moral leader will therefore wish to ensure that she is supported by a suitable educational system. Leadership is not a simple activity based solely on the display of personal charisma in a public setting, but a sophisticated activity involving a complex of related activities. Just as leadership itself emerges from a fundamental division of labour between leaders and followers in a society, so leadership itself requires a division of labour between the members of the elite who assist in leadership activities. This division of labour creates professions such as the religious priesthood, an incorruptible judiciary, and, above all, the teaching profession which imparts linguistic skills and provides the population as a whole with the cultural and historical context in which the leader's rhetoric can be understood.

It is in this respect that some of the deficiencies of contemporary Western leadership become most apparent. The defects of state education in Western countries – particularly the erosion of the core curriculum in primary and secondary schools – have received a good deal of media exposure, but characteristically the media have had few carefully thought-out improvements to suggest. Much of the spotlight has fallen on defects in the teaching of the 'three Rs', although the concomitant increase in truancy, juvenile crime and street violence almost certainly has more to do with defects in moral teaching instead. One serious problem appears to be that the decline in traditional religious instruction has left children (and a steadily growing number of young adults) without a command of language sufficient to allow them to articulate their feelings in a coherent way. According to the theories of Freud, for example, sex education at school should have liberated teenagers from any unhealthy feelings of guilt about relations with the opposite sex. When such feelings continue to arise, anger and confusion set in. Self-control, too, has been largely excluded from the curriculum – even though it causes teachers self-inflicted problems with lack of discipline in school. Without an ethic of self-control, the rational response to unwanted feelings of guilt is for teenagers to shift the responsibility on to others. Anger and violence are directed at parents, teachers and other authority figures. Ironically, the targeting of these authority figures is warranted, in a certain sense, because collectively, if not individually, it is deficient adult leadership which, through the weakness of its moral teaching, that has created the emotional crises with which these teenagers cannot cope. The inarticulate violence of youth is getting the message across, in a coded manner, to those who need to receive it, but the adult generation, reared on suspicion of leadership, is reluctant to take its responsibilities seriously.

OBJECTIONS TO THE MODEL

Finally, some possible objections to the model of leadership are noted. Four objections are considered.

1. **'It undermines the autonomy of the individual'** The force of this objection is weakened by the fact, already noted, that individualism is just a special case of the general leadership model in which each individual belongs to his or her own group. But a more vigorous defence can be mounted for the approach adopted here. The developmental view of human nature found in the social psychology literature – and especially works on educational psychology – emphasises that in many respects adults are just children grown older. 'The child is the father of the man', in other words. Children need parents and as they grow older and prepare to leave home they find role models elsewhere. This search for moral authority continues throughout adult life. For some the search takes a religious dimension; for academics it may become a search for abstract truth. But usually there is a human intermediary who plays a leadership role – the saintly priest, the eminent professor, and so on. The search for leadership is therefore a continuous aspect of human life.

2. **'Groups don't need leaders. Spontaneous order will emerge in a group because it is in everyone's interests for it to do so'** This view is closely identified with the later writings of Hayek (for example, Hayek, 1963). It is often asserted to be a method of addressing the problem of unintended consequences of human action, particularly in the provision of public goods where conventional market processes may be difficult to use. Unfortunately there is no formal model that has shown exactly how the emergence of spontaneous order occurs, or set out the conditions under which the mechanism will work and under which it will not. There are models that have a bearing on the problem, such as those of repeated games, or theories of focal points. Those who hold the faith that suitable models of this kind will be forthcoming may still like to give a provisional endorsement to the leadership approach, however. In critical situations leaders do indeed tend to emerge. There is a rational basis for this, for as the threat of descent into chaos becomes more real, the demand for leadership increases, and the rents that a leader can appropriate

increase. Although the responsibilities may be daunting, and the risks correspondingly high, the prospective returns are high as well. A leader therefore emerges to 'fill a gap in the market'. To this extent, the emergence of the leader may be identified with the emergence of spontaneous order. Whether the order persists depends, however, on the qualities of the leader; an able and committed leader may be able to stabilise the situation, whereas an incompetent or an opportunistic leader is likely to precipitate the extinction of the group.

3. **'It exalts the leader. In practice, leaders tend to be (or to become) corrupt'** The model only exalts *good* leaders, though. It provides a criterion by which the effectiveness of leaders can be judged in economic terms. It relates these to the qualifications that leaders require. It emphasises the need for the moral training of the leader. It also emphasises the role of status as a reward to encourage good leaders to come forward. In this context it may actually suggest a solution to the problems of finding high-quality leaders in contemporary Western countries in which leaders are typically offered difficult jobs, little training and limited rewards. Much of the problem stems from a lack of popular appreciation for the work that leaders have to do. This in turn reflects the paucity and the superficiality of intellectual discussion on the leadership issue.

4. **'It demeans ethics by reducing it to a utilitarian form. It inverts ends and means by turning ethics into a means of engineering improved economic performance'** This is not so. It has already been noted that the utilitarian framework is purely formal – 'utility' is simply shorthand for 'that which people maximise', whatever that happens to be. The model is essentially an exercise in positive economics. The model simply draws attention to the obvious fact that moral arguments are widely used to influence other people's behaviour, and to this extent are regularly employed as means, even though the arguments themselves clearly refer to ends.

SUMMARY AND CONCLUSION

When discussing business ethics, many people seem to be looking for an easy way of conferring legitimacy on corporate behaviour by keeping themselves up to date with the current fads and fancies in popular culture. This is certainly prudent business practice, because adverse ethical comments in the media can have a serious impact on perceptions of a company and its brands. This chapter has taken a rather different view of business ethics, though. It has focused on a traditional view of ethical values associated with the great world religions like Christianity and the great academic philosophers such as Aristotle and Kant. This view sees ethics as having a crucial role in maintaining social cohesion, and, by implication, business ethics is just one small part of it.

It has become something of a platitude to emphasise that the economy is 'socially embedded', but the truth of this proposition is not diminished by the frequency of its repetition. This chapter has examined one particular consequence of this – namely, that as social cohesion diminishes, the transaction costs of doing business rise. It has been suggested that something can be done about this – namely, steps can be taken to improve the quality of leadership. The idea of 'strong' leadership has negative connotations in Anglo-Saxon culture, and, to some extent, rightly so. What is required, theory suggests, is not so much strong leadership as simply good leadership – leadership which promotes shared morals of functional value to the community. Good leadership does not imply more coercion but less. For under good leadership people can be trusted, and because they can be trusted they can safely be given the freedom to decide for themselves. So far as business is concerned, good leadership generates a high-trust corporate culture within the firm, which allows employees to behave more entrepreneurially because they are not being constantly monitored and assessed on short-term results. Good leadership also generates good relations between firms, allowing them to cooperate in joint ventures – an important factor in a modern high-technology information-based economy. Finally, good leadership also leads to good relations between a firm and its customers. There is therefore no conflict between traditional moral values and a positive brand image. Indeed, so far as image is concerned, traditional values are likely to prove a better investment in the long run than a strategy of following contemporary fads and fashions, because over time the firm will be able to point to the consistency of its business ethics.

It needs to be emphasised that business ethics offers no 'quick fix' for contemporary social ills. The pay-off to ethical leadership is a long-run one. In the long run a prosperous economy requires a stable system of values that sustains a civil society. Without a civil society, transaction costs rise, and economic competitiveness declines. Once the value system has fallen into decline – as in the contemporary West – it requires a costly investment to rebuild it. The reaffirmation of functionally useful moral values will come as a 'culture shock' to middle-aged parents of the postwar 'youth' generation, to whom moral absolutes are simply a confidence trick perpetrated by discredited symbols of authority such as church and state. Changing the moral content of the school curriculum, restoring the objectivity and impar-

48   *The Economics of Ethical Leadership*

tiality of the news media, and introducing greater analytical rigour into intellectual debate on ethical issues will all damage established vested interests of one kind or another. There may also be specific implications for certain industries, or certain types of business practice, which have adverse short-run effects on profits. Against this can be set reduced expenditure on law and order, lower insurance premiums for theft and criminal damage, savings in social security payments on account of a smaller 'underclass', and higher productivity through greater commitment to work. This chapter does not specifically demonstrate that the long-run benefits of investing in ethical leadership will outweigh the short-run costs; but it does spell out the economic consequences of failing to respond to the contemporary challenge of rebuilding civil society.

References

Akerlof, G.A. (1982) 'Labour Contracts as Partial Gift Exchange', *Quarterly Journal of Economics*, 97, pp. 543–69.
Buckley, P.J. and Casson, M.C. (1993) 'Economics as an Imperialist Social Science', *Human Relations*, 46, pp. 1035–52.
Casson, M.C. (1991) *Economics of Business Culture: Game Theory, Transactions Costs and Economic Performance* (Oxford: Clarendon Press).
Casson, M.C. (1995) *Entrepreneurship and Business Culture* (Aldershot: Edward Elgar).
Casson, M.C. (1996) 'Economics and Anthropology: Reluctant Partners', *Human Relations* (forthcoming).
Frank, R.H. (1987) 'If *Homo Economicus* Could Choose His Own Utility Function, Would He Want One with a Conscience?', *American Economic Review*, 77, pp. 593–604.
Fukuyama, F. (1995) *Trust: The Social Virtues and the Creation of Prosperity* (London: Hamish Hamilton).
Hayek, F.A. von (1963) 'The Theory of Complex Phenomena', in M. Bunge (ed.), *The Critical Approach to Science and Philosophy: Essays in Honour of Karl Popper* (New York: Free Press of Glencoe).
Knight, F.H. (1935) *The Ethics of Competition* (London: George Allen & Unwin).
Smith, A. (1759) *The Theory of Moral Sentiments*, ed. D.D. Raphael and A.L. Macfie, Glasgow edition (Oxford: Oxford University Press, 1976).
Smith, A. (1776) *An Inquiry into the Nature and Causes of the Wealth of Nations*, ed. R.H. Campbell, A.S. Skinner and W.B. Todd, Glasgow edition (Oxford: Oxford University Press, 1976).
Weber, M. (1947) *The Theory of Social and Economic Organization*, trans. A.M. Henderson and T. Parsons, ed. T. Parsons (New York: Oxford University Press).

4 Cooperation, Contract Law and Economic Performance

Simon Deakin and Frank Wilkinson

INTRODUCTION

Economists have traditionally been suspicious of cooperation, regarding it as a species of collusion against the public interest. They are even more doubtful of the merits of institutional support for collective action, which they see as restricting competition and reducing economic welfare. In this respect, the views of Adam Smith are echoed in theories of our own time, of which Hayek's theory of spontaneous order has been particularly important. This is all in sharp contrast, however, to evidence of the competitive performance of economic systems which emerged in the postwar period to challenge the preeminent position of the Anglo-American economies. These systems, which include those of Germany, Japan and northern Italy, have developed systems of cooperation within and between firms which are supported by dense networks of institutions. Markets are regulated by commonly agreed rules, norms and standards. The result, in many cases, has been high rates of process and product innovation, high product quality, improved design and flexibility in meeting the changing requirements of consumers. The prolonged success of overtly cooperative productive systems appears to cast doubt on the negative attitude of economists to this form of economic organisation, and invites a reconsideration of the economic nature of cooperation. This is particularly important at the present time, because the pressure of 'globalisation' is leading many in the countries concerned to question the effectiveness of those institutional mechanisms through which cooperation was encouraged. Nor is there any shortage of those prepared to defend the so-called Anglo-American model and to argue for its superior survival value.

The purpose of this chapter is to reexamine the economic nature of cooperation and to explore its links with the institutional framework, and in particular with the normative structure for contracting which is provided by the system of contract law. In the following section we argue, first, that cooperation is a source of operational and dynamic efficiencies within productive systems and that cooperation, in this sense, should be thought of as a distinct mode of economic coordination which cannot be reduced to, or regarded as an outcome of, market-based competition. The next section then goes on to argue that the maintenance of cooperation presupposes the existence of rules and norms which embody cooperative values and which permit the emergence of trust between contracting parties. This theme is then developed by reference to the content and operation of systems of contract law. In particular, we explore the role played by notions of contractual 'good faith' in supporting cooperation in the civil law systems of mainland Europe. Our argument is illustrated by reference to the findings of an empirical study of relationships within vertical supply chains. We end with some conclusions on trust and the institutional framework.

COOPERATION AND ECONOMIC ORGANISATION

It is important at the outset to be clear about what we mean by the notion of 'cooperation', and how it is to be differentiated from that of 'competition'. At a basic level, cooperation describes an activity in which agents work together towards an agreed or common goal; competition, by contrast, concerns a process of rivalry between agents in the acquisition or distribution of resources. The two are not necessarily incompatible. According to classical political economy (and to latter-day neoliberals), the key to their reconciliation lies in the institution of the market. It is through market-based exchange that self-interest, or the pursuit of individual goals, becomes the mechanism by which society's material needs are also most efficiently met. Adam Smith recognised that in 'civilised societies' individuals stand 'at all times in need of the cooperation and assistance of the great multitudes' (1974, p. 118); however these needs are met 'not by the benevolence of the butcher, the brewer or the baker . . . but in exchange where they have regard for their own interest' (1974, p. 119). Self-interest thus provides the incentive for specialisation, exchange provides the opportunity, and the price system – the market – coordinates the individual production and consumption decisions of agents, thereby securing societal cooperation.

Cooperation is thus the consequence of competition; or, put slightly differently, competition is the basis for those forms of joint activity which are socially valuable. Such cooperation arises spontaneously, in the sense of being the consequence of the impersonal allocation of resources through the price mechanism. Where cooperation is *planned*, or deliberately brought about, it is likely to be the result of collusion or (in modern terminology) 'rent seeking' by organised groups aiming to capture a share of society's resources without contributing to the creation of wealth. At best, planned cooperation is a primitive form of economic coordination which lacks the potential for adaptation and learning which lies at the heart of Hayek's notion of competition as a process of discovery:

> Cooperation, like solidarity, presupposes a large measure of agreement on ends as well as on methods employed in their pursuit. It makes sense in a small group whose members share particular habits, knowledge and beliefs about possibilities. It makes hardly any sense when the problem is to adapt to unknown circumstances; yet it is this adaptation to the unknown on which the coordination of efforts in the extended order rests. Competition is a procedure of discovery, a procedure involved in all evolution, that led man unwittingly to respond to novel situations; and through further competition, not through agreement, we gradually increase our efficiency. (Hayek, 1988, p. 19)

But what this view of cooperation does not address is the question of joint labour within production, and the problems for distribution which it raises. Mainstream economic theory has sought to address the problem by arguing that factors of production are substitutes for each other. Thus it is supposed that the organiser of production is faced with a choice of production techniques composed of different amounts of labour and capital; the choice of which to use being determined by the relative prices of labour and capital. The problem of distribution is solved by the assumption of diminishing marginal rates of substitution between factors. However, nothing is said about the nature of the relationship between the factors of production once the technique has been chosen and production is under way: what, for example, does the notion of substitutability between factors of production mean when an operator is using a lathe to shape metal?

One of the first attempts to develop a distinctive economic theory of cooperation with particular reference to production was made by Edward Gibbon Wakefield (1835), an early critic of Adam Smith's treatment of the division of labour. Wakefield's editorial notes to the *Wealth of Nations* argued that Adam Smith, in his formulation of the division of labour, confused the categories of labour and employment, the latter meaning the work performed by labour. Wakefield pointed out that labour is naturally divided into pairs of hands so that the division of employment between many pairs of hands requires workers to work collectively: 'the greatest division of labour takes place amongst those exceedingly barbarous savages who never help each other, who work separately from each other; and the division of employment with all its great results, depends on cooperation' (Wakefield, 1835, p. xx). Wakefield went on: 'Cooperation appears to be of two distinct kinds, such cooperation as takes place when several people help each other in the same employment; secondly, such cooperation as takes place when several persons help each other with different employments. These may be termed simple cooperation and complex cooperation.' Cooperation is to be found not just in the workplace – 'the division of employment which takes place in a pin factory results from and is wholly dependent on the union, generally under one roof, of all the labour by which pins are made' – but more generally is 'dependent also upon the agreements, concert, or combinations of a general kind, in which the whole of society takes part' (ibid., p. 29).

What Wakefield was drawing attention to was, first, that in each stage of production, labour, equipment and material work in combination. None can operate without the others, so that the failure of any adequately to perform its productive functions lowers the joint product of the whole (see Wilkinson, 1983; Tarling and Wilkinson, 1987). The *operational efficiency* of productive systems – the effectiveness with which productive resources are utilised – therefore requires cooperation between the owners of different inputs. How effective this is depends on how well machines are designed and maintained, the suitability of the design of the product both to meet the requirement of the customer and for the ease of production, and how well workers perform their tasks from a technical point of view. The latter will depend on how well workers are trained, the degree of care and attention with which equipment is operated and materials and products are handled, and the timing of the flows of materials to semi-finished products at various stages of the production process. At each stage, the availability and communication of information between the agents concerned are essential. The sharing of information is important to ensure, for example, that all agents of production are equally well-informed about production techniques and how to operate them, and that components are designed and produced in such a way as to best fulfil their productive purpose. The availability of information about variations in the flow of materials, their specifications and quality, and the prompt reporting of and response to other problems impeding output and reducing product quality are also essential.

The sharing of market information is also of central importance in matching production to demand. The need continuously to adjust production to changing consumer demand necessitates cooperation in the supply chain, particularly in the rapid transmission of accurate information between buyer and supplier firms. To avoid producing unsaleable stock or allowing demand to go unsatisfied, responsive linkages within supply chains are needed; the more uncertain final demand is, the more important such close relationships become. Success in production and marketing also depends on access to information on the latest products, processes and forms of organisation. Here cooperation is important because of the problem-solving benefits of working together, and because the sharing of information increases the pace of diffusion of new processes and products, and hence the pace of technical progress of the productive system. The *operational efficiency* of a productive system, as opposed to a firm, therefore depends to an important extent on the generation and transmission of technical and market information; and its *dynamic efficiency*, the ability to introduce new and improved products, processes and forms of organisation, requires the generation and diffusion of new ideas and innovations.

Wakefield also drew attention to the importance of the organisational and institutional framework for securing cooperation. In this respect it is useful to distinguish between the *technical* and the *social* aspects of productive relations. The technical aspects concern the interlinkages between labour, equipment and materials in the production processes, and the exchange of technical and other information relating to production and the development of products and processes. These relations are therefore largely objective and impersonal associations, which are determined by the technicalities of products and of the methods by which they are produced. But in addition, relations between agents in the productive process are also made possible by, or shaped by, social and institutional structures which tend to vary considerably according to context. These social and institutional dimensions of the productive process play a central role in determining the effectiveness of technical cooperation, and hence of operational and dynamic efficiencies. Consequently, an understanding of the operations of the social and institutional aspects of production is central to an understanding of the determination of the competitive performance of productive systems.

One way of thinking about the institutional framework for production and exchange is to regard institutional forms as arising in response to the high *transaction costs* of conducting exchange within decentralised markets. Coase's seminal 1937 paper on the nature of the firm began by noting that 'an economist thinks of an economic system as coordinated by the price mechanism' (Coase, 1988, p. 34), but then posed the question, 'having regard to the fact that if production is regulated by price movements, production would be carried out without any organisation at all, well might we ask, "Why is there any organisation?"' (Coase, 1988, p. 36). The answer Coase gave was that economic organisation serves as an efficient way of overcoming costly impediments to the effective coordinating activities of markets. These arise from asymmetric bargaining power between trading partners created by such market imperfections as monopoly in supply and demand, the concentrated control of specific assets, privileged access to information, and difficulties in monitoring and securing performance. Institutions and organisations replicate the role of the market by neutralising the opportunistic exploitation of bargaining advantage.

From this perspective the development of managerial organisation is a defensive *reaction* to the transaction costs which may result from the opportunistic exploitation of bargaining advantage by trading partners. In other traditions in economics, of which those of Marx and Marshall are notable examples, organisational innovation plays a leading and *proactive* role in dictating the pace and direction of economic development. Marx followed Wakefield in explicitly recognising the importance of cooperation in his theories of the labour process and of surplus value (Marx, 1974, chs XIII–XV). He argued that cooperation in production originated when capitalist employers brought workers together in workshops under their command. Even with existing technology, workers increased their collective productivity by working in concert and this additional value was expropriated by capital. Assembling workers together also provided opportunities for the division of labour, the mechanisation of production and eventually the development of modern industry. In this process, cooperation changed from its simple form to a 'more specialised form based on the division of labour'; this was 'a technical necessity dictated by the very nature of the instruments of labour' (Marx, 1974, p.364). As part of this transformation, capital played a central innovating role in developing the social organisation within which cooperation evolved:

> A single violin player is his own conductor; an orchestra requires a separate one. The work of directing, superintending and adjusting becomes one of the functions of capital, from the moment that the labour comes under the control of capital [and] becomes cooperative. (Marx, 1974, p. 313)

In Marx's analysis the managerial *plan* coordinates production within the factory prior to the often chaotic and wasteful coordination of supply and demand by the market (Pagano, 1985). Distribution also involves a two-stage process in which the market and managerial control played a part but this time the market comes first. The money wage was seen by Marx as being determined by free market exchange after which, within the factory and under the control of the capitalist managers, additional value is extracted from labour: *surplus* value which constitutes profits.

Marshall similarly acknowledged the importance of cooperation in production in the sense that Marx used it (see Marshall, 1920, pp. 71–2, and especially footnote 2) but did not stay 'to consider all the implications of this argument' (1920, p. 72). He placed strong emphasis on the need for more sophisticated forms of coordination as the division of labour led to increasingly differentiated labour and machines (Marshall, 1947, Book IV, ch. VIII), and paid close attention to the role of organisation in the coordination of the increasingly specialised and mutually dependent productive activities of labour and machines. Thus, while Marshall saw freedom of industry and enterprise as a central motivating and integrating force, market success depended on increased specialisation and the development of more effective industrial organisation, a process driven by the entrepreneurial and innovating owner-manager who:

> is the organiser in command of capital, who bears the uninsurable risk. He takes complex decisions with limited information. Superintendence is only a small part of this: coordination, imagination and risk bearing are fundamental. (O'Brien, 1990, pp. 72–3)

In much of economics, then, the central question of how to secure cooperation in production has been subsumed in theories of market exchange, on the one hand, and of managerial authority, on the other. Both the invisible hand of the market and the visible hand of management serve to coordinate and control the resources of production. In modern neoclassical economics, the market remains the principal coordinating device, with managerial organisation a reaction to the failure of markets to coordinate costlessly. By contrast, for the Marshallian and Marxist schools, markets and hierarchy are more clearly seen as complementary forms of governance or regulation, and capitalist management takes the lead in directing the organisation. But even then, many non-Marxist economists would agree about the central importance of the market in determining income distribution. Marshall, for example, dismissed Marx's argument that the employment relationship was essentially exploitative by arguing that employees were protected by competition between employers for labour. He countered Marx's claim that capitalist employers reap the benefits of cooperation between workers as surplus value by arguing that, 'so long as there is active competition between employers, each will be forced to pay as wages the equivalent of the net value that the 100 men, working cooperatively, add to the product' (1920, pp. 71–2).

In transaction cost economics, too, the market constantly reappears as the source of allocative efficiencies, notwithstanding attempts to develop a meaningful economic theory of institutions. The firm is, it seems, an institution of the market, but at the same time separate from it. One implication of Coasian analysis, extensively developed by Williamson (1985, 1996), is that high transaction costs may effectively reduce the scope of operation of the 'ordering principle' of the price mechanism; its effect must then be replicated by other organisational and institutional means if efficiency is to be achieved. However, some accounts in new institutional economics muddy the waters by seeking to maintain that 'firms are formed by and revised in markets' (Klein, Crawford and Alchian, 1978). The logical enough conclusion, for some, is that the firm is, in essence, a kind of market, in which an equilibrium is brought about through contractual exchange (Alchian and Demsetz, 1972; Jensen and Meckling, 1976).

But this seems incompatible with Coase's original insistence that the 'distinguishing mark of the firm is the *supersession* of the price mechanism' (Coase, 1988, p. 36 emphasis added). The appropriate conclusion to be drawn from such a characterisation is that cooperation in both intra-firm and inter-firm relations constitutes a distinct *mode of coordination* involving elements of hierarchy and mutual dependence between employer and employee, on the one hand, and the joint planning of product and process innovation on the other (Deakin and Wilkinson, 1996).

The central question to be addressed, then, is how precisely are cooperative relations maintained given the divergent interests of the contracting parties, in circumstances where the allocative mechanism of the price system operates distantly, at best. Much attention has recently focused on the role of *trust* as a mechanism for enhancing contractual security and facilitating long-term cooperation. One set of explanations sees trust as derived from interpersonal relations or cultural factors. Trust may be expected to emerge, then, within small communities or familial groups which share a common set of ethical values or moral principles (Fukuyama, 1995). Economic explanations, by contrast, see trust largely as the expression of the self-interested strategies of individual agents (Dasgupta, 1988), although it is arguable that this form of 'calculative trust is a contradiction in terms' (Williamson, 1996, p. 256). Game theory and principal–agent theory have provided extensive formal analysis of the strategies and incentive structures through which contracting parties can lend credibility to their mutual promises of future action. The guiding assumption here is that the parties will observe their respective contractual commitments as long as they calculate that it is in their self-interest to do so, but no further. This approach can be extended to incorporate a role for social norms, including those deriving from business ethics. Social norms and ethical values are seen as emerging on the basis of repeated exchange between self-interested agents; they are simply the expression, at any given time, of the evolution of business practice (Schotter, 1981).

While these approaches undoubtedly have certain insights to offer into the self-enforcing aspects of contracts, they neglect any role which may be played by more formal modes of economic governance, in particular the firm and the legal system. We now turn to a closer consideration of the role which may be played, in this respect, by the system of law governing commercial relationships.

COOPERATION AND CONTRACT LAW

According to Hayek, the market order is underpinned by a system of law whose function is to express and protect rights of property and contract. The 'spontaneous order' of the market (or, in Hayek's terminology, *catallaxy*) rests on the 'abstract rules of just conduct', or the rules of private law including those of the law of contract:

> It would . . . seem that wherever a Great Society has arisen, it has been made possible by a system of rules of just conduct which included what David Hume called 'the three fundamental laws of nature, *that of stability of possession, of its transference by consent*, and *of the performance of promises*', or . . . the essential content of all contemporary systems of private law. (Hayek, 1976, p. 40)

The principal function of private law is to provide a framework within which economic activity may be coordinated through individual action. In contrast to public or regulatory law which is 'designed to achieve particular ends, to supplement positive orders that something should be done or that particular results should be achieved' (Hayek, 1976, p. 125), private law does not seek to bring about a particular end-state or distribution of resources. In that sense, it is complementary to a market order in which the function of competition is to operate as a 'process of discovery'.

Hayek does not attempt to argue that there is no role whatsoever for public or regulatory law in relation to the market order. The issue, rather, is to identify the legitimate sphere of regulation. Forms of economic organisation – 'the family, the farm, the plant, the firm, the corporation and the various associations, and all the public institutions including government' – fulfil various economic functions, but 'in turn are integrated into a more comprehensive spontaneous order', that is to say, the spontaneous order of society (Hayek, 1976, p. 46). Hence, there is a need for a form of public law which underpins the internal relations of hierarchy and command within such organisations. What is illegitimate, in Hayek's view, is to apply this form of legal ordering to the regulation of spontaneous orders, such as the market. 'Specific commands ("interference") in a catallaxy create disorder and can never be just' (1976, pp. 128–9). Equally, 'attempts to "correct" the market order lead to its destruction' (Hayek, 1976, p. 142). This is because regulations which seek to correct for 'market failure', in an attempt to bring about a more allocatively efficient state of the world, merely block the *process* of competition as discovery which provides the means by which dispersed knowledge and information are put to use:

> the gist of the argument against 'interference' or 'intervention' in the market order . . . is that, although we can endeavour to improve a spontaneous order by revising the general rules on which it rests, and can supplement its results by the efforts of various organisations, we cannot improve the results by specific commands that deprive its members of the possibility of using their knowledge for their own purposes (Hayek, 1973, pp. 50–1).

Hayek's argument would seem to leave little or no space for the imposition of restrictions upon freedom of contract, even of the kind which might be justified by appeals to informal business ethics, let alone attempts to regulate private contractual power through law. His analysis has particular resonance within systems of common law, which have a tendency to view regulatory interventions (such as those of employment law or consumer law) as alien intrusions into the body of private law. Hayek's strictures against trade union legislation were anticipated by Sir Frederick Pollock's description of the Trade Disputes Act 1906 as 'a violent empirical operation on the body politic' (Pollock, 1908, p. v). But it is not just regulatory legislation which struggles for acceptance; the English judges have only recently refused to give legal effect to a contractual obligation between commercial parties to negotiate towards an agreement in good faith. The effect of the decision of the House of Lords in *Walford v. Miles*[1] is that a duty to negotiate *voluntarily undertaken by the parties themselves* could not be enforced in the courts, on the grounds of uncertainty. Still less would an English court acknowledge the existence of a general *implied* duty to bargain in good faith in commercial relations. Although this idea has been accepted in certain instances (see Brownsword, 1997), there has been strong resistance to its adoption in commercial relations which contain no element of inequality of bargaining power.[2] It has been suggested that notwithstanding its limitations, the 'classical' or minimalist model of contract law is capable of being effectively used in the majority of commercial transactions whether they are short-term or long-term, precisely because it gives the parties substantial scope to make their own agreement and to exclude or to enhance the power of court-based remedies as they see fit: 'apart from being aware of the reasons why parties to long term contracts express their obligations in broad, flexible terms and giving effect to these clauses, long term contracts do not demand distinctive regulation by the courts or by [the legislature]' (McKendrick, 1995, p. 333).

It is interesting, then, to find that the idea of contractual good faith, which the English courts find so puzzling, plays a central role in the commercial law of the civilian systems of mainland Europe, and that one of its principal applications concerns long-term relations between firms. In Germany, Article 242 of the Civil Code (the *Bürgerliches Gesetzbuch* or BGB) has come to have an extensive influence throughout the body of commercial contract law. The immediate aim of Article 242 is 'to spell out what performance entails, for example, to show that one need not accept delivery at an inconvenient time' (Leser, 1982, p. 135), but through the interpretations of the courts its function has become one of 'giving legal force to broad ethical values' (ibid., p. 138). One of the most important areas in which Article 242 has been applied is to require parties to renegotiate long-term contracts which have been subject to an unanticipated event, such as an unexpected rise in prices or fall in demand, in such a way as to go far beyond what would normally be permitted by the common law doctrine of frustration, which relieves the parties from future performance but only in a much more restricted range of circumstances (Dawson, 1983, 1984). In Italian contract law, similarly, it has been said that the application of the notion of good faith means that performance of contractual obligations

must take place with the loyal and honest cooperation of the parties to achieve the reciprocal benefits agreed in the contract. Only in that way can the contract play its part as a useful private mechanism in the context of the 'social solidarity' which is the inescapable duty of all citizens under article 2 of the [1949] Constitution. (Criscuoli and Pugsley, 1991, p. 142)

The role of good faith in these systems is not confined to this high level of legal abstraction. In Germany, it operates at the micro level of inter-firm relations by virtue of the close relationship between the Civil Code, legislation governing terms in standard-form contracts, and the contents of the standard-form contracts themselves which are agreed at industry level. The general effect is to confer a very high level of stability upon the normative framework within which inter-firm relations are conducted. Firms rarely seek to vary either the standard-term agreements which derive from the trade association or those implied terms which operate as a matter of law; indeed, there is considerable doubt as to whether they may, legally, contract out of those norms which the courts would read into the contract (Casper, 1997). This is in stark contrast to the position under English law, where the parties to commercial agreements enjoy, from this point of view, almost complete freedom of contract: judicially implied terms and the clauses of standard-term agreements operate only at the level of default rules which can be varied or omitted as the parties wish. The principal difference between the systems, then, resides not so much in the 'quantity' or 'weight' of legal intervention (assuming that this can be evaluated in any relevant way), but in the way in which the different elements of the institutional framework – legal doctrine, industry-level standards, individual contractual agreements – relate to one another. In Germany the relationship between the levels is one of a high degree of functional interdependence, with normative influences flowing in both directions so that the legal system is affected by the content of agreements as well as vice versa. In Italy, despite the operation of a similar principle of good faith at the level of contract law, the perceived expense and rigidity of the court system means that it is less relied on by firms, which tend instead to make use of softer industry-level standards and conventional understandings of good business practice. In Britain, neither legal doctrine nor the terms of industry-level assocations are particularly important by comparison with the scope given to individual parties to 'make their own agreements'. But the question must be whether the autonomy enjoyed by contracting parties in the British system is more apparent than real. Is it possible, in a 'voluntarist' system such as the British, for firms to achieve the kind of extended collaboration which is more actively encouraged in systems which clothe the values of cooperation in institutional form?

This question was investigated as part of the Cambridge study of vertical inter-firm contracting in the mid-1990s.[3] Case studies of contractual practice were carried out for two contrasting engineering sectors (mining machinery and kitchen equipment) in three countries (Germany, Britain and Italy). It was found that the institutional framework was a much more important source of differences in contractual form and performance outcomes than the differences between the two sectors in terms of market structure, ease of entry and exit, stability of demand and technological requirements. The study found, first of all, that differences in the institutional framework for contracting (as described above) were reflected in the types of contracts which firms normally used for their long-term trading relationships with buyers and suppliers. Contracts in Germany tended to be longer-term, in the sense of spanning a number of discrete exchanges; they also tended to be more complex, in the sense of making provision for future contingencies. Hardship clauses, requiring the parties to renegotiate the contract in the event of changed circumstaces, were common in Germany, but were almost unknown in the other two countries. In both Britain and Italy, most agreements tended to be order-specific or, at best, were loose 'framework' or 'requirement' contracts under which the buyer could place orders as required. British firms were the least likely to have formal performance standards based on audits and rating systems incorporated into contracts.

A further difference related to the role of standard-form agreements. In Britain, in particular, it was common for larger buyer firms to seek to customise the normal industry-level terms, often insisting on the insertion of terms which exposed their subcontractors and suppliers to a high level of risk. Suppliers reported that they were obliged to accept this practice as a condition of continuing to do business with these customers. Instability in this aspect of the institutional framework was put down to the effects of the sharp recession of the early 1990s and also to privatisation in the electricity and mining industries, which had led to a reassessment of previously established standard-form agreements.

In each country, firms could be seen to use contracts as mechanisms for future planning and, to a lesser extent, as means for inducing future performance through the possibility of legal sanctions. However, the relationship between formal contracts and flexibility in performance differed between the three countries. The predominant British strategy could be described as *flexibility outside contract*, in the sense that informal contacts and understandings often arose independently of, and often in contradiction to, the terms of an agreement. In Germany, on the other hand, the approach could be described as *flexibility beyond contract*, where flexibility took account of the contract in the sense of filling in gaps or providing for additional elements of performance. In Italy, the absence of 'hard' standards and the cost of using the legal system to enforce contracts was made up for, in part, by the presence of widely accepted social norms governing quality and reliability and by collective provision of public goods, as well as by an implicit threat to cease trading with any firm which failed to match up to these expectations. The apparent advantages, in the British system, of minimal regulation, had to be weighed against the increased costs to firms which arose from the absence of collective provision (in relation, for example, to skills training) and the tendency for certain low-trust practices, such as late payment of debts, to become acceptable.

This can be seen from a striking finding to the effect that the use of the legal system to resolve disputes, with all the costs which it would entail, was least likely in the most highly juridified environment, namely that of the German firms. Contrary to some earlier studies which suggested that legal formality was often negligible or non-existent in buyer–supplier relations

(Macaulay, 1963), the firms in the Cambridge study almost all said that they contracted on the basis of a written and legally binding agreement (even if, in some cases, the agreement was only an order form; but not much should be read into this last point, as respondents who used such documents were almost invariably aware that they constituted contracts). The only exception related to a number of British kitchen furniture firms, who dispensed with formal documentation altogether in favour of informal understandings. German respondents made the most frequent references to the role of normative influences, in particular the standard-form contracts of industry-level trade assocations, in shaping contractual practice; they expressed the greatest confidence in their ability to predict the level of legal costs; and they were the most likely to carry insurance against legal liability. They were also the least likely to take legal action for breach of contract, even to recover debts. By contrast, legal action for non-payment of the agreed price was regarded as highly likely in Britain in both the sectors studied, but in particular in the kitchen furniture sector which exhibited the lowest level of contract formality of any of the sectors studied. A number of British firms in both sectors complained about the practice of late payment of debts and many looked on legal action to claim the price as a matter of first, rather than last, resort.

The Cambridge study also provides some pointers to the relationship between contract form and economic performance. Importantly, no significant correlations were found between the adoption by *individual* firms of one of the features of close cooperation (such as financial assistance, quality audits or longer-term contracts) and their performance as measured by increases in turnover and/or employment in the five years before the date of the interview. Both within the sample as a whole, and within individual countries, the incidence of 'relational' contracting was randomly distributed among successful and less successful firms. However, this is not the whole story, since the findings also indicate significant differences at the level of *industries* in the competitiveness of firms. These results suggest that the location of a firm makes an important difference to its performance in terms of employment and turnover, and may also affect its ability to offer stable employment to a larger number of workers: 39 per cent of the British firms reported growth of turnover in real terms in the period in question as opposed to 61 per cent of German and 50 per cent of Italian firms. In relation to employment, 27 per cent of British firms reported a rise, compared to 53 per cent of German firms and 67 per cent of Italian firms. Across the British sample as a whole, performance with regard to employment was polarised between a substantial group reporting rapid growth, at one extreme, and one reporting rapid decline at the other. Another interpretation of the British data would be that improved turnover was often accompanied by downsizing of the workforce.

A far larger percentage of British firms than in either of the other two countries had no overseas customers, although, at the opposite end of the scale, a sizeable group of British firms had more than half of its customers overseas. In other words, a small group of highly successful firms at one extreme is set against a long tail of underperformers at the other. While the best British firms compete more than effectively with their overseas counterparts, the average level of performance is lower. Industry-level data confirm this picture: import penetration was lower and the proportion of domestic production exported was higher in Germany than in Britain in the period covered for both the industries in the survey.[4]

Within industries, then, the *general* level of performance of firms differed; in Germany, the institutional framework, by requiring firms to come up to a certain quality threshold as a *de facto* precondition of entry to the trade, improved the level of performance of average firms, and thereby enhanced the capacity of the system as a whole in two ways: it was better able to meet domestic requirements and to build up a large export capacity. This suggests that the export performance of firms is linked not only to the nature of consumer demand in their domestic markets, but also to the domestic institutional conditions under which production takes place. The variations in performance within each system reflect the managerial and other capabilities of individual firms; the institutional influences which serve to promote quality in a given system are necessary but not sufficient conditions for its achievement at the level of the firm. But even if individual firms vary in their capacity to compete, it is still the case that such institutional support is a prerequisite for the enhanced competitiveness of the system *as a whole*.

CONCLUSION: TRUST AND THE INSTITUTIONAL FRAMEWORK

In Hayek's account, private law underpins the ordering principle of the market by protecting the personal domain of each individual agent and securing the conditions upon which exchange can take place, thereby releasing resources to more general use and initiating the process of market discovery through competition. Restraints on freedom of disposition and freedom of contract, unless they have as their purpose the control of collusion and other forms of anti-competitive behaviour (see Hayek, 1979, p. 15), are to be condemned. We must put aside, on this occasion, certain powerful critiques of this position – such as the observation that the regulatory effort needed to put in place a functioning market order may involve the state in forms of intervention at least as extensive as those which Hayekians associate with state management of the economy (see McCormick, 1986). For present purposes, we may focus on Hayek's account of cooperation. Hayek's caricature of planned cooperation as a primitive form of coordination is contradicted by the evidence that high-trust relations, both within and between firms, are an important source of competitive advantage, and that these relations, in turn, rest upon an institutional framework of a particular kind.

The hallmark of high-trust productive systems is that the parties give open-ended commitments to cooperate in order to achieve returns which can only be expected to mature over a long period. The complexity of the network of relationships within a productive system and the intensity of the competitive pressures to which producers are subject mean that the single workplace or even the single firm is unlikely to provide a secure enough base for creating and maintaining the long-term commitments necessary for establishing and sustaining trust and cooperation. The importance of the institutional framework lies in its capacity to generate the circumstances under which relations based on trust can emerge. The more effective it is in this respect, the more successful it will be in improving the availability of information and lifting the costs of conflict, monitoring and risk from individual firms. In effect, the *hardware* of trust is established by investment in supportive laws, rules, norms and standards, while the *software* of trust is developed by a learning process by which the reliability of these norms from the point of view of the parties to trading relationships is established. But both elements are needed if productive systems are to survive and grow.

This is not to suggest that systems based on rigid institutional norms, in which values of good business practice are embodied, necessarily enjoy a competitive advantage. Normative systems must themselves evolve to meet changing circumstances, or they will threaten the stability of the productive organisations which rely upon them. But this is quite different from the argument that, under the pressure of 'globalisation', national economies are moving in the direction charted by the Anglo-American model. The increasing interpenetration of economic activity has so far done little to reduce the diversity of institutional forms within developed economies.

A consideration of the conditions necessary for creating high-trust relationships suggests that the problem extends beyond the workplace to include the network of linkages which constitute the productive system and to the economic environment in which the productive system is embedded. The creation of high-trust relationships is inhibited by two types of uncertainty: social and economic. Social uncertainty could be countered by extending the range of theory, or by contracts or by the establishing of rules, standards and norms to rule out practices which created social uncertainty.

Such arrangements could also prove useful in countering economic uncertainty. However, the consequence of economic change may be so all-embracing that wider national and international policies, rules, norms, standards and institutions may be necessary to constrain its potentially disruptive effects and to guide it into creative channels.

There can be no doubt that the adversarial relations generated by deregulation are inimical to the development of trust and cooperation. Neoliberal solutions are now being pressed on the economies which took the lead in demonstrating the competitive advantage of cooperative forms of production organisation. There is no convincing evidence to suggest that the Anglo-American economies have managed to escape from their long-term decline through an intensified dose of the adversarialism to which that decline can be largely attributed in the first place. If those countries which demonstrated the advantage of trust in productive relations decide to go down the neoliberal route, the effects can only be guessed at. But it would not be surprising if they included growing inequality, poverty and productive inefficiency.

Notes

1. [1992] 2 AC 128.
2. The one area, above all, in which the concept of good faith has entered the common law concerns contracts covered by the Unfair Terms in Consumer Contracts Regulations 1995, a measure which implements a European directive based largely on German law.
3. See Arrighetti, Bachmann and Deakin, 1997; Lane, 1997; Burchell and Wilkinson, 1997; Deakin, Lane and Wilkinson, 1997; Deakin and Wilkinson, 1997. The account of the research in the text, below, draws on these papers, to which the reader is referred for a more detailed account of the methodology employed.
4. See Deakin, Lane and Wilkinson, 1997, and Deakin and Wilkinson, 1997, for the relevant details.

References

Alchian, A. and Demsetz, H. (1972) 'Production, Information Costs, and Economic Organisation', *American Economic Review*, 62, pp. 777–95.
Arrighetti, A., Bachmann, R. and Deakin, S. (1997) 'Contract Law, Social Norms and Inter-Firm Cooperation', *Cambridge Journal of Economics*, 21, pp. 171–96.
Brownsword, R. (1997) 'Contract Law, Cooperation, and Good Faith: The Movement from Static to Dynamic Market-Individualism', in S. Deakin and J. Michie (eds), *Contracts, Cooperation and Competition* (Oxford: Clarendon Press).

Burchell, B. and Wilkinson, F. (1997) 'Trust, Business Relationships and the Con-
tractual Environment', *Cambridge Journal of Economics*, 21, pp. 217–38.
Casper, S. (1997) 'National Institutional Frameworks and Innovative Industrial
Organisation: Supplier Relationships in the United States and Germany', in T.
Kochan and K. Wever (eds), *Mutual Learning* (forthcoming); paper presented to
the ESRC Centre for Business Research seminar, February 1997.
Coase, R.H. (1937) 'The Nature of the Firm', *Economica* (NS), 4, pp. 386–405.
Coase, R.H. (1988) *The Firm, the Market and the Law* (Chicago, Ill: University of
Chicago Press).
Criscuoli, G. and Pugsley, D. (1991) *The Italian Law of Contract* (Naples: Jovene).
Dasgupta, P. (1988) 'Trust as a Commodity', in D. Gambetta (ed.), *Trust: Making
and Breaking Cooperative Relations* (Oxford: Blackwell).
Dawson, J. (1983) 'Judicial Revision of Frustrated Contracts: Germany', *Boston
University Law Review*, vol. 63, pp. 1039–68.
Dawson, J. (1984) 'Judicial Revision of Frustrated Contracts: USA', *Boston Univer-
sity Law Review*, vol. 64, pp. 1–38.
Deakin, S. and Wilkinson, F. (1996) 'Contracts, Cooperation and Trust: The Role of
the Institutional Framework', in D. Campbell and P. Vincent-Jones (eds), *Contract
and Economic Organisation Socio-Legal Initiatives* (Aldershot: Dartmouth).
Deakin, S. and Wilkinson, F. (1997) 'Contract Law and the Economics of Inter-
Organisational Trust', in C. Lane and R. Bachmann (eds), *Trust Within and Be-
tween Organisations* (Oxford: Oxford University Press).
Deakin, S., Lane, C. and Wilkinson, F. (1997) 'Performance Standards in Supplier
Relations: Relational Strategies, Organisational Processes and Institutional
Structures', paper presented to the EMOT Workshop on Performance Standards,
Wissenschaftszentrum Berlin, January 1997.
Fukuyama, F. (1995) *Trust: The Social Virtues and the Creation of Property* (Lon-
don: Hamish Hamilton).
Hayek, F. (1973) *Rules and Order* (London: Routledge).
Hayek, F. (1976) *Law, Legislation and Liberty vol.2: The Mirage of Social Justice.*
(London: Routledge).
Hayek, F. (1979) *The Political Order of a Free People* (London: Routledge).
Hayek, F. (1988) *Socialism: The Fatal Conceit* (London: Routledge).
Jensen, M. and Meckling, W. (1976) 'Theory of the Firm: Managerial Behaviour,
Agency Costs and Ownership Structure', *Journal of Financial Economics*, 3, pp.
305–60.
Klein, B., Crawford, R.G., Alchian, A. (1978) 'Vertical Integration, Appropriable
Rents and the Competetive Contracting Process', *Journal of Law and Economics*,
vol. 21, pp. 297–326.
Lane, C. (1997) 'The Social Regulation of Inter-Firm Relations in Britain and Ger-
many: Market Rules, Legal Norms and Technical Standards', *Cambridge Journal
of Economics*, 21, pp. 197–216.
Leser, H. (1982) 'The Principle of Good Faith: Article 242 BGB', in N. Horn, H.
Kotz and H. Leser, trans. T. Weir, *German Private and Commercial Law: An In-
troduction* (Oxford: Clarendon Press).
Macaulay, S. (1963) 'Non-contractual Relations in Business: A Preliminary
Study', *American Sociological Review*, 45, pp. 55–69.
McCormick, N. (1986) 'Spontaneous Order and the Rule of Law: Some Problems',
Jahrbuch des öffentlichen Rechts der Gegenwart, 35, pp. 1–12.

McKendrick, E. (1995) 'The Regulation of Long-term Contracts in English Law.' in J. Beatson and D. Friedmann (eds), *Good Faith and Fault in Contract Law* (Oxford: Clarendon Press).

Marshall, A. (1920) *Industry and Trade* (London: Macmillan).

Marshall, A. (1947) *Principles of Economics*, 8th edn (London: Macmillan).

Marx, K. (1974) *Capital* (London: Lawrence & Wishart).

O'Brien, D. (1990) 'Marshall's Industrial Analysis', *Scottish Journal of Political Economy*, 37, pp. 61–84.

Pagano, U. (1985) *Work and Welfare in Economic Theory* (Oxford: Blackwell).

Pollock, F. (1908) *Law of Torts*, 8th edn (London: Stevens).

Schotter, M. (1981) *The Economic Theory of Social Institutions* (Cambridge: CUP).

Smith, A. (1974) *An Inquiry into the Nature and Causes of the Wealth of Nations* (Harmondsworth: Penguin).

Tarling, R. and Wilkinson, F. (1987) 'The Level, Structure and Flexibility of Costs', in R. Tarling and F. Wilkinson (eds), *Flexibility in Labour Markets* (London: Academic Press).

Wakefield, E. (1835) *Notes to A. Smith, An Inquiry into the Nature and Causes of The Wealth of Nations* (London: Knight).

Wilkinson, F. (1983) 'Productive Systems', *Cambridge Journal of Economics*, 7, pp. 413–29.

Williamson, O. (1983) 'Credible Commitments: Using Hostages to Support Exchange', *American Economic Review*, 73, pp. 519–40.

Williamson, O. (1985) *The Economic Institutions of Capitalism* (New York: Free Press).

Williamson, O. (1996) *The Mechanisms of Governance* (Oxford: Oxford University Press).

5 The Role of Voluntary Codes of Practice in Setting Ethics

Adrian Cadbury

BACKGROUND

Having spent a good deal of my time since 1992 on codes of practice, I am understandably deeply interested in whether they work! This seems to me to be the first question to be attempted, before moving on to whether they advance standards of behaviour in an ethical sense. I take 'voluntary' to cover all forms of code which are not statutorily enforced. While the chapter will touch on the, perhaps surprisingly, wide range of codes which fall under this definition of voluntary, it will focus on those like the *Code of Best Practice* of the Committee on the Financial Aspects of Corporate Governance (referred to as the 'Corporate Governance Committee') and on company codes.

What is it that such codes aim to do, to whom are they addressed, what is their nature and how far can they be said to achieve their objectives? Quite apart from assessing whether those of us involved in these matters have been wasting time and paper, an important reason why this issue of the effectiveness of voluntary codes deserves debate is that it is an approach which is neither understood nor accepted by our partners in the European Union. Matters which are dealt with in the UK under the *Takeover Code* or the *British Codes of Advertising and Sales Promotion* come under the law on the continent of Europe.[1] The advantages which, in the UK, we claim for codes – speed of resolution, swift response to changing issues, avoidance of the costs (and frequently the irrelevance) of the legal system – carry no weight in the rest of Europe, largely because they are outside the experience of those who have always worked in a regulatory climate. The code approach will not survive within the EU unless and until a more compelling case can be made for it.

NATURE OF CODES

International Codes

Codes can be divided by the audiences which they seek to address. There are international codes, such as *The Code of Ethics on International Business for Christians, Muslims and Jews – The Interfaith Declaration* (1993). Other examples at this level include the *Minnesota Principles* (1994) and the *Caux Roundtable Principles for Business* (1992). They are a response to a shrinking world and to the emergence of global markets. Their aim is explicitly to raise standards of business behaviour and to overcome national differences of view as to where the ethical boundaries of business behaviour lie. The Interfaith Declaration, for example, states:

> This Declaration is offered to business people, business organisations, and those who advise companies as a basis for sound ethical business practice. (Appendix)

Such codes score highly on ethical purpose, but have no effective mechanism for encouraging compliance. Their practical consequence lies in their contribution to a worldwide understanding of ethical principles.

National Codes

At the next level come codes which are devised to meet particular issues within national boundaries, although their influence may spread more widely. Current examples are the *Code of Best Practice of the Corporate Governance Committee* and the *Code of Practice on Directors' Remuneration* (1995). Another example from a different field is the *Report of the Committee on Standards in Public Life* (Nolan Committee, 1995). In addition, however, there is a wide range of other codes applying to specific trades, to commercial services like advertising and to business situations such as take-overs and mergers.

The ethical content of these codes reflects their purpose. The Nolan Committee's first report set out a code of conduct for MPs. It was, therefore, designed to establish what was and what was not acceptable parliamentary behaviour and so it had a high ethical content. That report also serves as a reminder that what is acceptable changes through time and these shifts in perception are not always obvious to those to whom they apply. Equally, codes of conduct for those selling second-hand cars, for estate agents or for those advertising to the public have an ethical side to them, but their primary purpose is to promote consumer confidence in the activities concerned and perhaps to act as an insurance against potential statutory regulation. They are aimed at raising standards of business behaviour for understandable commercial reasons; any lifting of ethical standards is a by-product of this aim.

Club Rules

There is, however, a subset of this category of code which deserves consideration. These are what might be termed 'club rules'. The City of London, to use a shorthand expression for the financial services centred there, worked in the past to an unwritten code. The City's system of self-regulation, in so far as it existed, was largely exercised through peer pressure along the lines of a traditional English club. The rules of the club were never codified and were set by example. They depended on the lead given, as to standards of conduct, by the heads of City firms and by their own maintenance of these standards. The penalty for breach of the rules was expulsion from the club and exclusion from City activities; a somewhat similar sanction to that which can be applied under the Takeover Code.

The advantages and disadvantages of the club approach and the reasons why it failed to survive in the City are worth touching on. Its plus was that it side-stepped the costs and inefficiencies of an external regulatory structure. The rules could be applied speedily and the sanctions against transgression were effective. The downside of governance by a club is that the rules are likely to reflect what suits the members, rather than those who in commercial terms are their clients, that they may be used to exclude 'outsiders' and that they will fail to move with the times.

From an ethical point of view, the City's code of conduct was open to question. It sanctioned, in the past, such practices as rigging the market for new issues and more enduringly insider dealing. Rigging the market came to a head with the Steam Loop case of 1890. The City's argument to the court was a familiar one – it was accepted practice; everyone did it. As one of the defendants put it,

> You have only to ask anyone about new companies, if it [that is, creating a false premium in their shares] is not a necessity. (Dennett, 1989, p. 102)

The judge took a very different view:

> I do say, that if persons, for their own purposes of speculation, create an artificial price in the market by transactions which are not real, but are made

at a nominal premium merely for the purpose of inducing the public to take shares, they are guilty of as gross a fraud as has ever been committed. (Dennett, 1989, p. 103)

William May of Slaughter and May, one of the defendants, described this decision as a 'magnificent miscarriage of justice' (Dennett, 1989, p. 104). The reality was that the City's code had failed to keep pace with the movement of opinion as to where the balance should be struck between the smooth working of the capital market and the interests of those who made their living from that market on the one hand and the right to fair dealing and to objective information of those who invested in the market on the other. Clubs live in their own world and may fail to perceive that the boundaries within which they carry on their being have shifted. The need for that perception applies far more widely, hence the importance of independent members on boards of all kinds.

The other reflection on the ethics of the City club rules is that they seem to have taken as their text, 'Thou shalt not muzzle the ox when he treadeth out the corn' (Deuteronomy 25: 4). Thus the rules on insider dealing were designed not to stop the practice, but to keep it under control. Since those working in City firms were privy to market-sensitive information, it was accepted that they would use it for their own benefit and the rules were aimed at not allowing such self-serving to get out of hand.

What broke the club system was the rapid expansion in the numbers of those employed in the financial services sector, which meant that the personal influence of the heads of City firms, mainly partnerships, was diluted and no more formal methods of conveying what standards were expected of the members of their staff were put in its place. At the same time many of these new entrants had different goals and views about how to achieve them from those of their predecessors. Finally, there was the internationalisation of the City and an influx of foreign firms – clubs depend for their cohesion on shared values.

Company Codes

Company codes summarise the standards of conduct expected of the employees of an individual firm. They need to be seen in the context of the broader levels of code just described. Thus a travel agency will draw up its own code in the light of the code for its industry. Codes at the national and at the company level should be mutually reinforcing, with company codes addressing those issues particularly pertinent to the nature of their business; for example, retailers' codes will cover inducements to buyers and the codes of financial service firms' exposure to risk. The report of the Corporate Governance Committee gave its support to company codes, stating:

It is important that all employees should know what standards are expected of them. We regard it as good practice for boards of directors to draw up codes of ethics or statements of business practice and to publish them both internally and externally. (para. 4.29, p. 26)

AIMS OF NATIONAL AND COMPANY CODES

Code of Best Practice

Focusing now on codes such as the one published by the Corporate Governance Committee and company codes, what are their respective aims? In the case of the Corporate Governance Committee, the concern of its sponsors – the Financial Reporting Council, the London Stock Exchange and the leading accountancy firms – was the perceived lack of confidence in company reports and accounts and the audit statements attached to them. This followed some failures of prominent firms whose financial reports prior to their collapse appeared to give no forewarning of the true state of their affairs. Thus a simple test of the effectiveness of the Code of Best Practice of the Corporate Governance Committee would be the degree to which investor confidence in London as a financial centre improved in the wake of the committee's work.

What, however, transpired was that events like the Maxwell affair, the failure of the BCCI Bank and the growing controversy over directors' pay unexpectedly pushed the committee's deliberations into the limelight. Although set up to make recommendations on the financial aspects of corporate governance, the committee was increasingly expected to broaden its agenda. What had looked at the outset like a technical report to be published and then decently laid to rest came to have a wider significance.

A point to keep in mind over this shift in the role of the committee is that the code was addressed to boards of directors, a group which had had no direct hand in establishing the committee. The committee did make recommendations to the accounting profession and to shareholders, but the heart of its report was the Code of Best Practice. The code had to attract the support of those who were being asked to follow it, even though they had not commissioned it. This is contrary to the general rule that those who are expected to abide by codes should initiate them.

In judging the committee's effectiveness, a broader test than simply its effect on investor confidence has to be applied. Against that background, the aims of the Code of Best Practice could be summarised as providing a checklist for boards of directors to measure their standing in matters of governance and an agenda for shareholders in their dialogues with boards. The code is a set of governance principles or guidelines based literally on best UK practice. It provided a lead as to the standards expected of company boards at a time of uncertainty and this is why it was not dismissed out of hand by those who might otherwise have considered it unwarranted or irrelevant. An ethical element runs through those standards, but it was not the committee's purpose to set ethical benchmarks, nor would it have been the right body to do so, given that it was constituted for a different task.

Company Codes

Turning now to company codes, they are drawn up to provide guidance to employees. They aim to assist those working in a company to know what standards of conduct are expected of them and how to deal with the kind of problems which they may come across in the course of their duties. Thus they need to be individually drafted, preferably with an input from those to whom they will apply.

From a company's point of view, codes of conduct are a form of safeguard for their reputation. They strengthen what are otherwise unwritten rules of behaviour, picked up by observation of the way things are done in a particular business environment. The issues addressed by company codes will have an ethical content and those which are specifically labelled codes of ethics clearly do have the raising of ethical standards as an aim. The general test for company codes, however, has to be how far they are adhered to and whether they assist employees in knowing how to act when faced with uncertainty as to the right course to take.

COMPLIANCE

Code of Best Practice

This leads on to the whole question of compliance – how far do codes influence the thinking and actions of those to whom they are addressed? The Corporate Governance Committee's Code of Best Practice had the support of the London Stock Exchange in respect of publicly quoted companies and all of the broadly similar codes drawn up in other countries, except the *Vienot Report* (CNPF/AFEP, 1995) in France, have received similar backing.

The listing obligation which the Stock Exchange introduced on the publication of the Code of Best Practice centred on disclosure. To retain their listing on the London Stock Exchange, publicly quoted companies registered in this country have had, since mid-1993, to make a statement of how far they comply with the code and to give reasons for areas of non-compliance. Companies do not have to comply; the requirement is to make a compliance statement. Compliance itself is a matter between boards and their shareholders. The code is not prescriptive. It recognises the wide diversity of companies, of boards of directors and of their chairpersons. The code sets out governance principles and it is for boards to implement those principles in ways which make sense in their particular circumstances and which carry the support of their shareholders.

Fears were expressed at the outset that, although companies had the freedom not to comply with sections of the code, non-compliance, however rational, might affect their share price adversely. This problem does not seem to have arisen in practice. Smaller firms, in particular, found that they could opt out of those parts of the code which they felt added no value to their system of governance, without any damage to their share price, provided that they explained their reasons for non-compliance.

Although the focus was on compliance by quoted companies, the committee's report added, 'we would encourage as many other companies as possible to aim at meeting its requirements' (para. 3.1, p. 16). The degree to which this encouragement has been followed would be hard to determine, but reasons for non-quoted companies to follow the code could include that the code guidelines made business sense, that the company had its sights on becoming listed at a future date and that compliance would give assurance to employees, creditors, suppliers or customers that the business was soundly directed and controlled.

The essential point is that the committee is not the arbiter of whether the code has been effectively followed. Companies have to satisfy their shareholders, not the committee. The committee has relied on what might best be called 'market regulation' to bring about acceptance of its recommendations. By that is meant that it will prove to be in the self-interest of boards to comply and therefore in the interests of their shareholders to encourage them to do so. The foundation of the code and of the committee's other proposals is the need for disclosure. Those with rights and responsibilities towards companies can only exercise them effectively if they have the information which they need in order to do so. This theme of the necessity for openness, for transparency, runs through codes of all kinds at all levels.

There is an important difference of principle between the Corporate Governance Committee's Code and the *Code of Practice on Directors' Remuneration*. The latter code recommended not only that the London Stock Exchange should make it a listing obligation for companies to publish a compliance statement in respect of Section A of the code, but also that there should be 'a specific obligation to comply with the provisions in Section B of the Code . . . and with provision C10 of the Code' (para. 2.4, p. 13). There is, therefore, a mandatory element in the Remuneration Code, not present in the Governance Code.

Company Codes

Compliance with company codes will reflect their purpose and the manner in which they have been drawn up. If their purpose is largely protective, that is to say, codes handed down from on high to be called on in defence of the board in case of need, there will be little incentive for those to whom they are directed to take note of them. The same could be said for codes taken off the shelf, so to speak. On the other hand, there are cogent reasons for following codes which address issues of concern to those to whom they apply and which they have had a hand in formulating. The motives for complying with company codes will thus turn on their nature, on the reasons for introducing them and the degree to which they are part of the mainstream of the business, for example, by featuring in the appraisal or promotion process.

SETTING OF STANDARDS

Before considering in more detail the effect of codes on governance standards, it is appropriate to reflect on how the standards to which boards work are determined. Companies operate within boundaries which are set externally and internally. First, there stands the law and the regulations which apply to companies. Then, for quoted companies, there are the shareholders to whom the directors report on their stewardship in general meeting. More generally, there is the influence of public opinion, expressed by employees, customers and the media, in defining what is or is not acceptable behaviour for a particular company at a particular time. The views of shareholders and of the public as to the appropriateness of a company's standards of behaviour move with the times. A clear example of this kind of shift has been the relatively recent building-in of environmental considerations into the standards by which the companies are judged.

Internally, boards of directors are responsible for setting the standards of governance and conduct which apply in their enterprises. While the prime responsibility for business standards lies with boards, shareholders, those who advise shareholders, those who comment on company matters and the wider public have their part to play in defining the boundaries of acceptable conduct. To take a specific example, a Board of Trade enquiry found Robert Maxwell unfit to head a public company. Yet directors joined his board, shareholders invested in his businesses and banks lent him money. They did not have to support him in these ways, but they chose to do so. By setting aside the rules under which the enquiry had judged him, they substituted a lower level of business conduct in their place and thus contributed to a reduction in accepted standards.

Whether as a consequence or as a cause of the growing interest in corporate governance, specialised agencies have been called into being to advise investors in particular, but the public in general as well, on what standards of conduct to expect from companies and their boards. Pensions and Investment Research Consultants, for example, provide pension funds with advice on governance issues and on how to vote at general meetings. Single-interest groups call for consumer boycotts of companies which offend the particular interest which they represent. There is more media coverage and more critical media coverage of company affairs than in the past.

Corporate governance has become an accepted subject for academic research, research which will in its turn influence the definition, setting and monitoring of standards. Organisations such as Public Concern at Work[2] have been formed to respond to the enquiries of those who wish to raise doubts about the acceptability of practices at their place of work, but have been unable to do so through the normal channels. On the international scene, Transparency International[3] was launched in 1993 and its initial task was to collate codes of conduct from around the world and to encourage firms to draw them up because, in their words, 'we believe these to be essential in the implementation of strategies against corruption'. Employee, public and shareholder opinion is thus being mobilised to influence business standards in a more organised way than in the past.

Against that background, have business standards changed? Standards are never static, because they reflect shifts in where the line should be drawn between acceptable and unacceptable behaviour in relation to various aspects of business conduct. The controversy in the UK in the 1990s over directors' pay is an example of an economic and ethical issue in flux. It is to be hoped that out of that debate, clearer guidelines will emerge over how executive remuneration should be set and over the limits within which executive pay packages should fall. A major change in attitudes in this matter has been the increasing accent on bonus and incentive payments of all kinds. Competitive pressures and pay for performance are bound to have their effect on business behaviour – that is what they are designed to do – but it needs to be appreciated that their consequences go beyond forming a basis for setting remuneration.

An extreme example of the degree to which the emphasis on winning has altered standards of acceptability was Boesky's 1986 Commencement Address to the University of California at Berkeley, when he said:

> Greed is all right . . . I want you to know that. I think greed is healthy. You can be greedy and feel good about yourself.[4]

The change in standards is exemplified more by the choice which the university authorities made, by inviting Boesky to give the address and thus set the tone for students about to embark on their courses, than by his expression of his personal philosophy. Codes, therefore, need to take account of the current competitive climate with its emphasis on winning and should aim to ensure that it is not at all costs.

EFFECTS OF CODES

Quoted Companies

The Committee on the Financial Aspects of Corporate Governance published its *Monitor on Compliance* with the Code of Best Practice in May 1995. This set out the degree to which the code recommendations had been put into effect by quoted companies. In doing so, it established a benchmark against which future changes in governance structures and processes can be assessed. By its nature, a monitor of this kind captures changes in the structure of boards rather than changes in board process, although the committee's aim was to influence both. It is not possible to answer the question of how far the response by companies to the code represents an acceptance of the spirit of the committee's recommendations and not just of their form. I would argue, however, that when a board, for example, splits the posts of chairman and of chief executive, or establishes properly constituted board committees, these structural changes alter the way in which the board works, regardless of the motives of the board in instituting such changes. Structure affects process.

Another conclusion to be drawn from the Monitor was the amount of useful information which the boards of quoted companies are now disseminating through their statements of compliance about the way in which their enterprises are governed. This information has never been available before and it forms the raw material from which governance standards can be assessed and raised. I wrote in my preface to the Monitor:

From the Committee's viewpoint, the response to our recommendations has been heartening. Appropriate governance systems cannot of themselves guarantee board effectiveness and accountability, but they improve the chances of achieving them. Real progress in raising governance standards is being made and the task now is to maintain the momentum. (p. 8)

Shareholder Accountability

The question remains of who is the arbiter in the matter of standards of governance and who is to judge whether they are ethically acceptable. In respect of quoted companies, the responsibility for setting standards rests primarily with the board of directors, but it is also in the hands of shareholders. This in turn raises the issue of shareholder accountability. The institutions collectively own around 70 per cent of the equity of UK companies. The thrust of the governance movement has been to increase the accountability of directors to investors, but to whom are the investors answerable? The chain of accountability cannot end with boards.

Institutional investors are investing other people's money and should be using their influence with the companies in which they hold shares to promote the causes of those on whose behalf they are investing. As a pensioner, I may be primarily interested in the level of my pension, but I am also interested in the quality and nature of the society into which I am retiring. When a single investing institution has the casting vote over whether or not Granada should take over Forte, the least it should do is to declare the policy on which its voting is based beforehand – one of the recommendations in our committee's report which has up to now been largely ignored – or at best find some way of sounding out opinion among those whose funds they are managing. Investing institutions have the power to influence the conduct of the companies in which they invest and if they consulted those on whose behalf they are acting, I would expect ethical issues to move up their list of priorities.

The key in all this is disclosure. The more that companies are open about their aims and activities, the more possible it is for society to influence them in ways which it sees fit at the time, and the more those with responsibilities for the conduct of companies, like institutional investors, will weigh up the wider consequences of their policies. Openness and ethics go together and codes are a route to openness.

Company Codes

The degree to which company codes of conduct are effective will depend on the motivation for introducing them and the manner in which they were drawn up, as we have seen. If they are drawn up in good faith and backed by example from the top, they have two important attributes. First, they can act as a practical guide to individuals faced with uncertainty about the course of action they should take, and second, they give individuals, whose judgement is questioned or who question the decisions of others (normally their superiors), a firm basis on which to stand their ground. I, therefore, have no doubt as to the capability of codes to buttress individual consciences and to promote ethical standards of conduct within a firm. The importance which Transparency International attaches to company codes is evidence in support of that view.

A company code which is cynically introduced as window dressing is likely to have the effect of debasing standards, because it will be seen to reflect the motives of those who put it in place. Sadder still is when the same outcome derives perhaps from misunderstanding. An account of the General Electric price-fixing case in the 1950s runs as follows:

> [S]ome of those who signed 20.5 [the rule against price fixing] simply did not believe that it was to be taken seriously. They assumed that 20.5 was mere window dressing; that it was on the books solely to provide legal protection for the company and for the higher-ups; that meeting illegally with competitors was recognised and accepted as standard practice within the company; and that often when a ranking executive ordered a subordinate executive to comply with 20.5, he was actually ordering him to violate it. (Brooks, 1963, p. 145)

The result of this confusion was gaol for some of the 'higher-ups'.

This brings us to the key issue of the words used in codes. One of the bases for their importance lies in their use as a guide for individuals faced with uncertainty. When attempting to provide such guidance in my former company, I always had in mind the isolated manager in Nigeria or Indonesia. To say 'Thou shalt neither accept nor offer bribes' is of no help to him or her, unless you define what those sonorous terms mean in as culture-free a way as possible.

Practical Guidance

I, therefore, set out two practical rules of thumb to test whether a payment made, or gift received, was acceptable from the company's point of view. For payments, the rule was that they had to be on the face of the invoice, that is to say, that they had to go through the books. Some curious payments, by my standards, were made within this rule, but they were properly accounted for and backhand payments in cash and kind were, as far as I know, avoided. Accounting for payments may not be sufficient as an ethical test, but payments which are outside the company's system and control will almost certainly be both corrupt and corrupting.

On gifts, the test was, 'Would you mind having the gift written up in the company newspaper?' A gift becomes a bribe when it puts recipients under an obligation which could override their duty to the company. There is no set tariff which can measure this degree of obligation, but those who receive gifts and their colleagues can measure it precisely. We are back to disclosure. The logic behind these rules of conduct is, once again, that openness and ethics go together and that actions are unethical if they will not stand scrutiny.

As Chairman of Cadbury Schweppes, I drafted a brief statement of what I thought the company stood for, entitled *The Character of the Company*. This was circulated round the company at home and abroad and formed the basis of discussions with groups of employees when I visited company sites. As a result of those discussions, the wording reflected the views of as wide a sample of the international workforce as possible. In this way, a sense of ownership of the statement was gained throughout the enterprise and it dealt with matters which were important to those who read it. In addition, the discussions gave me the opportunity to answer questions about the way in which I thought we in the company should handle difficult issues. The aim was to achieve as wide a degree of agreement as possible on how best to resolve the kind of problems which confront companies in balancing their duties to people, the community and the business. It also meant that individuals faced with decisions, but with no one on hand to whom they could turn for advice, would have a lead as to the course they should take, whether or not in the event they chose to take it.

When I first proposed attempting to set down what the company stood for and then getting agreement to it, some board members were sceptical of its usefulness and said it would simply be filed away. In the event, the degree to which the statement was valued and called on seemed to be a function of distance from the perceived seat of authority. It was the smaller business units, geographically furthest from the head office in the UK, who particularly felt that it filled a need and it was those lower down in the hierarchy who turned to it most often.

Although *The Character of the Company* was not a code as such, it was a statement of values and values are important both in their own right and because they are the glue which holds an organisation together in an increasingly fragmented world. Drafting a code is hard work, even though there are guides to doing so provided by bodies like the Institute of Business Ethics (see Wright, this volume). The point to keep in mind is that what may seem platitudinous to those drawing up a code can prove invaluable to those down the line who look to that code for a lead in times of uncertainty, especially if they have had a hand in its content.

I believe, therefore, that company codes are important in raising standards of conduct and in maintaining them. Their effectiveness depends on example from the top and on their wording providing unambiguous advice to those who turn to them for practical guidance.

CONCLUSION

Statutory or Voluntary?

I will touch on three points in conclusion. First, why not enforce codes such as the Governance Committee's Code of Best Practice statutorily? Statutory enforcement of a code ensures, as far as is feasible, compliance by those unlikely to heed a voluntary code. It also underlines the significance to society of the issues addressed by the code and so affects public attitudes; legal intervention in matters of race relations is an example of such raising of public awareness. Voluntary codes, on the other hand, have the advantage of not requiring enforcement agencies, of being able to respond to new issues as they arise and of being able to demand observance of the spirit as well as the letter of the code. Their effectiveness depends on the degree to which they are backed by the relevant constituencies; in the case of the Code of Best Practice, these were boards of directors, shareholders and informed opinion.

The particular problem which a statutory code of corporate governance would face is that it is difficult to legislate for good governance. A statutory code would tend to focus on governance structure. But if separation of the posts of chairman and of chief executive was, for example, made a legal requirement, then provided a board gave the titles to two different directors it would have met the law. This would be so, regardless of whether a real separation of powers had taken place. The Code of Best Practice's recommendation that 'There should be a clearly accepted division of responsibilities at the head of a company, which will ensure a balance of power and authority' (para. 4.9, p. 21) is not only a stricter test of separation than simply giving two directors different titles, it is open to probing by shareholders and other interested parties. If the statutory test is met, further debate is effectively closed off.

Equally, the Code of Best Practice can refer to the need for non-executive directors to be sufficient in calibre and number for their views to carry weight with a board. A word like 'calibre' may have no meaning in law, but it is readily comprehended by shareholders and by those who comment on company affairs. A legal code would have to concentrate on the framework of corporate

governance, when the heart of the matter is how boards act within that framework and the quality of the individuals who make up boards.

The Code of Best Practice was drawn up to give guidance to boards, shareholders and the accounting profession and to strengthen confidence in the
corporate system. It has an ethical content, but that was not central to its aim.
Where codes are more directly concerned with setting standards of business
conduct, there is a fundamental argument in favour of the voluntary approach.
The danger of relying too much on statutory regulation in the corporate field
is that it may lead to business and personal morality being considered as distinct and separate. If standards of business conduct are thought of as being
primarily set by the law, then compliance with the law may come to be seen
as all that is required, even though conforming to the law would normally
count as a minimum requirement, setting the floor to acceptable conduct. If
business standards are to rise, in response to the expectations which society
has of business, then personal morality has to give the lead to business morality; the two should not be divorced. If the two do become seen as separate,
then an increase in statutory intervention could lower standards of business
ethics, as regulatory standards came to replace personal standards. Whatever
their limitations, the club rules, to which I referred earlier, recognised the importance of individual heads of enterprises giving a lead over the standards
expected of those working for them, a lead based on their own moral standards.

The limitations to the City's system of club rules and its eventual breakdown does not mean that the club approach should be dismissed out of
hand. Clubs have the means to set standards, to enforce them effectively
and to react swiftly to new challenges. Club members need, however, to
have interests and values in common and this restricts club size. The
dangers to the club approach are that the members may use the club and its
rules to further their own interests at the expense of everyone else's and
indeed that they may not even recognise the extent to which they have conflicts of interest. Two ways of minimising these potential disadvantages
are first to have independent outsiders on the club's ruling body and second
to require members formally to register their interests. Above all clubs
take their lead from the top and so the quality of their leadership is all-
important. As they say in India, 'As are the rulers, so are the ruled.'

Limits to Codes

A second, and quite different, point is that codes like the Code of Best
Practice can be misunderstood and misused. An example of misuse is that
some public sector organisations have appropriated the code, but made it
in effect mandatory. Guidelines have been turned into commandments.

This goes against the whole approach of the code and blurs its essentially non-prescriptive nature.

The code is misunderstood if it is taken as offering the main line of defence against disasters such as the reckless trading which brought down Barings. The response to Barings in some quarters has been to regard it as representing a failure of the control system, to which the solution is to tighten the control screw. Reliable systems of internal financial control are essential and form part of the code, but there are limits to their effectiveness. Beyond those limits and reinforcing them, organisations rely on trust, on the moral standards of individuals. Codes cannot replace a due process of selection and training of those whom an organisation needs to trust. An enterprise has to have confidence in the standards of conduct and judgement of the individuals to whom it gives power of decision. This confidence can only come from ensuring that these decision makers know what is expected of them and it can only be maintained through personal contact. The human side of an enterprise cannot be left to codes.

Ethical Standards

Finally, I have said little about ethics, because of the nature of the code with which I have been most closely involved. The Code of Best Practice is, however, addressed to boards of directors and so it is logical to raise the question of how far ethical standards in business matter. They clearly matter to society. Distrust is a barrier to the flow of trade and of information. If all business had to be based on contract, the pace of progress would be unimaginably slow. Equally, regulation is costly, to an extent that those who ultimately pay for it are usually unaware.

Ethical standards matter to companies. If unethical practices are ignored or condoned in a business, there is no means of knowing where the line between acceptable and unacceptable behaviour is to be drawn. The danger is that this uncertainty will result in a downward slide in standards, which may in turn become cumulative through time and lead to disaster. A further consideration for a business is its need to attract able recruits to its ranks. A company whose ethical standards are seen to be uncertain has to be at a disadvantage in recruitment, against those with higher reputations and against other occupations which are ranked further up the ethical scale than business. Thus business standards matter to individual companies and to the company sector in aggregate. The development of company codes is, therefore, to be encouraged with the objects of contributing to the debate on the place of ethics in business and of raising standards of business conduct. In the end business morality is personal morality writ large. As Thoreau (1849) said:

> It is true enough said that a corporation has no conscience. But a corporation of conscientious men is a corporation with a conscience.
>
>   (H.D. Thoreau, 1849, Resistance to Civil Government, p. 227)

Notes

1. Details of the *Takeover Code* are found in Stedman (1993), while the *British Codes of Advertising and Sales Promotion* are available from the Advertising Standard Authority. The Takeover Panel is the regulatory body which publishes and administers the City Code on Takeovers and Mergers.
2. Public Concern at Work: Lincoln's Inn House, 42 Kingsway, London WC2B 6EX.
3. Transparency International: Hardenbergplatz 2, D-10623 Berlin, Germany. More details of Transparency International can be found at their World Wide Web site at 'http://www. transparency. de/'.
4. Ivan F. Boesky, Commencement Address, School of Business Administration, University of California at Berkeley, 18 May 1986. Quoted in *Columbia Dictionary of Quotations*, Columbia University Press, 1993.

References

Brooks, J. (1963) *The Fate of the Edsel and Other Business Adventures* (London: Gollancz).

Caux Round Table (1994) *Caux Round Table Principles for Business*. This is available from *Business Ethics Magazine*. Also available on the World Wide Web at 'http://stthomas.edu/www/mccr_http/Prin4bus.htm'.

CNPF/AFEP (1995) *Vienot Report* (Paris: Editions Techniques Professionelles).

Committee on the Financial Aspects of Corporate Governance [Cadbury Report] (1992) *Report with Code of Best Practice* (London: Gee Publishing).

Committee on the Financial Aspects of Corporate Governance (1995) *Compliance with the Code of Best Practice* [Greenbury Report] (1995) (London: Gee Publishing).

Dennet, L. (1989) *Slaughter and May: A Century in the City* (Cambridge: Granta Editions).

Minnesota Centre for Corporate Responsibility (1992) *The Minnesota Principles: Towards an Ethical Basis for Global Business.* (Minnesota: Minnesota Centre for Corporate Responsibility). Also available on the World Wide Web at 'http://stthomas.edu/www/mccr_http/Mn_prin.htm'.

Nolan Committee (1995) *First Report on the Committee on Standards in Public Life*, CM 2850, May 1995 (London: HMSO).

St. George's House, Windsor and the Al Albait Foundation, Amman (1993) *An Interfaith Declaration: a Code of Ethics on International Business for Christians, Muslims and Jews.* Reprinted in *Business Ethics – a European Review*, 5(1) (1996), pp. 55–7. Also available on the World Wide Web at 'http://www. transparency.de/sourcebook/Part_C/cvL/18.htm'.

Stedman, G. (1993) *Takeovers* (London: Longman).

Study Group on Directors' Remuneration (1995) *Directors' Remuneration: Report of a Study Group Chaired by Sir Richard Greenbury*, 17 July 1995. (London: Gee Publishing).

Thoreau, H.D. (1849) *Walden and, Resistance to Civil Government: Authoritative Texts, Journal Reviews, and Essays in Criticism*, ed. by William Rossi (New York: Norton, 1992).

6 Government and Business Ethics

Norman Barry

INTRODUCTION

Since the collapse of Communism there has been a dramatic change in the relationship between intellectual opinion and the market. The well-established errors of central planning and the spread of market methods of resource allocation throughout the world have brought about a new type of social and economic criticism of capitalism. Although the price system reigns supreme it is now argued that there are different types of capitalism and that we should not assume that the familiar Anglo-American model is either uniquely efficient or, in a moral sense, the most pleasing. We are now told[1] that there are competing types of capitalism and, although they all depend to a great extent on competition, private property and the signals of the market to allocate resources, the way these institutional arrangements are organised indicates differing social forms. Thus we have, amongst other phenomena, the 'social market economy' (which originated in postwar West Germany), East Asian capitalism, 'stakeholder' capitalism, and the various types of socially concerned market theories that derive from American business ethics.

The role of government is important here because, although few people expect it to run the economy in a direct sense, there seems to be an obligation imposed on it to implement, or at least encourage, one of these models. The theory of spontaneous order (Hayek, 1973, 1982) supposes that any economic order which develops naturally when people transact under the rule of law has an almost *a priori* entitlement to our approbation, yet this approval does not always extend to the Anglo-American model of business enterprise. However uncoerced its emergence may have been, and however consistent its basic features are with the Western social and moral tradition, it has certain economic and ethical features which cry out for government correction. And normally the rectification is claimed to be consistent with the basic elements of capitalism. The aim of reformers is not to replace the market, or even to reject all of the inequalities that it generates, but to sanitise it and to make its unavoidable inegalitarian features consistent with some compelling moral goal.

But not only does this corrective purpose have a moral rationale, it is also thought to be conducive to economic efficiency in the conventional sense. Thus the alternative forms of capitalism are thought to be better able to cope with the exigencies of the present and the future than the Anglo-American model. They are predicted to survive the test of evolution and those economic regimes that fail to adapt to the movement of the new *Zeitgeist* will be condemned to economic decline as well as moral obloquy.

The particular errors that the critics of Anglo-American capitalism have in mind relate to its corporate organisation, its method of finance (primarily through the stock market), its approach to industrial change via the takeover mechanism and its obsession with shareholder value as the sole guide to economic efficiency. These phenomena are said to derive from a potentially malevolent form of self-interest; the agents in this form of capitalism apparently are egoists and display an almost deliberate insouciance in the face of legitimate moral claims from the victims of its remorseless allocative process. Similarly, it shows an indifference to the adverse effect that individualism has on the integrative role of 'community' in social and economic life (see Etzioni, 1963).

Indeed some early defenders of capitalism said its success was due precisely to its rejection of certain moral standards – standards that have their origin in religion but which have been easily assimilated by secular, non-individualistic morality. Bernard Mandeville, in his notorious *Fable of the Bees* (first published in 1705), said that: 'The grand principle that makes us social creatures, the solid basis, the life and support of trade and employment, without exception is evil' (Mandeville in Kaye, 1924, p. 369). It was he who made the famous contrast between virtue and commerce and argued that morality had to be suspended if economic success were to be achieved. In a famous phrase he said that the public good depends on private vice (p. 36), though it should be said that Mandeville's parody was addressed to an excessive moralism which was dominating public opinion during his lifetime.

Most contemporary defenders of capitalism would not go as far as Mandeville but they would insist that morality should be limited to those conventional rules that make the system predictable for transactors, and which guarantee them security in their possessions. If they follow these rules they are absolved from any further moral duties (of a compulsory type). It is certainly true that the frenetic world of the 1980s had Mandevillian features and it is undeniable that advocates of Anglo-American capitalism maintain that the imposition of 'higher' moral duties on transactors seriously inhibits the allocative operation of the system. They are regarded as, at most, *supererogatory* duties, that is, desirable but not morally compelling.

Any defence, however modest, of Anglo-American capitalism must counter the charges that it encourages immorality, and that it is ultimately self-destructive and will not survive the evolutionary process. But we must be clear in our minds about its basic features and be fully aware of the rationale for the familiar institutions it has developed. The alternative views of corporate organisation, of industrial change and development, of the relationships between employer and employee and between individuals and their communities, have to counter some sophisticated and critical theories of the role of government which have been developed by advocates of Anglo-American capitalism (especially, Friedman, 1962). Indeed, it is their serious analysis of the role of government in society that underlies the defenders' critique of the suggestion that the state should have an extensive role in the moral environment of business.

ANGLO-AMERICAN CAPITALISM

This form of economic organisation is individualistic in two important senses. In an economic sense its rationale rests on the claim that self-interested behaviour produces, in a utilitarian way, the best possible allocation of resources: it satisfies the demands of anonymous agents better than any known alternatives. In a world in which knowledge is dispersed, constantly changing, and often 'tacit', that is, impossible to articulate in a precise and replicable form, only the market can coordinate the information on which efficiency depends (see Kirzner, 1973). In a metaphor made famous by Adam Smith, these striving and self-interested individuals are led 'as if by an invisible hand' to produce a benign social outcome which is no part of anyone's deliberate intention. In a phrase which has as much relevance to contemporary criticisms of capitalism as it does to old-fashioned central planning, he said: 'I have never known much good done by those who affect to trade for the public good' (Smith, 1976, pp. 28–30). From the perspective described by a theory of universal self-interest, there is no reason at all to suppose that those charged with the responsibility of managing an economy, or enjoined to participate in it in a non-profit-maximising way so as to achieve higher goals, will be imbued with the necessary altruistic motivations. Indeed, those often inspired by business ethics to recommend companies to behave in socially responsible ways stand to gain most from non-profit-maximising behaviour, for example, managements that resist takeovers and in other ways pretend to act for the interests of the community rather than the shareholder. There is a temptation for all agents to behave opportunistically whenever the immediate constraints of the market are removed or attenuated. Indeed, 'legislated' business ethics is often implemented at the behest of self-interested groups adversely affected by economic change.

Of course, the controversial word in all this is 'profit', whether it is understood in the simplistic way as returns to owners (shareholders) or, more accurately, as the reward for spotting gaps in the market and exploiting the advantages of knowledge that one or more persons may have over others in a market process (see Kirzner, 1995). Even those who favour resource allocation by the market often wince at 'excess' profit and believe that it is not required, at least to the extent that it obtains in Anglo-American capitalism, to spur people into innovative activities. Most business ethicists seem to think that price should equal long-run cost (in almost a physical sense); but if this is so, and any earnings that exceed this are to be eliminated because they are somehow exploitative, then it is difficult to see what creativity there could be in the market. Yet all economic progress depends on 'discovery', that is, hitting on some new way of doing things, anticipating consumer demand, or combining existing assets in novel ways. This form of entrepreneurship is not necessarily limited to the Schumpeterian type that breaks up prevailing industrial forms with a completely new technique but it is also that form which constantly coordinates activity, perhaps in financial markets (as in the discovery of the much maligned 'junk bond') or in management itself. If the activity is genuinely creative then the innovators are surely entitled, in the full moral sense, to the reward which it earns.[2]

Of course, in financial markets especially, where the exploitation of scarce information sometimes resembles deception, *caveat emptor* may be an inadequate guarantee that a proper moral decision has been reached. But business ethics errs when it tries to establish a kind of epistemological egalitarianism, a situation in which no one is at a disadvantage through lack of information. The attempt to try to create artificially a perfect market in which each transactor is fully informed of all possible outcomes would provide no incentive to innovate at all.

As we know from elementary political economy, a perfectly competitive market never, or only rarely, obtains in the real world and the attempt to provide a surrogate for it inevitably coagulates the flow of information on which economic progress depends. The desire to charge government with the responsibility of ensuring heavy regulation, especially of the securities market, the product market and all things to do with the environment, are examples of this phenomenon. Much of this is not to protect transactors, or innocent bystanders, from wrong-doing but to provide impossibly high standards of 'fairness' and safety. It is also the case that such regulation often encourages 'rent-seeking' by government employees, that is, the diversion of the extra value created in an economic enterprise to the regulators, who secure high salaries and improved career prospects.

It should be clear that the kind of morality that obtains in typically Anglo-American markets is utilitarian. Good consequences are likely to occur when the government limits itself to the enforcement of general rules of just conduct. It does not try to influence the outcome of the process, or to ensure superficially more appealing goals, such as guaranteeing 'level playing fields' in financial markets, or socially just distributions of income.

Almost all the considerations relevant to these arguments turn upon questions of knowledge. It is maintained by defenders of the Anglo-American model that governments can never have the knowledge to bring about the proposed morally desirable ends and cannot guarantee that they represent the genuine ends of the community (especially in the anonymous markets of Britain and the USA) rather than the purposes of organised groups. Indeed, when certain of these goals are imposed on business, often at the request of its personnel (especially if they are non-owners), the result is that business takes on a welfare role; but this is properly the responsibility of government, not business.

However, the morality that obtains in the free market is not exclusively utilitarian (see Frey, 1985). After all, it is not for nothing that the rules that govern the Paris Bourse are called 'les principes des deontologies'. The Kantian, or deontological, morality of 'duty', which implies that there are certain, universally valid, rules (justice is probably the best example) which we ought to follow regardless of the beneficial consequences that might or might not accrue from their observation, applies just as much to business as it does to other aspects of life. The rules of fair play and the importance of trust in business dealings are often cited as examples; they restrain agents from the pursuit of immediate acts of gratification, even though these might have some vague utilitarian rationale. It is true that in the long run immorality in business will not pay, but in non-repeatable transactions it does, and it is here that deontological constraints are compelling.

Only in examples such as the demand that firms pay a 'just' or a minimum wage, where this is different from that determined by the marginal productivity of the worker, do we find deontological principles in open conflict with utility. For the observed consequences of this, in terms of the loss in economic efficiency, are clear enough. It is also the case that governments are alluding to deontological principles whenever they make a minimum wage obligatory.

It could also be argued that the adverse consequences of such action are not the only considerations that tell against it, for it would also be pertinent to suggest that the inhibitions to employment brought about by minimum wage laws constitute an *unjust* denial of the right for each person to sell his or her labour in the market. It would be a most peculiar moral argument that this disadvantage is somehow compensated for by the increased well-being of those who remain in employment at the decreed higher wage. Only in cases of monopsony (a single buyer of labour) do ethics provide an uncontroversial injunction for government to interfere in wage determination. In most cases we cannot read anything moral into the market's determination of wages for they are not fixed by any one person whose actions can be labelled 'right' or 'wrong', or 'just' or 'unjust'.

THE SOCIAL MARKET ECONOMY

Still, undoubtedly the market produces outcomes which many people find offensive and various adjectives have been used to describe ethically inspired modifications to its rigour. The most popular to emerge since the 1970s has been the ideal of the social market economy. In a trivial sense it is true that all markets are social markets in that they contain features which are clearly not reducible to individual choice. Markets can only function in conformity to a system of rules which people did not specifically create. These rules, embodying contract, respect for legitimately acquired property, trust and the principles of fair play, are the product of history and a myriad of social arrangements and interactions which defy analysis in pure utility-maximising terms. Undoubtedly government has a duty to maintain this system, and even modify it in the light of new circumstances. It must act especially to preserve its liberty-enhancing features when they are threatened by such things as the spontaneous emergence of monopoly power.

However, recently the expression the 'social market economy' has been used in more substantive, and controversial, ways. It is much more likely to refer to a system of rules, practices and government policies which goes beyond the protection of the immediate transactors (owners, workers, consumers and so on) in a market process and it aims at making the market serve 'society', a phenomenon not reducible to identifiable agents. It is here that the doctrine of communitarianism becomes important because it specifically rejects the major metaphysics of neoclassical economics, that is, the idea that a person can be abstracted from his social circumstances and treated as a utility-maximiser detached from all extra-economic social obligations. The communitarian approach validates an extensive role for government in the preservation of those social institutions and practices which are thought to be vulnerable to the ravages of the market.

We can see some of the strengths and weaknesses of the doctrine of the social market economy, and its connection with communitarianism, by retracing its origins and development in postwar West Germany. It began with the ideas of an important group of thinkers, including Walter Eucken, Wilhelm Ropke and the West German Economics Minister (and later Chancellor) Ludwig Erhard (see Barry, 1993). There was a specific ethical impulse behind the social market (and the related, though more free market, ideals of *Ordoliberalism*[3]). Although its theorists were concerned with the utilitarian advantages of the market they were equally cognisant of certain tendencies in it which required government attention if they were not to prove fatal to the free order itself. They had themselves witnessed in the early part of the twentieth century the mutation of the market towards a heavily cartelised system (and other market-closing phenomena) which had undermined liberty. Therefore there was a role for government, not in directly maximising utility or welfare, but in preserving the Kantian ideal of liberty under law, though this was given a communitarian twist. Thus a freely contracting society must be prevented from undermining the ideal of contract itself. A law that inhibited a voluntary, market-closing contract would not count as a dereliction of liberty if it were designed to protect the *order* of freedom. Still, government policy should be *marktkonform*, that is, it must be designed to preserve the market order, not eliminate it.

The immediate policy implication of the social market theory was the construction of a competition policy that outlawed all cartels and monopolies. There was also a communitarian aspect to this since it led to the well-known distaste for the takeover mechanism in the German economy, though no doubt this hostility was originally inspired by the (now mistaken) theory that corporate raiding leads to the concentration of industry. Indeed, West Germany hardly needed laws against this activity; communal resentment against takeovers seemed to be a sufficient deterrent. Perhaps all this led to attitudes of cooperation between workers and management and the absence of adversarial attitudes on the part of managements to owners.

The original idea of the social market was not confined to a demand to cut back on state welfare spending. Disquiet is being expressed at the style of German business – especially its limited concern for shareholder value. It was this that distinguished it from the orthodoxy of Anglo-American economic styles and was one reason why it has always been admired by critics of the latter. The takeover method is even creeping into German business practice.

The original social market doctrine had both economic and moral aspects. With regard to the former, German business was thought to be less short-term in outlook and better able to embark on investment projects that did not show an immediate return. In fact, early social market spokesmen strongly advised governments to devise competition policies which discouraged managements from constantly looking at the share price and taking actions to deter a takeover specialist. The moral aspect was linked to this, for what critics of Anglo-American capitalism admired about the German system was its apparent cooperativeness. Employers, workers and members of the community were thought to be engaged in a common enterprise, an engagement which deterred any of these from behaving in an opportunistic manner. This contrasts nicely with the more open and pluralistic Anglo-American system which leaves it to the market to coordinate the various groups in the economy, which are unlikely to have common purposes beyond the need to follow general rules of just conduct. In this system, coordination is the aim rather than the pursuit of a common purpose.

However, the current fashion for the social market seems to be a little behind developments in Germany itself, for there commentators are beginning to look more favourably at the Anglo-American model. Leaving aside the enormous welfare costs of the system, its business rationale is now being questioned. The neglect of shareholder value and the sometimes 'cosy' relationships between owners and managers are blamed for the current inflexibility of the German economy.[4] Banks have an inordinate influence over business decisions through the *de facto* concentration of ownership; and this is mainly how takeovers are resisted.

There are, in fact, good ethical and social reasons why governments in Anglo-American-style economies should be sceptical of the advice frequently offered by business ethics about economic management. The main argument is that these societies normally lack a common good, at least the sort that would validate a serious attenuation of the profit motive. In countries such as Germany (and Japan especially) it might be true that certain goals can secure common agreement and that these do enable their economies to be successful despite the serious modification to individualism that their versions of capitalism encourage. It might even be true that they refute a common Anglo-American assumption that capital flows automatically to where the returns are highest, although recent evidence of German overseas investment seems to confirm neoclassical orthodoxy.

However, in the absence of such unifying ideals, or a common scale of values, it is more likely that the imposition of specific goals on business will lead to rent-seeking and opportunism on the part of market participants. These problems and controversies can be seen when we analyse the role of the corporation in capitalist societies.

THE CORPORATION

It is the corporation that has aroused perhaps the most controversy in Anglo-American economies, and brought about unfavourable comparisons between the familiar version in more or less *laissez-faire* economies and the form that it takes in alternative versions of capitalism. In the USA and in Britain it has traditionally been thought of as a powerful institution, resistant both to the corrective mechanisms of the market and to the regulatory endeavours of the state. It is argued that it holds great power over its employees (indeed, the 'master–servant' relationship is sometimes openly used in its description) and, in its multinational manifestation, it is accused of exploiting the Third World in the remorseless pursuit of profit. Still, it is unlikely that in the late 1990s anyone holds the view that the corporation is invulnerable to any pressures, either from the market or the state. Even J.K. Galbraith (1996), who pioneered the radical critique, no longer believes the corporation to be immortal and indestructible: a view which is scarcely tenable in the light of clear evidence of the demise of once-great industrial enterprises, the rapid rise of new companies and the emergence of intense global competition.

Many critics of the corporation have argued that the state has a 'right' to control the institution because it only exists by the state's permission. It is said that its major features, notably entity status, the ability to sue in its collective capacity, more or less permanent life and, most importantly, limited liability, were granted by statute law so that it (morally) owes something to society in return for these privileges. There is a body of thought, though, that plausibly urges the counter-claim that the corporate form could, and did, emerge spontaneously through contracting under common law (see Hessen, 1979). In this explanation, the corporation has no more rights than those possessed by individual agents. This, of course, means that it can never be criminally liable for wrongdoings, for the feature of *mens rea*, which is required for a criminal conviction, can only be attributed to individuals. One of the attempts to moralise the corporation in recent years has taken the form of charging it with such things as 'reckless homicide', corporate manslaughter and corporate theft (see Barry, 1991, 1995a).

Whatever the rights and wrongs of these particular arguments, the corporation is a special type of economic institution. In a curious way it is a non-market phenomenon.[5] In perfectly competitive equilibrium there would be no firms or corporations; each agent would contract to perform specific tasks so that there would be no such thing as economic power deriving from non-individualistic economic forms. The corporation emerged because of the immense transaction costs involved in multilateral contracting (though these costs are declining with the advent of modern technology). To the extent that the corporation has the power of command over its members (who can only express their dissent by, ultimately, leaving it), and may occasionally have monopoly advantages, it has always provoked hostility.

Thus, although criticism of the corporation is now somewhat muted (at least compared to comments made in the 1960s), it continues, and quite radical suggestions are made for reforms to the institution. It is not always clear whether these are to be made by corporations themselves, fulfilling a type of supererogatory duty, or are to be mandated by government. But the suggestions always involve a departure from the traditional model of the corporation as a device to maximise shareholder value.

The corporation emerged as a consequence of the division of labour; the owners of capital appointed 'specialists', managers, who could handle the assets more efficiently than they could. At the heart of the Anglo-American model of the corporation is the separation between ownership and control and the subtle principal–agent relationship between shareholders and managers that this requires. The latter are supposed to act exclusively in the interests of the former. This is important for business ethics since most of the supererogatory duties that are said to be owed by business to the community are addressed to managers rather than owners. If these duties are taken as seriously as business ethicists demand they would affect the profitability of the firm. In such circumstances the only sanction the shareholder has is to sell his or her stock in the company; hence the takeover mechanism.

The rationale for the corporation is that it provides returns to shareholders. It rests, in theory, securely in the property rights structure of Anglo-American capitalism. Property rights here do not simply imply possession of assets,[6] they also involve the freedom to use them in ways that derive ultimately from the rights-bearers' choices. In the context of the corporation they involve control rights. Thus owners can not only claim the residual, they can also determine the ultimate policy of the company, most importantly the hiring of the board of directors.

This is the utilitarian model of the corporation. It exists primarily to serve the interests of its owners; but the specialisation and innovative activity that the corporate form generates is also ultimately of benefit to the anonymous members of market society. Since the rise of institutional ownership and the relative decline of the private shareholder, almost everybody in society, through investment in pension funds, insurance policies and so on, is in some way dependent on its success. The critics of the corporation tend to concentrate on two interrelated areas: they stress its social responsibility and they wish to widen the range of personnel (beyond its formal owners) who may be said to have an interest in its functioning and a share in its well-being. Each of these concerns reflects a serious departure from the individualistic, market-driven and property rights model of the corporation. The ethical rationale for these departures seems to be a rather unstable combination of deontological and communitarian considerations.

The critical analysis is buttressed by examples from economies which, although they have corporations with the familiar features, seem not to be entirely market-driven and not exclusively concerned with returns to owners. In some non-Western capitalist economies, notably Japan, the returns to owners are minimal and the control rights derisory. Despite these somewhat unpromising lessons for Western economies, the critics are, presumably, recommending an important role for government in restructuring the corporation on these alien lines, or at least encouraging its development away from the standard individualistic, property rights model.

The case of Italian corporations is especially important for it illustrates a different ethical experience. There, close-knit families seem to dominate even publicly quoted enterprises and are able to resist outsiders. According to Fukuyama (1995), the notion of trust is limited to family members and Italian business ethics lacks that universalist implication which is such a feature of Anglo-American capitalism. Thus although the family members owe strict duties to each other they seem not to recognise obligations beyond the immediate kin group. Whether this inhibits corporate growth is a moot point, as is the question of the acceptability of this type of business morality. But certainly Italian business has produced business actions as ethically condemnable as any in the Anglo-American model. Indeed, the very impenetrability of corporate life there hardly makes it a system worthy of imitation. And the involvement of Italian business with government, through complex family and other intimate connections, is not something to be universally recommended.

CORPORATE SOCIAL RESPONSIBILITY

The demand that corporations be socially responsible does not necessarily undermine the property rights model but the way that the concept has been expanded by business ethics probably does.[7] Implicit in this expansion has been the suggestion that if the corporation does not fulfil its social duties then there is a role for government to enforce them: presumably on the ground that the corporation owes its existence to the state and this 'permission' can be legitimately withdrawn. The harmless, indeed trivial, sense of social responsibility is that corporations, and businesses of any size, should obey the law and social conventions in their activities.[8] At the minimum they should avoid inflicting harm. Here their moral duties are no different from those that apply to private agents and, although there may be some dispute as to what a social and moral convention might imply in a particular case, the minimal moral duties of business are clear enough.

Still, it is true that, because of the all-powerful influence of the profit motive, public-good problems might arise in an acute form where business is concerned. We can see this in the familiar problem of the environment. Pollution itself is not necessarily harmful, it is the *additional* polluter who causes the problem. To avoid harm by voluntary methods would require a great deal of cooperation on the part of business agents; and it is especially difficult to achieve in Anglo-American economies, where transactors normally deal at 'arm's length'. In such circumstances morality will not pay, despite the mantra of business ethicists that it always does. Defectors from putative 'no excessive pollution' agreements are hard to identify and punish, making it inevitable that the state will be involved in the enforcement of a moral duty. Thus even the minimal standards implied in the arm's length model may not be self-enforcing.

The important point about this morality is that although it does not involve the imposition of any special duties on business, government might simply be an efficient way of enforcing conventional moral standards. However, the social responsibility of business thesis now embraces supererogatory duties, actions that involve doing a positive good rather than merely refraining from inflicting harm.

Sometimes the differences between the two forms of duty are confused so that what is really a duty of 'imperfect' obligation is presented as a compelling moral demand. We can see this in the case of safety. It is true that there is a duty on business to avoid producing dangerous products. It is also true that the market, and the law especially, may be slow to correct errors in production. It is obvious that business ethics will concentrate on particular cases of harm and on those individuals whose interests are adversely affected (and their lives possibly lost) before information about faulty products circulates. But there is no such thing as a perfectly safe product, and the attempt to achieve perfect safety would price most goods out of the market for ordinary people. Indeed, as Wildavsky (1988) has persuasively argued, a certain amount of risk is essential if we are to increase safety.

In addition, there is the moral claim that people are responsible agents who can weigh up for themselves the advantages and disadvantages of various choices. After all, this is the basis of *caveat emptor*, a legal principle that has been badly compromised in the rash of product liability suits in America. Of course, there are marginal cases where producers do not provide adequate information on which consumers can make rational choices.

Cigarette advertising in its early days is perhaps a good example of the competing principles at work.

In fact, the paternalism that economic liberals so often complain of in government regulation is primarily a result of common law decisions. Thus in America, contract law, which assumes a certain amount of minimum rationality on the part of consumers, has effectively been replaced by tort law; the latter is now imposing excessive burdens on producers. Compliance is both difficult and costly. If there is a role for government in this area it might well be to provide legislation which weighs carefully the demand for genuine risk avoidance with the need to provide a framework within which business can innovate with some security.

But even more questionable are the demands that corporations should implement policies, dictated by moral principles, that would clearly involve them in loss, or reduced profit. They are simply attempts to sanitise the aggressive, individualistic image of Anglo-American capitalism. Examples are the claims that firms should practise affirmative action in the workplace when this would lead to inefficiency in the labour market, to pay workers above their marginal product in order to satisfy highly contestable theories of social justice and to act in the interests of the community through various charitable acts.

Henry Manne (1972) gives a good example of the problems that arise when firms try to meet the last of these demands. In the 1970s Coca-Cola opened a plant in Florida which was, unavoidably, rather an unpleasant place to work. The workers were immigrants who had come from Third World countries where conditions were much worse. However, to satisfy the demands of business ethics and, no doubt, to gain some credit from the public, the company operated a kind of private enterprise welfare system. Predictably, this involved Coca-Cola in extra costs, resulting in reduced employment prospects for newcomers. Yet what was noticed was the 'socially responsible' behaviour of the company; what was not so visible was the increased unemployment it brought about. There would be many more examples of this phenomenon if government were to impose extensive social responsibilities on business.

At the fundamental level this sort of business ethics threatens the viability of commerce, for the purpose, or *telos*, of an enterprise is to increase value for its owners, not to advance social justice (although that may be a legitimate function of a democratic government). To maximise owner value requires the efficient use of a company's assets, its property. To the extent that these assets are diverted into socially responsible actions (in the supererogatory sense), then a company cannot adequately fulfil its primary function.

Equally important is the question: to whom are these duties (of imperfect obligation) addressed? Is it the managers or the owners? As one would expect from basic political economy, the managements are not averse to taking on a moral role since it is not normally their assets that are being depleted when business pursues the expanded version of social responsibility. Indeed, to the extent that supererogatory duties are embraced by managements they are in breach of the principal–agent relationship. And when they so act it could be another example of opportunistic behaviour. It is presumably less taxing, and morally more pleasing, to act on behalf of the community than to work to increase shareholder value. Anyway, in a market economy, socially responsible behaviour (in the expanded sense) is more feasible the less competitive an industry is. The most socially responsible business agent will be a monopolist who donates most of his profits to charity: a nice irony for business ethics.

STAKEHOLDER CAPITALISM

The attenuation of property rights is taken to its logical conclusion in the theory of stakeholder capitalism. The idea behind it is that those who have an interest in a company are not just the owners. Other people, for example, workers, suppliers and members of the community in which it is situated, have made investments of a non-pecuniary kind and are entitled to consideration, perhaps even a voice equal to that of shareholders, when important decisions are to be made. In an explicitly Kantian theory, Evan and Freeman (1993) write that: 'The very purpose of the firm is to serve stakeholder interests' (p. 79). Those who put up the capital have no special rights. There is a 'perfect' obligation to serve stakeholders and this overrides any other duty, such as the maximisation of profits.

In a trivial sense, there is some merit in stakeholder theory. People other than shareholders have an interest in a firm and it would be a foolish owner who gave them no consideration. Workers may have 'firm-specific' human capital, which is highly vulnerable in the event of a takeover (see Ricketts, 1994). Any owner who treated these workers in a cavalier manner would find it difficult to attract special sorts of human capital in the future. It is even possible to write special employment contracts that protect firm-specific human capital from the unpredictability of the market. There are other devices that have been invented to protect the interests of stakeholders without undermining the property rights basis of the firm.

But the theory of stakeholder capitalism goes beyond these prudential measures. What it wants to do is to 'politicise' the firm so that decision making becomes subject to endless negotiating between interested parties. It is no coincidence that the term 'constituencies' is used by business ethics to describe the interests that should be taken into account in corporate strategy. There is, however, no natural limit to the range of stakeholder interests; almost any group can establish a plausible claim to a 'voice' in decision making.

Furthermore, the claims of the various groups are almost certain to conflict. The Anglo-American model of capitalism is pluralistic and to this extent it reflects the structure of Western society. Outside the purpose of maximising shareholder value, from which anonymous people benefit, there is little need for further agreement. There is, however, the problem for stakeholder theory of how the claims of the interested parties are to be accommodated, if the verdict of the price mechanism is to be qualified by morality. There is rarely a scale of values which can order coherently rival claims. The market may be a crude moral substitute for the exquisite harmony of communitarian-inspired stakeholder theory but it is the only one that makes any kind of sense in our inevitably pluralistic world. How are we to decide the conflicting claims of competing stakeholders in plant relocation decisions? Should we bow to the wishes of present (and loyal) employees and not move to a new (more profitable area) or must we cater for the future employment prospects of those living near the proposed site? After all, the latter are stakeholders in society, and have a claim in economics (though in stakeholder theory that should not be decisive). Evan and Freeman are aware of the problem of resolving conflicting demands. They make the slightly comic suggestion that every company should (presumably by law) have a 'metaphysical director' (1993, p. 83) who, being a disinterested party, can objectively make decisions that take all stakeholders into account. But this is simply rent-seeking by philosophers.

One wonders who would ever invest in a company that handled assets in this fashion. If such a procedure were to be imposed by government, then all the bargaining that takes place politically at the national level would transfer to the local economic level. From the investment strike that would undoubtedly result from such a procedure Evan and Freeman would discover that owners are a little more important than they originally thought.

FINANCIAL MARKETS AND INSIDER DEALING

It is in financial and capital markets where the most notorious business scandals have occurred in the Anglo-American economies and it is here that the most insistent demands for government action have been made. Most of the legislative initiatives are based on (perhaps inchoate and not well-articulated) theories of justice and fairness. However, government-inspired measures to guarantee equity have often produced efficiency problems and compromised the rule of law. Governments will want to eliminate fraud, deception and other types of criminality but in going too far in the pursuit of justice they might well inhibit the search for information that is such a crucial feature of capital markets.

Until quite recently dubious practices, such as insider dealing (Barry, 1996a), in financial markets were policed by the institutions themselves, with the possible (and not too successful) recourse to common law remedies. Now the area is almost entirely regulated by statutory law (criminal in Britain and a combination of criminal and civil law in the USA). No doubt, the legislative innovations have been part of the drive to encourage a wider spread of private share ownership. It was felt that people would be deterred from investment in the stock market without legal protection from exploitation by well-informed professionals. Insider dealing has always been a minor issue in Europe since industrial finance there is much less dependent on the stock market. Indeed, it might be thought that the complex system of interlocking directorships that operates outside the Anglo-American economies would make insider dealing very difficult to police (Germany had no law against the practice until the country was compelled to adopt the European Directive). Insider dealing is closely linked to takeovers since vast amounts of money can be made if price-sensitive information is used for investment decisions made in advance of a public announcement of a takeover bid.

The economic and moral problems of insider dealing involve questions of entrepreneurship within the firm and the claims to property rights arising out of it, the relationships between company owners and employees, the conditions which are necessary to ensure fairness to all participants, and the effect of regulation on the rule of law. If capital markets are to operate efficiently the prices of shares must accurately reflect underlying economic values.[9] Because information is so valuable it is the methods that are used to acquire it which provoke intense debate. Of course, if markets were in perfect equilibrium there would be no problem; every participant would be fully informed of all relevant economic data, hence there would be no ignorance to exploit. As in other fields in business ethics, the problems arise because markets are imperfect. It is this phenomenon that creates the opportunities for immoral behaviour.

A glance at the famous case in the USA[10] that gave rise to the current plethora of law and regulation there (and which was to a qualified extent mimicked in Britain) reveals almost all the problems. It illustrates almost perfectly the theoretical issues. In 1966 the employees of a none-too-successful company, Texas Gulf Sulphur, made an important mineral discovery in Canada. The information was not immediately revealed, giving time for the employees to invest heavily in the company's stock. They were eventually charged with a civil law offence through an innovative and, some critics plausibly claimed, unpredictable, interpretation of the 1934 Securities and Exchange Act. They were made to return their 'illicit' gains but, more importantly, the event was followed by criminalisation of the offence and greatly increased civil penalties for offenders; in Britain it is exclusively a criminal offence and there is no institution equivalent to the US Securities and Exchange Commission (SEC) to police the capital markets.

The economic and moral questions that arose out of the case can be easily summarised. Were not the company employees entitled to the gains as a reward for their entrepreneurship or is all knowledge owned exclusively by the company? Were the employees in breach of a fiduciary duty to their employers? Did they have an unfair advantage over other investors because of their possession of vital information? Did the activity of the SEC involve a threat to the rule of law on the ground that the agents could not have reasonably predicted how the regulations would affect them? And does this type of regulatory activity inhibit the search for knowledge, so reducing the efficiency of the market?

It is noticeable that the really outrageous cases of insider dealing, for example, those involving Dennis Levine and Ivan Boesky, did not create any serious problems since they illegally used confidential information about takeovers (there is a minor equivalent to the Levine–Boesky affair in Britain, that which involved Collier, an employee of Morgan Grenfell, who similarly traded on knowledge of a takeover (see Hannigan, 1988, ch. 1)). Those involved in these cases were in clear breach of fiduciary duty, a matter that could perhaps be better dealt with by an improved system of private law.

The most important issue in insider dealing is knowledge. It is a type of property but, unlike things like the office furniture, the nature of company information is not easy to establish and it is also difficult to determine when a theft of it has occurred. Much will depend on the state of the positive law, but even here there can be moral disputes. Is it fair that the law should assign property rights in such a way that the discoverers of vital information have no claim on its use? In a perfectly free market contracts between a company and its employees would determine the rights of ownership and it might be the case that some of these agreements would grant property rights in information to employees so that internal entrepreneurship could be encouraged. Discoverers of knowledge might have the right to use it and pass it on to others (which is how many cases of insider dealing occur). In fact, before statutory regulation there were few examples of firms deliberately restricting the use of confidential information (though there were some law suits for breach of fiduciary duty (Hannigan, 1988, ch. 5)).

Those who favour the removal of criminal restraints on the activity do so for straightforward utilitarian reasons.[11] If insider dealing is allowed then information will circulate much more quickly and the capital market will more accurately reflect underlying economic values. Even if the profits are 'unjust' (by perhaps controversial moral criteria) they will be quickly dissipated without regulation; whereas if there are legal restraints much greater profits will accrue to those who are prepared to violate them. But the major argument against regulation is that it inhibits entrepreneurship within the firm. Normal emoluments, in the form of salary, bonuses, stock options and so on, may not be adequate incentives to encourage innovative activity. The right to trade on 'privileged' information may be necessary if internal entrepreneurship is to flourish. Outside shareholders will eventually gain from the rise in share prices.[12]

This is all very well if the news is good (an oil strike or an impending takeover) but if the news is bad (a projected fall in profits or bankruptcy) then outside stockholders may justifiably feel that they have been used, in a decidedly un-Kantian way, merely as means to the ends of others. Also, the permission to trade on inside information may encourage employees to play the market and perhaps deliberately circulate false information. The temptation to 'short' the stock might be irresistible.

Perhaps the really crucial moral question is whether insider dealing always involves a breach of fiduciary duty. It clearly does when, say, financial intermediaries reveal information about takeovers. However, in case law, in the USA especially (with some modification from Supreme Court decisions), the notion of fiduciary duty has been stretched so as to include people who have no real connection with the original company. Current law in Britain (see Macqueen, 1994) is so potentially severe that market traders may be inhibited from their research activities through fear of becoming insiders.

The most unsatisfactory justification for heavy government regulation of capital markets derives from attempts to establish a 'level playing field'. Outside the imaginary world of perfect competition, information will always be asymmetric and money will be made from its use. As long as opportunities are open to people to acquire information, disparities will be gradually, or even rapidly, competed away. It is the job of market researchers to ferret out information not obtainable from publicly disclosed documents (for example, company reports) and as long as no contracts are breached then immorality will not have taken place. The advantages that company employees have are only unfair if they derive from the breach of a *clear* fiduciary duty.

The threat to the rule of law in the attempt to police insider dealing derives largely from the problems involved in regulating what is a difficult offence to define and where it is often almost impossible to determine who has been directly harmed. Insider dealing is not a classic example of a 'victimless' crime since some people have been cheated when a breach of fiduciary duty occurs. But it is obviously not as straightforward as murder, robbery or rape. It is the case that much of government regulation through the positive law has produced great uncertainty (and probably an efficiency-reducing increase of risk aversion) for market traders.

The fact that in Britain policing the activity is entirely through the criminal law has caused much controversy. The burden of proof in criminal cases is higher than in civil ones so that prosecutions do not often succeed; the activity therefore goes on. The current law in this country, the Criminal Justice Act 1993 is, superficially, quite draconian but it offers so many defences to the accused that it is unlikely to be effective. Furthermore, the significance of the defences will depend a great deal on judicial interpretation and this adds another layer of uncertainty to an already indeterminate legal framework.

A plausible suggestion is that insider dealing should be decriminalised and made a civil offence. There should be a statutory body like the Securities and Exchange Commission (SEC) to police it. The trouble with this is that such bodies invariably expand their powers; this has certainly been the case in the USA where the SEC has become a serious impediment to market research. A better approach might be to try to make improvements on the remedies that were always available under private law. There have historically been cases where aggrieved shareholders have sought remedies for breach of contract by their employees but they did not succeed,[13] largely because the courts were not prepared to enforce vaguely defined, and possibly onerous, duties on company employees.

Historically, informal action was taken against wrongdoers. But as the market has become more anonymous these pressures have become less effective so that the demands for decisive regulatory action will continue. A possible solution might be for government to legislate on the nature of fiduciary duties and to make it easier for private persons to sue for their breach. In such a world it might be feasible to maintain an efficient information-gathering system while eliminating obvious cases of wrongdoing. At present we seem to have the worst of both worlds: a regulatory system which, if enforced rigorously, would inhibit the growth of knowledge and therefore undermine the capacity of the capital market to transmit it accurately, and a criminal order that allows the real offenders to escape justice.

An additional disincentive to the emergence of efficient markets is the fact that the current law embodies regulations that apply across Europe so that competition for the supply of efficient capital markets has been all but eliminated.

All these arguments have a special, if not peculiar, resonance to Anglo-American economies which rely heavily on the stock market for investment. The agents in them are thought to be obsessively concerned with maximising shareholder value. Critics of this type of economic organisation say that it leads to short-termism and the neglect of projects which, although potentially valuable, are not noticed by the market. The dispute between advocates of the two approaches comes to a head with the question of the takeover mechanism as a method of disciplining managements and realising long-term economic value. But takeovers also have a moral aspect: they are thought to exemplify in a spectacular way the individualism (and greed) of Anglo-American economies, and they encourage cavalier treatment of communities and employees in the remorseless pursuit of shareholder value. There may be a kind of harmony between economics and business ethics here. Government action to limit takeovers (and the alleged power of the City of London) might produce long-term growth and it might also generate those communal values which are apparently destroyed in Anglo-American capitalism.

TAKEOVERS AND THEIR RATIONALE

The hostile takeover is probably the most controversial and least popular aspect of Anglo-American capitalism. Other successful capitalist economies make little use of it and seem to avoid the disruption to orderly life, career patterns and community values that it is said to entail (see Hoffman *et al.*, 1987; and Barry, 1996b). However, there is a rationale to it, one which is fully consistent with the economic culture of Anglo-American capitalism. It has not, on the whole, been economically harmful and, given the individualism and relative anonymity that underlines the system, it is possibly the only mechanism that can bring about necessary industrial change.

To put it loosely, it is the response to the absence of specific common economic purposes that makes takeovers necessary. It is not that agents in Anglo-American economies are incapable of cooperating under *informal* rules and practices, although the excessive legalism of the American economy and the resource costs that it involves is beginning to worry observers, but it is the case that the public interest tends to emerge from the dispersed actions of transactors rather than being the product of *deliberate* cooperation.

The need for the mechanism arises partly out of the separation between ownership and control. Owners hire managers to handle their assets but there is no incentive for those whom they hire to behave efficiently, unless they are major shareholders themselves. They might behave opportunistically: without constant monitoring they tend to divert resources to themselves (rent-seeking). They will perhaps not discover entrepreneurial opportunities if there is little incentive beyond their normal salaries. To the extent that a takeover produces a reorganisation of assets and a better use of resources it is itself an example of entrepreneurship. In these circumstances the obsession with shareholder value is actually quite rational, for given the culture of Anglo-American capitalism, that is the only measure of success.

Not all takeovers are economically valuable and it is important to make a distinction between those that take place as a consequence of expansionism driven by managements, and those that come about through the desire to maximise shareholder value. For example, in the 1960s and 1970s (in the USA especially) there was considerable empire-building by companies. Instead of returning excess cash to shareholders,[14] managements embarked on costly programmes of buying up companies, and these were often unrelated to the activities of the original purchasing corporation. Thus unwieldy conglomerates were built up. It is not surprising that alert individuals should see the opportunity for increasing value by breaking up these inefficient operations. The takeover boom of the 1980s was therefore different from earlier examples of industrial reorganisation because it restored ultimate power to the owners.

Contrary to many critics' expectations, and predictions found in the history of economic thought, the reorganisation did not lead to the concentration of industry (see Goldstein, 1995) but the reverse. Indeed, management buyouts brought about a partial return to that ideal of Adam Smith – the owner-managed enterprise. Certainly the slimming down of American business that took place in the 1980s has made the US economy highly competitive. Furthermore, there is little evidence that the takeover system led to a decline in investment. Fear of a takeover did not deter managers from making long-term commitments; research by Michael Jensen (see Jensen, 1988) has shown that the market valued companies highly when they embarked on heavy investment programmes.

Innovative methods were discovered in the financing of hostile takeovers and they aroused great economic and moral controversy, largely because they involved debt. The development of the notorious 'junk bond' was actually an example of entrepreneurship. Michael Milken noticed that the credit ratings of the New York agencies were highly conservative, and inaccurate. They refused to give ratings to up-and-coming enterprises. However, he discovered that the default rate was actually quite low on these 'risky' bonds and he managed to secure loans, at high rates of interest, for companies which had good prospects. The same technique was applied with success to the financing of takeovers. So, far from the boom of the 1980s producing a mere shuffling of paper it added value. Whatever wrongs Milken may have committed, and there are now doubts about the validity of his convictions, there were very serious ethical shortcomings in the way he was persecuted by the authorities[15] and little understanding of what he was doing.

None of this is meant to imply that takeovers do not involve problems. Some of the methods used may be dubious and there are sometimes serious doubts about who made the entrepreneurial discovery. The Guinness case is the classic example. It looks as if it was James Gulliver who noticed that Distillers was inefficiently managed and conjectured that if the assets were reorganised value could be added. In a particularly bruising battle his discovery was apparently 'stolen' by Ernest Saunders who led the bid for the Guinness company. Saunders and others were convicted of various criminal offences, although there is now some doubt about the justice of this. Still, it is an interesting question as to whether in a moral sense it was Gulliver who was entitled to the rewards of entrepreneurship.[16] Thus even if Saunders had behaved with perfect propriety his action could still have been morally condemnable since it was Gulliver who had been originally alert to the opportunity; though how a government could enforce a property right arising out of this activity is difficult to say.

It might be the case that the social market economy has managed industrial change without the disruption that the takeover mechanism involves. Perhaps there is not that tension between owners and managers that seems to be endemic to the Anglo-American system. It may be the case that the heavy involvement of the banks in the management of German companies precludes the need for market incentives to discipline managers. It might even be true that the social market economy has produced such a spirit of cooperation that opportunism, which often gives rise to takeovers, is rare.

These questions are unanswerable but it is perhaps apposite to make some sceptical observations on the suggested reforms to the takeover mechanism. The major recommendation for Britain is that takeovers and mergers (of a certain size) should be permitted only if they are in the 'public interest'. Under current British law and practice, takeovers are only forbidden if they are against the public interest, for example, if they would lead to monopoly power or some other market-closing arrangement.

Obviously it is relatively easy to satisfy the negative requirement but the positive standard, that a takeover should advance the public good, is a much more controversial request. The public interest is a highly emotive term: it is supposed to indicate those things that we share as members of the public, as opposed to those that we have as members of private groups (see Barry, 1995b, ch. 10). But it can only be used in an uncontroversial sense in relation to the familiar public goods and, in the general social sphere, to the interest each citizen and economic transactor has in a stable and predictable legal order that protects contract and property.

If we are to ask potential bidders to satisfy inherently disputable criteria in takeovers then economic rationality will quickly give way to party-political bickering. It is almost certain that decisions will not be taken in the public interest but at the behest of private groups who stand to be adversely affected by a corporate reorganisation. In a response to the 1980s, most of the American states passed anti-takeover laws. But the legislation was a result of intense lobbying by managements and leaders of community groups.

CONCLUSION

Despite the obvious differences in the various forms of capitalism they do have some common features. There is perhaps a generic moral code to which they all conform, parts of which are embodied in positive law. This code covers such things as the sanctity of the person, the freedom to trade and to innovate, respect for legitimately acquired property and the more-or-less inviolability of contract. Indeed, most of the business scandals that have occurred involved breaches of the generic code and are not always ethically controversial: they are straightforward crimes. It is also the case that economies which have been recommended for their more appealing moral systems have produced examples of immoral behaviour which are at least as gross as any on Wall Street or in the City of London. Japan is an obvious example,[17] for its intimate, communal business morality functions as an *instrumental* device to secure certain national economic goals rather than as a moral model to be imitated. It is not an example of strict Kantian ethics.

From this it follows that the primary role of government in business morality is to enforce the generic moral code rather than to encourage the fulfilment of supererogatory moral duties. They are inherently disputable and are likely to have a detrimental effect on the primary purpose of Anglo-American business, which is to maximise owner value. The attempt to transplant differing business practices, by coercive law, to environments which do not have the appropriate cultural backdrop could have adverse conse-

108   *Government and Business Ethics*

quences for prosperity. The morality of Anglo-American business is essentially universalistic;[18] its rules apply to all who engage in transactions. It is for this sound moral reason that attempts to impose alien moral cultures on its agents should be resisted. The social market economy, and other varieties of capitalism recommended by business ethics, may be quite inappropriate for countries that lack the necessary elements of social cohesion for their successful adoption. Anyway, are we not witnessing a retreat from the social market economy and other versions of capitalism which are the traditional rivals of the Anglo-American model?

Notes

1. For a comparison between the Anglo-American model and those of Europe (especially Germany's system), see Albert (1993). Albert is convinced that what he calls the 'Rhineland' model will dominate world capitalism. Some of his predictions have already been falsified. See also Hutton (1995) for a thoroughly misleading account of British capitalism.
2. For the argument that there is a moral claim, via the 'finders keepers' principle, to discovered things, see Kirzner (1989).
3. *Ordoliberals* overlapped with the social market school but they were more interested in making the capitalist system work better than in welfare policy, see Barry (1989).
4. See D. Walker, 'A Shock to the System', in *Financial Times*, 6 August 1993.
5. Throughout we treat corporations as if they were the same as firms. For a ground-breaking analysis of the firm, see Coase (1937).
6. Though it is sometimes argued that shareholders do not properly own the firm, in the sense that they can do what they like with it; they merely own the shares.
7. There are many books that argue a positive case for corporate social responsibility; see especially, Donaldson (1982).
8. Milton Friedman (1993) has produced the most cogent argument against the demand for corporations to be socially responsible.
9. The best economic analysis, from an opponent of statutory regulation, is Manne (1966).
10. *Securities and Exchange Commission* v. *Texas Gulf Sulphur Company* (1968).
11. Henry Manne (1970) wrote: 'Morals, someone once said, are a private luxury. Carried into the area of serious debate on public policy, moral arguments are either frequently a sham or a refuge for the intellectually bankrupt.'
12. In fact, this could be a reason for not trading on inside information. The employees might be entitled to the full profit from their internal entrepreneurship but some of it is paid to the owners in the form of higher share prices; see Ricketts (1994). Still, maybe they would still demand the right to trade on inside information because they could not trust the owners to pay them their 'just' returns in the form of higher salaries, bonuses and so on.

13. The leading case is *Percival* v. *Wright* (1902).
14. This is the 'free cash flow theory' pioneered by Jensen; see Jensen (1988).
15. See Fischel (1995). For a defence of Milken in the context of 'Austrian' economics, see Barry (1991).
16. This point is raised by Ricketts (1992), who points to a difference between the moral claim arising out of a discovery and the ability to profit from it. There may be two different people involved here.
17. For Japan, see Flaherty and Hiroyuki (1988). There have been many Japanese scandals in the securities market; see *Financial Times*, 4 September 1991.
18. This universalism was applied perhaps inappropriately when the US Congress tried to stamp out bribery by American business agents overseas with the passing of the United States Foreign Corrupt Practices Act 1977. In some business cultures bribery is endemic.

References

Albert, M. (1993) *Capitalism versus Capitalism* (London: Whurr).
Barry, N. (1989) 'The Political and Economic Thought of German Neo-Liberalism', in A. Peacock and H. Willgerodt (eds), *German Liberalism and the Social Market Economy* (London: Macmillan).
Barry, N. (1991) *The Morality of Business Enterprise* (Aberdeen: Aberdeen University Press).
Barry, N. (1993) 'The Social Market Economy', *Social Philosophy and Policy*, 2, pp. 1–25.
Barry, N. (1995a) 'What Moral Constraints for Business?', in A. Hamlin and S. Brittan (eds), *Market Capitalism and Moral Values* (Aldershot: Edward Elgar).
Barry, N. (1995b) *An Introduction to Modern Political Theory* (London: Macmillan).
Barry, N. (1996a) *Insider Dealing* (London: Foundation for Business Responsibilities).
Barry, N. (1996b) 'Rational Barbarians: Innovators in the Corporate World', in N. Kuenssberg and A. Lomas (eds), *The David Hume Institute: The First Decade* (Edinburgh: Edinburgh University Press).
Coase, R.H. (1937) 'The Nature of the Firm', *Economica*, 4, pp. 386–405.
Donaldson, T. (1982) *Corporations and Morality* (Englewood Cliffs, NJ: Prentice-Hall).
Etzioni, A. (1963) *The Spirit of Community* (New York: Crown).
Evan, W. and Freeman, E. (1993) 'A Stakeholder Theory of the Modern Corporation; Kantian Capitalism', in T. Beauchamp and N. Bowie (eds), *Ethical Theory and Business*, 4th ed (Englewood Cliffs, NJ: Prentice-Hall).
Fischel, D. (1995) *Payback: The Conspiracy to Destroy Michael Milken and His Financial Revolution* (New York: Harper).
Flaherty, M. and Hiroyuki, I. (1988) 'The Banking–Industrial Complex', in D. Okimoto and T. Roblen (eds), *Inside the Japanese System* (Stanford, Calif.: Stanford University Press).
Frey, R. (ed.) (1985) *Utility and Rights* (Oxford: Blackwell).
Friedman, M. (1962) *Capitalism and Freedom* (Chicago, Ill: University of Chicago Press).
Friedman, M. (1993) 'The Social Responsibility of Business is to Increase its Profits', in T. Beauchamp and N. Bowie (eds), *Ethical Theory and Business*, 4th edn (Englewood Cliffs, NJ: Prentice-Hall).

Fukuyama, F. (1995) *Trust* (London: Hamish Hamilton).

Galbraith, J.K. (1996) *The Good Society* (London: Sinclair Stevenson).

Goldstein, H. (1995) 'Junk Bonds and Corporate America', *Critical Review*, 9, pp. 403–19.

Hannigan, B. (1988) *Insider Dealing* (London: Kluwer).

Hayek, F.A. (1973) *Rules and Order* (London: Routledge & Kegan Paul).

Hayek, F.A. (1982) 'The Tradition of Spontaneous Order', *Literature of Liberty*, 5, pp. 7–58.

Hessen, R. (1979) *In Defense of the Corporation* (San Francisco: Hoover Institution).

Hoffman, M., Frederick, R. and Petty, E. (eds) (1987) *The Ethics of Organizational Transformation* (New York: Quorum Books).

Hutton, W. (1995) *The State We're In* (London: Jonathan Cape).

Jensen, M. (1988) 'Takeovers: Their Causes and Consequences', *Journal of Economic Perspectives*, 2, pp. 21–48.

Kirzner, I. (1973) *Competition and Entrepreneurship* (Chicago, Ill: University of Chicago Press).

Kirzner, I. (1989) *Discovery, Capitalism and Distributive Justice* (Oxford: Clarendon Press).

Kirzner, I. (1995)'The Morality of Pure Profit', *Journal des Economistes*, 2, pp. 315–27.

Macqueen, H. (ed.) (1994) *Insider Dealing* (Edinburgh: David Hume Institute).

Mandeville, B. de (1924) *The Fable of the Bees*, ed. F.B. Kaye, (Oxford: Clarendon Press). First published 1705.

Manne, H. (1966) *Insider Trading and the Stock Market* (New York: Collier–Macmillan).

Manne, H. (1970) 'Insider Trading and the Law Professors', *Vanderbilt Law Review*, 23, p. 549.

Manne, H. (1972) *The Modern Corporation and Social Responsibility* (Washington, DC: American Enterprise Institute).

Smith, A. (1976) *The Wealth of Nations*, ed. R. Campbell, A. Skinner and W. Todd (Oxford: Clarendon Press). First published 1776.

Ricketts, M. (1992) 'Kirzner's Theory of Entrepreneurship', in B. Caldwell and S. Bohm (eds), *Austrian Economics: Tensions and New Directions* (London: Kluwer).

Ricketts, M. (1994) *The Economics of Business Enterprise*, 2nd edn (Brighton: Wheatsheaf).

Wildavsky, A. (1988) *Searching for Safety* (New Brunswick, NJ: Transaction Books).

7 Evidence of a New Environmental Ethic: Assessing the Trend towards Investor and Consumer Activism

Maurie Cohen

INTRODUCTION

For corporate managers throughout most of Western Europe and North America the environment initially emerged as a strategic consideration during the early 1970s. During this decade, the political systems of the world's advanced nations, acting in response to both public demands and the objective criteria of serious ecological deterioration, developed the first generation of comprehensive industrial, agricultural and vehicular emission standards. Enforcement of these regulations was originally situated within existing public health agencies, but as the scope and complexity of environmental dilemmas became apparent, national and local governments found it necessary to create separate bureaucracies to assume these responsibilities (Lundqvist, 1980; Vogel, 1986; Hays, 1987).

During this first wave of modern environmentalism, the regulatory context for industry, while at times contentious, was relatively predictable. New legislative initiatives emerged regularly throughout the 1970s, progressing through political channels corporate managers understood well. The business community was able to deploy familiar tactics, principally the application of pressure on public officeholders, to defend themselves from overly stringent environmental controls. Once government imposed a new regulation, corporate objections based on financial hardship and technological unfeasibility – as in the case of American automobile emission standards – often proved effective in delaying actual implementation (see, in particular, Schnaiberg, 1980; Hawkins, 1984). When contesting these issues in the public arena, firms regularly threatened to relocate their operations or to reduce employment in order to intimidate local communities from pressing too aggressively for environmental controls on manufacturing activities (Kazis and Grossman, 1982; Nelkin and Brown, 1984; Robinson, 1991). This relatively comfortable situation for industry, however, began to change during the later part of the 1980s. In most advanced nations a recognition began to build that, despite modest improvements in water and air quality, the earlier generation of environmental regulations was inadequate (Commoner, 1990; Weale, 1992). Concentrating this awareness was the emergence of a whole new array of ecological concerns that, because of their transboundary characteristics and embeddedness in contemporary economic systems, defied traditional, largely localised mitigation strategies. Acid rain, the precursor of this new generation of problems, was joined on the international environmental agenda by ozone depletion, toxic chemical contamination, declining biodiversity and global warming.

These issues, because they cut to the organisational core of modern industrial society, represented a qualitatively different form of ecological deterioration. Particularly in the case of greenhouse gas emissions (for example, carbon dioxide, methane), substantive reductions cannot be achieved with end-of-pipe solutions, the sorts of technologies that provided the preferred interventions during the earlier phase of environmental correction. In this case, strategies that fail to curb economic growth and resource consumption – in both developed and developing nations – are unlikely to be effective in the long run. At this point in time, it appears that progress on climate change will require the negotiation of a broad international treaty to limit economic expansion and to reconcile thorny disputes concerning global equity.[1]

It is thus apparent that the past two decades have brought profound changes to the way in which the most economically and politically capable countries in the world address the adverse environmental conditions caused by the high-consumption lifestyles to which their residents have become accustomed. The intention of this chapter is to explore how these changes in the environmental policy domain have generated new and profound challenges for corporate managers. The following section examines the reasons why the current array of ecological problems differs so sharply from the customary air and water pollution controversies that catapulted the environment to prominence in the early 1970s. This chapter's third section introduces the notion of the 'operational milieu' as a conceptual mechanism for understanding the context in which firms are being forced to improve their environmental performance. The fourth section explores the reasons for the rise in ecological consciousness that is evident across the community of advanced nations and asserts that this awareness is not likely to be a passing phenomenon. Despite its enduring qualities, there is considerable diversity in the ecological consciousness being expressed in these countries and the fifth section analyses these differences. The concluding section demonstrates that this pressure to meet higher standards of ecological responsibility should not be viewed in isolation, but rather as part of a more expansive movement to make managers accountable for quality and excellence.

THE NEW CLASS OF ECOLOGICAL DILEMMAS

Contemporary ecological dilemmas such as global warming are fundamentally different from the problems that characterised the 1970s on at least four levels. First, the new generation of concerns entails a much greater role for *scientific expertise* and as such embodies considerable uncertainty regarding risk to human health and natural systems. The previous environmental era was marked by efforts to regulate pollutants that were, for the most part, objectively experienced by members of the lay public. Obnoxious emissions emanating from industrial facilities or vehicle tailpipes had a sensory reality (that is, experienced through normal sight or smell) that did not require specialised training and sophisticated equipment to ascertain. Further, the implications of these hazards were often encountered in an immediate and personal manner; for instance, prohibitions on swimming due to the presence of toxic chemicals in local rivers and lakes were not uncommon.

Second, the most serious consequences of global warming (and most other modern environmental problems) are *latent* and not likely to become apparent for at least another generation into the future. In this sense, climate change does not pose an immediate threat to personal livelihoods. This characteristic, coupled with the severity of the lifestyle changes necessary in the world's most affluent nations to achieve any appreciable reductions in greenhouse gas emissions, has made it difficult to mobilise sufficient political support for mitigation initiatives outside the realm of ideologically committed environmentalists.

Third, due to its *global scale*, progress toward remediation of climate change does not lend itself to localised initiatives to reduce greenhouse gas emissions, but instead is dependent on the successful implementation of comprehensive international agreements. The atmosphere is essentially a 'commons' and meaningful solutions must entail the negotiation of complex conventions by all the nations of the world. In the absence of such a formal structure, any reductions achieved by one country will be neutralised by increased industrial activity undertaken elsewhere. This feature of the climate change dilemma seems, by most reasonable and informed assessments, to place demands on the current international political system that exceed its capabilities for reaching successful resolution.

Finally, the scope of global warming appears so daunting and the requisite 'technological fix' so remote that a certain *resignation* has become manifest among both political actors and members of the general public. The inability of any single nation to advance a strategy able to achieve appreciable improvement has led many countries to acquiesce to the inevitability of environmental harm. In the eyes of many observers it may simply be preferable, for instance, to abandon certain low-lying communities to inundation and to build massive sea-walls along other coastal areas. In some countries, especially those situated in extreme latitudes (for example, Canada and the Scandinavian nations), any remorse over climate change has been moderated by the possible economic benefits that may accrue from a more temperate climate and an extended agricultural season.

While these factors point to the fact that the new generation of ecological threats is appreciably different from that of the 1970s, it is also true that calls to challenge poor environmental performance have begun arising from unfamiliar quarters. For example, activist organisations that had previously limited their sphere of operation to protests in opposition to nuclear power have started to focus their attention on more general forms of corporate environmental abuse. Consumer boycotts, first targeted towards firms that traded in sentimentalised species such as seals, elephants and whales are now being mobilised in opposition to the activities of other economic sectors (for example, pharmaceuticals, cosmetics) and these actions have the potential to inflict serious economic damage. Perhaps most troublesome to corporate managers has been the revolution taking shape within their own ranks in the form of pressure from shareholders and employees urging more responsible behaviour. These attacks on organisational integrity emanate from recondite sources and tend to proceed in unpredictable directions due to their dependence on media attentiveness. Often intangible and difficult to discern, the sources of outrage typically form and then dissolve, only to coalesce again in response to some stimulus over which firms have little control. Such threats, because of their quixotic and variable quality, can be frustrating for managers because they do not lend themselves to customary contingency planning techniques.

Though a variety of social trends is responsible for this new ecological consciousness, a series of major industrial accidents at now infamous locations such as Seveso, Three Mile Island, Bhopal, Chernobyl and Valdez has helped to catalyse them into a broad movement for social change.[2] This series of catastrophic events provoked unprecedented indignation because the disasters were not simply ecological abuses in the conventional sense. Rather, these tragedies highlighted in salient form large corporations' lack of public accountability and the virtual powerlessness of political systems to manage effectively the risks of modern industrial economies. This realisation, combined with the demise of Cold War tensions, the eroding influence of organised labour, the personal uncertainty created by economic globalisation and the discredited status of Marxian analysis as an alternative to orthodox political discourse, has elevated the environment to a position in which it has become an important element of comprehensive social critique (see, for example, Giddens, 1991; Beck, 1992; Goldblatt, 1996).

These changes have their origins deep within the body of contemporary society and managers' concerns about the sources of these new threats to organisational integrity are not illusory. Sizeable segments of the population in advanced nations are demanding that central components of the business community conform to an enhanced environmental ethic, one that requires fundamental alterations in how economic institutions relate to the larger society. This chapter is devoted to an exploration of these issues. In developing this analysis, the current account attempts to place prevailing unease about declining biodiversity, diminishing stratospheric ozone levels and increasing carbon dioxide emissions into a broader context of social and demographic change. Treated in this manner, it will become apparent that the pressure managers are currently facing to improve environmental performance is not likely to disappear. Though fluctuations in the intensity of these demands are inevitable, the general direction is resolute.

THE OPERATIONAL MILIEU FOR FIRMS

Business strategies are formulated as responses to dynamic situational factors, some of which are discrete and obvious, while others tend to permeate more subtly the boundaries separating firms from society. Because of the multiplicity of variables that must be reconciled, managers make decisions heuristically in response to perceived changes in what can be described as the *operational milieu*. As depicted in Figure 7.1, the operational milieu is structured and tempered by three domains of individual and institutional actors: fiscal stakeholders, consumers and voters. These actors are not anchored to single domains, but invariably move from one realm to another as they reconstitute themselves for different activities. Transitions, for example from fiscal stakeholder to consumer, are becoming increasingly common as the boundaries between the different domains become less clearly defined. Nonetheless, the techniques appropriate for affecting change in the operational milieu will differ markedly based on the domain in which an actor is operating at a particular point in time. Furthermore, certain actors are likely to possess comparative advantages that enhance their perfor-

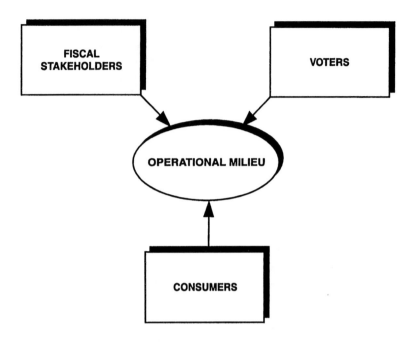

Figure 7.1   Operational milieu

mance in one setting and this will encourage them to privilege one domain over the others.

The relative strength of each of the domains to shape the operational milieu is regularly subject to realignments. As the result of demographic and attitudinal shifts in the world's most affluent nations, the comparative influence of the domains has gradually changed in important ways during the past several decades. The following section describes how these adjustments have led to the application of new techniques for promoting corporate ecological improvements. This discussion is necessarily informed by the author's more intimate familiarity with the American context, though an effort is made to draw parallels with the developing situation in Europe.

Fiscal Stakeholder Domain

The fiscal stakeholder domain comprises employees, investors and financial institutions, each of which plays a different role in shaping the operational milieu. While pressure from employees (more particularly, from their labour organisations) can still be an important mechanism for drawing attention to issues that impinge on working conditions (for example, compensation, health and safety), activism on the part of both institutional and individual investors has of late become the most prevalent channel for fiscal stakeholders to press forward the cause of corporate reform. In the United States, many of these initiatives have been launched by pension funds, mutual funds, and philanthropic foundations which have acquired large corporate equity holdings (Davis and Thompson, 1994; Pozen, 1994; Hawley, 1995; Smith, 1996).

The proportion of the average American firm's equity under the control of institutional investors increased from 16 per cent in 1965 to 43 per cent in 1986, and among the country's 1000 largest corporations, institutional holdings in 1993 reached 56 per cent (Davis and Thompson, 1994). This change in ownership distribution has enabled these institutions to overcome the problems of atomisation that prevented small individual investors from challenging managers' authority. Some observers assert that because these entities control sizeable blocks of major corporations' shares, this wave of fiduciary activism by institutional investors represents a transition towards 'relationship' investing, an emergent form of social and economic organisation that re-establishes the linkages between owners and managers. From a related perspective, Hawley (1995) suggests this development is part of a process in which corporate property is being 'semi-socialised'.

This form of fiduciary activism originated during the aftermath of the 1980s takeover frenzy. Institutional investors, because of the large size of their holdings, began experiencing difficulties profitably divesting themselves of underperforming companies. The pension funds that faced this problem most acutely were the California Public Employees Retirement System (CalPERS), the New York State Public Employees Retirement System (NYPERS), and the Wisconsin Investment Board. As a result, these three funds played important roles in leading the trend among institutional investors from, in Hirschman's (1970) terms, an exit to a voice strategy. As Davis and Thompson (1994) observe:

> The increased size of institutional investors' holdings limited their ability to divest from firms with which they were dissatisfied. Previously institutions that were dissatisfied with management would typically do the Wall Street Walk and sell their stake rather than confront management. When one's stake is large enough, however, selling out depresses the share price and harms the seller, in addition, for the largest funds, the number of alternative investments is limited. (p. 154)

While in some cases, the recent influence of institutional investors has been described as 'proxy power', the real authority of fiduciary activism cannot be judged in terms of the number of ballot measures management is forced to face. When an institutional investor (or more likely a coalition of such interests) begins to demonstrate dissatisfaction, proactive managers retain considerable discretion over how to defuse the matter before it escalates to a proxy vote.[3] In this reconstituted operational milieu, corporate managers have become adept at engaging in negotiations with powerful shareholders to resolve outstanding concerns rather than submitting the matter to a referendum.

Related to the fiduciary activism being pursued by large pension funds is the trend towards ethical investment by smaller shareholders who participate in mutual funds targeted toward specific agendas (Rosen, Sandler, and Shani, 1991).[4] Portfolio managers of these funds screen corporations on their performance before declaring their shares acceptable for acquisition. For instance, some funds refuse to commit any portion of their portfolios to firms that fail to include minority representation on their boards of directors. When applied widely, the use of such screens can measurably depress the share value of those firms whose operating practices contravene investors' standards of acceptability. Pioneered in the United States, such socially responsible investment programmes have also begun to attract larger slices of the mutual fund markets in Europe. As these investment vehicles have grown in popularity, their managers have acquired greater power to influence corporate managers' decisions.

Importantly for current purposes, fiduciary activism by pension and mutual funds has begun to extend beyond prosaic issues of corporate governance to encompass sensitive policies with respect to social issues and environmental management. A frequent tool of these reform initiatives has been the use of codes of conduct to encourage managers to steer corporations in particular directions. These codes are essentially extra-legal protocols designed to elicit ethical commitments from targeted firms and have been used to promote such issues as gender and racial equity, military disarmament, prohibition of child labour, protection of indigenous populations and commitment to local communities. This device initially captured attention as part of the effort to further the cause of political reform in South Africa. In 1977, Leon Sullivan, a Philadelphia minister and General Motors board member, formulated a code of conduct – subsequently known as the Sullivan Principles – that encouraged American firms operating in South Africa to design employment policies to promote racial equality (Paul, 1989; Gray and Karp, 1993).[5] The Sullivan Principles, which were endorsed by General Motors, Citibank, and several other large multinational corporations, were intended to provide a constructive approach for alleviating pressure on American firms to withdraw from South Africa. In more recent years, with the dissolution of legally enforced apartheid in South Africa, environmental activists campaigning for more ecologically responsible corporate behaviour have continued the use of this mechanism of moral suasion.

The favoured approach of pension and mutual funds committed to an agenda calling for enhanced corporate ecological responsibility has been to urge firms to endorse voluntarily the CERES Principles (Figure 7.2) developed by the United States-based Coalition for Environmentally Responsible Economies (Sanyal and Neves, 1991; Hoffman, 1996). This particular code, originally known as the Valdez Principles in ignominious recognition of the 1989 Alaska oil spill, is a ten-point list of guidelines specifically conceived to enhance the environmental stewardship of endorsing firms. The CERES Principles are constructed quite broadly and their specific objectives include the sustainable use of natural resources, the provision of compensation to individuals harmed by corporate activities, and the disclosure of hazards to employees and members of the public. By the end of 1995, more than fifty *Fortune 500* companies – including General Motors, Sun Oil, Bethlehem Steel, and Polaroid – had endorsed this code of conduct (Bavaria, 1996).

Consumer Domain

Consumers, through their purchase selections, have access to potentially powerful tools for altering the operational milieu. The most effective approach available to consumers interested in promoting corporate reform is the boycott. For instance, Friedman (1995) cites evidence suggesting that boycotts are the expression of consumer protest that managers perceive as most effective, largely because such actions pose grave threats to firm survival. Though consumer boycotts can be difficult and expensive to organise, this form of collective action has come to be deployed with some frequency, especially by environmental activists. According to one estimate from the United States, organisations committed to environmental protection and animal rights launched more than 100 boycotts between 1987 and 1991. Specific boycott targets have been fur manufacturers, firms associated with the nuclear power industry, pharmaceutical and personal care product companies, and pulp and paper processors engaged in abusive land management practices. For animal rights activists, facilities using animals for laboratory testing purposes have been found to be particularly objectionable. As Friedman (1995) notes, 'Organizations like Earth Island Institute, People for the Ethical Treatment of Animals, Earth First!, and the Rainforest Action Network did not exist fifteen years ago, but they now constitute major players in consumer protest actions against perceived corporate abuses of the environment' (p. 197).

Figure 7.2 The CERES principles

By adopting these Principles, we publicly affirm our belief that corporations have a responsibility for the environment, and must conduct all aspects of their business as responsible stewards of the environment in a manner that protects the Earth. We believe the corporations must not compromise the ability of future generations to sustain themselves. We will update our practices constantly in light of advances in technology and new understandings in health and environmental science. In collaboration with CERES, we will promote a dynamic process to ensure that the Principles are interpreted in a way that accommodates changing technologies and environmental realities. We intend to make consistent, measurable progress in implementing these Principles and to apply them to all aspects of our operations throughout the world.

1. PROTECTION OF THE BIOSPHERE

We will reduce and make continual progress towards eliminating the release of any substance that may cause environmental damage to the air, water, or earth or its inhabitants. We will safeguard all habitats affected by our operations and will protect open spaces and wilderness, while preserving biodiversity.

2. SUSTAINABLE USE OF NATURAL RESOURCES

We will make sustainable use of renewable natural resources, such as water, soils, and forests. We will conserve non-renewable natural resources through efficient use and careful planning.

3. REDUCTION AND DISPOSAL OF WASTES

We will reduce and where possible eliminate waste through source reduction and recycling. All waste will be handled and disposed of through safe and responsible methods.

4. ENERGY CONSERVATION

We will conserve energy and improve the energy efficiency of our internal operations and of the goods and services we sell. We will make every effort to use environmentally safe and sustainable energy sources.

5. RISK REDUCTION

We will strive to minimize the environmental, health, and safety risks to our employees and communities in which we operate through safe technologies, facilities, and operating procedures, and by being prepared for emergencies.

6. SAFE PRODUCTS AND SERVICES

We will reduce and where possible eliminate the use, manufacture, or sale of products and services that cause environmental damage or health or safety hazards. We will inform our customers of the environmental impacts of our products or services and try to correct unsafe use.

7. ENVIRONMENTAL RESTORATION

We will promptly and responsibly correct conditions we have caused that endanger health, safety, or the environment. To the extent feasible, we will redress injuries we have caused to persons or damage we have caused to the environment and will restore the environment.

8. INFORMING THE PUBLIC

We will inform in a timely manner everyone who may be affected by conditions caused by our company that might endanger health, safety, or the environment. We will regularly seek advice and counsel through dialogue with persons in communities near our facilities. We will not take any action against employees for reporting dangerous incidents or conditions to management or to appropriate authorities.

9. MANAGEMENT COMMITMENT

We will implement these Principles and sustain a process that ensures that the Board of Directors and Chief Executive Officer are fully informed about pertinent environmental issues and are fully responsible for environmental policy. In selecting our Board of Directors, we will consider demonstrated environmental commitment as a factor.

10. AUDITS AND REPORTS

We will conduct an annual self-evaluation of our progress in implementing these Principles. We will support the timely creation of generally accepted environmental audit procedures. We will annually complete the CERES Report, which will be made available to the public.

DISCLAIMER

These Principles establish an environmental ethic with criteria by which investors and others can assess the environmental performance of companies. Companies that endorse these Principles pledge to go voluntarily beyond the requirements of the law. The terms 'may' and 'might' in Principles one and eight are not meant to encompass every imaginable consequences, no matter how remote. Rather, these Principles obligate endorsers to behave as prudent persons who are not governed by conflicting interests and who possess a strong commitment to environmental excellence and to human health and safety. These Principles are not intended to create new legal liabilities, expand existing rights or obligations, waive legal defences, or otherwise affect the legal position of any endorsing company, and are not intended to be used against an endorser in any legal proceeding for any purpose.

(Reproduced by kind permission)

In the United States, the effectiveness of boycotts has been enhanced by the establishment of resource centres such as the Institute for Consumer Responsibility and Co-Op America that track the initiatives of a vast number of decentralised groups. Boycott organisers have achieved several noteworthy successes, the most prominent of which was the effort to assure the provision of so-called dolphin-safe tuna.[6] However, consumer-based efforts for corporate reform do not have to impart actual market consequences to prove effective, as often the threat of a boycott can be sufficient to achieve the activists' objectives. For instance, Benetton acceded within two months to the pressure of animal rights groups critical of the Italian fashion company's use of laboratory animals to test a new line of cosmetics. From these experiences, many shrewd boycott leaders have come to realise that campaigns no longer need to be launched as protracted protests involving some degree of consumer sacrifice, but rather should be structured to derive maximum media exposure for the promoting group's claims.

Organised actions have not been the only mechanism used by consumers to spur changes in corporate behaviour. Individual shoppers, even in the absence of formal prodding from boycott organisers, have demonstrated a willingness to modify their personal purchasing habits to favour more ecologically benign products. For instance, many consumers have expressed an increased willingness to pay a premium for organically produced foodstuffs (see, for example, Hammitt, 1990). The shift towards greater environmental consciousness has also prompted many firms to devote attention to so-called eco-marketing and 'green labelling' programmes as a means of securing competitive advantages (Salzhauer, 1991). According to Davis (1992), 'nearly ten per cent of all new products introduced [in the United States] in 1990 were identified *by their manufacturer* as "green" or otherwise "environmentally friendly"' (italics in original). This number of newly launched 'green' products was more than double that of the previous year and 2000 per cent greater than in 1985.

While some important achievements have been realised – for example, replacement of certain hazardous production technologies, reductions of ecologically harmful extraction practices and decreases in the use of extraneous packaging materials – most firms approach ecological marketing with instrumental intentions and structure their interventions to achieve maximum promotional benefits.[7] Further complicating progress on this front has been the rampant use of disingenuous assertions of ecological integrity by corporate advertisers and the difficulties regulatory agencies have encountered designing appropriate standards to assure the legitimacy of environmental claims (Kangun, Carlson, and Grove, 1991; Davis, 1992; Welsh, 1993; Scammon and Mayer, 1995). Many managers operate from the premise that questionable advertisements constitute acceptable marketing behaviour, placing on government and advocacy organisations the burden of disproving the assertions. For instance, Dow began promoting its plastic bags in the United States as 'photodegradable', suggesting the product would decompose in sunlight once discarded at disposal facilities. In reality, these conditions are not generally attainable because landfilled refuse is covered with soil and other debris. Ultimately, the company was forced to retract this claim, but this action did not occur until after the Environmental Defense Fund and the Environmental Action Foundation had launched a public protest.[8] Such situations, combined with several high-profile media campaigns aimed at discrediting firms typically held in high public regard for their ecological accomplishments (for example, the Body Shop, Ben & Jerry's Ice Cream), have undermined consumer confidence in environmental marketing initiatives (Mayer, Scammon and Zick, 1993; Davis, 1994).

Far more radical behaviour by individual consumers to alter the operational milieu is represented by a small minority of people in the world's most affluent countries who have deliberately and freely adopted less consumption-oriented lifestyles. These so-called voluntary simplifiers are variously committed to relaxing their dependence on consumerism and to reorganising their lives to promote less intensive resource utilisation (Elgin, 1993; Dominguez and Robin, 1993). While current estimates in the United States place the number of people who have adopted voluntary simplicity in one form or another at no more than 10 per cent of the national population, the movement of increasing numbers of people in this direction would have truly widespread consequences for economic and social life. Some individuals who identify with this lifestyle might consider themselves to be 'societal drop-outs', but most voluntary simplifiers continue to function quite actively in mainstream society (Goldberg, 1995; Schor, 1996). In order to buffer the intrusive effects of advertising, mass consumption and community values that celebrate rampant acquisition, many of these people avoid watching television and form support groups of like-minded people to insulate themselves from consumerist influences.

Political Domain

Participation in democratic processes through the familiar practices of mobilising publics and voting for elected representatives can promote changes in the political realm that reorient the operational milieu. This particular domain for securing ecological improvement, pursued aggressively by advocacy organisations in most advanced nations during the 1970s and

1980s, has typically involved lobbying governments for stricter regulations and more vigorous enforcement. While certain elements of the environmental agenda have been institutionalised in government procedures, there is accumulating evidence to suggest that further opportunities for progress are limited and that this era of environmentalism is drawing to a close.

Indications of the declining attractiveness of the political option to effect changes in the operational milieu capable of promoting ecological improvement can be gleaned from the ebbing fortunes of environmental advocacy organisations. Despite notable accomplishments in many Western European nations during the 1980s, the Green parties' ecological agenda has become frayed in recent years and this form of political expression is facing an uncertain future (Jahn, 1993; Bramwell, 1994). On the other side of the Atlantic Ocean, institutionalised American environmentalism – as represented by mail order membership associations such as the Sierra Club – is casting about for a redefined role that will enable it to transcend the familiar political battlefields (Gottlieb, 1993; Dowie, 1995). The conventional groups' leadership role has been eclipsed by newer organisations representative of a more professional type of ecological activism that owes its success to astute scientific expertise (for example, the Natural Resources Defense Council, the Environmental Defense Fund).[9] An additional factor that has worked to press the mainstream groups to the periphery is the emergence of a vast network of agile grassroots organisations committed to the cause of environmental justice and the eradication of social inequalities in the distribution of industrial hazards (Bullard, 1994; Cable and Cable, 1995).

This discussion suggests that fundamental adjustments have occurred in the relative influence of the three domains that shape the operational milieu, most particularly in terms of how ecological concerns receive public expression. The political domain has receded from its dominant position, partly due to environmental proponents' realisation that this channel is losing its viability. This awareness is grounded in the fact that the fortunes of existing political elites are predicated on preservation of the prevailing economic system and these groups are unlikely to champion interventions that would jeopardise its survival. As a result, in most advanced nations, environmental activists have shifted their attention from the political domain to the fiscal stakeholder and consumer domains and have begun to formulate a more comprehensive critique of societal organisation. This has meant that the signals urging reform have begun to come from less familiar directions and managers are correct in sensing that the relative strength of the domains shaping the operational milieu has changed. The character of the new generation of ecological dilemmas, coupled with the realisation that problems such as global warming cannot be resolved through conventional measures, has been critical in forcing this realignment. However, less acknowledged social and demographic factors have also played important roles in encouraging firms to improve their environmental performance and it is to these issues that the next section turns its attention.

THE RISE OF ECOLOGICAL CONSCIOUSNESS IN ADVANCED NATIONS

To be sure, crucial structural and legal adjustments in economically advanced nations are to some extent responsible for the rise of the new sorts of environmental activism described above. For instance, changes in share ownership patterns and revised regulations have facilitated the reform initiatives currently being advanced by pension funds in the United States and elsewhere. Additionally, the increased willingness of individuals in these countries to invest in mutual funds, as opposed to assembling their own portfolios, has enabled small investors to overcome the collective-action problems of highly dispersed and differentiated ownership. However, the scope of activism, particularly by institutions such as the California Public Employees Retirement System (CalPERS), extends beyond narrow issues of corporate governance that would ensure improved investment returns. Important segments of the financial communities in economically advanced nations have embraced a progressive constellation of social, political, environmental and ethical commitments traditionally beyond shareholders' interests. Furthermore, consumer demands for less ecologically destructive products cannot be attributed in broad terms to regulatory interventions. Rather, these developments suggest a critical reorientation of societal objectives, characteristics that are most readily examined by adopting a comparative analytic framework. While it would be an overstatement to claim that such adjustments have touched all members of this group of elite countries, it is not unreasonable to assert that these new values have become manifest, to a varying degree, within virtually all of these societies.

To shed light on the sources of this apparent reorientation of priorities towards environmental protection in advanced societies and to explain the opening of new channels for expressing these concerns, the work of political scientist Ronald Inglehart (1977, 1990) offers a useful point of departure. Since the latter part of the 1970s Inglehart has been examining cultural change and the emergence of new value commitments within a broad cross-section of advanced nations. Inglehart and his associates have set themselves the task of regularly administering a series of opinion surveys, the results from which indicate that Western European and North American societies are experiencing an intergenerational value shift. This realignment involves a transition away from traditional values of economic security to a new constellation of preferences that places greater emphasis on quality of life. This evolution is occurring, Inglehart contends, because the generations of people that experienced the relative scarcity of the pre-Second World War years have values that more strongly favour economic growth and material consumption. As these age groups are replaced by younger cohorts which have reached adulthood since the Second World War, during a period of unprecedented wealth creation throughout all advanced nations, there has been a gradual societal transformation toward so-called 'postmaterialism'. In a Maslowian sense, Inglehart's thesis posits that now that advanced nations have largely satisfied their publics' material needs, an emphasis on personal freedom, education and self-expression has become more pronounced. The continued advance of this process of generational replacement in future decades means that the proportion of the population in these countries with postmaterial values can be expected to exert increasing influence on the character of their societies.

According to Inglehart, the trend toward postmaterialism can be witnessed in several indicators. First, declining birth rates in the world's most affluent countries are interpreted as reflections of increasing female equality and women's desire to forsake family responsibilities in favour of alternative endeavours. Second, this gradual value realignment is evident in the declining effectiveness of conventional incentives to motivate people to work long hours and engage in consumption-intensive behaviours. Third, survey responses suggest that the publics of advanced societies express an increasing demand to protect freedom of speech. Finally, individuals in the world's wealthiest nations are becoming more interested in participatory forms of governance that devolve responsibility to local communities and enable them to engage in the decision processes of other institutions.

While these trends are familiar to most social scientists, Inglehart does not rely purely on anecdotal evidence to support his contentions. Rather he has, for the past twenty years, been subjecting his survey results to extensive statistical analyses to disprove assertions that these trends are spurious. For instance, some critics have argued that what Inglehart identifies as intergenerational value shifts are simply life-cycle effects. In other words, people may indicate less materialistic leanings when they are younger, but these inclinations disappear as the more youthful cohorts age. Another major criticism has focused on the observation that Inglehart is confusing period effects with intergenerational shifts. This claim contends that postmaterialism rises during periods of prosperity, but erodes when economic fortunes reverse. Inglehart has consistently confronted his critics and mobilised evidence to refute their assertions, but these efforts have not defused entirely the controversy that surrounds this thesis.

In order to highlight the efficacy of Inglehart's theory, it is useful to consider some actual data. According to one of the most recent cross-national surveys of public opinion in a sample of advanced nations, The Netherlands has the most postmaterial public (refer to Figure 7.3). In other words, these results suggest that the intergenerational value shift has progressed furthest in this society and the Dutch population expresses a pronounced willingness to adopt new lifestyle commitments. Among the countries at the other extreme of this distribution we find Portugal, Spain and Ireland. The publics of these countries continue to place high priority on traditional goals of economic growth and security, a result that can be interpreted as the outcome of their lagging developmental status.

Inglehart's more recent research attempts to explicitly link trends towards increasing postmaterial values with public willingness to support environmental protection (refer to Figure 7.4).[10] The sample of countries appears to disaggregate into four roughly discrete clusters. First, the publics of The Netherlands and Sweden are both strongly postmaterial and this is combined in each of these societies with keen support for the environment. The second cluster, comprising such nations as the United States, Germany (West) and Italy, combines moderate postmaterialism with comparably modest support for environmental protection. In the context of the stage-model strictures of Inglehart's thesis, these countries are expected to progress along the path previously established by the most advanced societies. In other words, as the processes of intergenerational replacement continue, these nations can be expected to experience an increase in both their incidences of postmaterialism and ecological consciousness. Third, the countries located on this sample's lower-income tier (Ireland, Spain and Portugal) have yet to make the transition to postmaterialism and their low incidences of ecological consciousness are indicative of this lagging status.

Problematic for the view that environmentalism is merely one form of expression for postmaterialism is the evidence provided in Figure 7.4 for Norway and Japan (and to a lesser extent for Denmark). Interestingly, these countries are among the group of nations that environmental policy experts generally acknowledge as having made the most commendable strides towards ecological improvement since the 1980s. To discover that these environmentally sound countries have a negative correlation between postmaterialism and ecological consciousness must be viewed as a curious result. At first glance, these countries may represent aberrations that should not be used to discount more general connections between postmaterialism

128

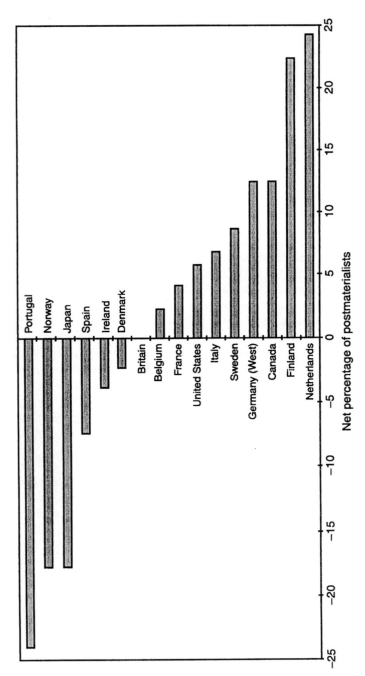

Figure 7.3 Postmaterialism in selected OECD countries, 1990
Source: Adapted from Inglehart (1995).

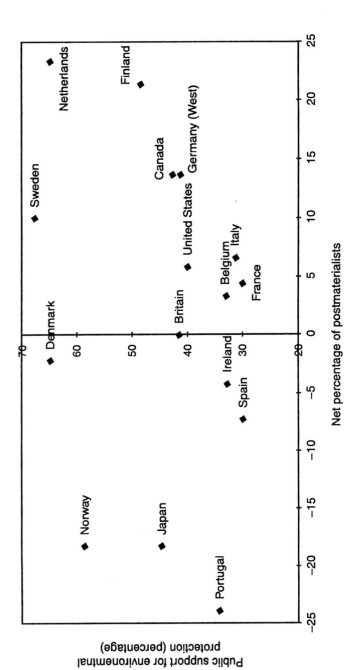

Figure 7.4 Postmaterialism and environmentalism
Source: Adapted from Inglehart (1995).

and environmentalism. However, upon more detailed consideration, the vanguard positions of Norway and Japan raise critical questions for an exclusively Inglehart-inspired explanation for rising ecological consciousness in advanced nations that cannot be summarily dismissed.

How are we to account for the seeming contradictory quality of these findings regarding the relationship between postmaterial values and environmentalism? Are we to presume that there are, in fact, two trajectories along which advanced nations can proceed that entail rises in ecological consciousness? On one hand, the path seemingly taken by The Netherlands and Sweden presupposes postmaterialism as the engine of environmental improvement. On the other hand, there appears to be an alternative route, as charted by Norway and Japan, that suggests societies can progress environmentally without having to undergo an intergenerational value shift towards increasing emphasis on quality of life and self-expression.

Clearly, Inglehart's postmaterialism thesis offers only a partial explanation for recent trends of widening public support for environmental protection in advanced nations. There exists a range of societies for which the gradual emergence of postmaterial values provides a credible explanation for ascending ecological consciousness. This more restrained application of the theory suggests that the relatively similar developmental experiences shared by these countries support critical suppositions undergirding the notion of postmaterialism. However, the existence of important anomalies such as Norway and Japan – countries that, in the absence of postmaterialism, evidence relatively high levels of public support for environmental protection and commendable ecological progress – contravenes key contentions of Inglehart's thesis. A comprehensive explanation for the spreading pattern of ecological consciousness across a broad array of affluent countries appears to be more complex than the advent of a new constellation of values arising out of post-Second World War prosperity.

To supplement postmaterialism as the rationale for the emergence of environmentalism in advanced nations it is necessary to look more deeply at the specific characteristics that define the social, political, economic and cultural contexts of individual societies. Such a methodology might, in the end, reveal meaningful explanations for the rise of ecological consciousness in recent decades, but it also runs the risk of producing idiosyncratic accounts of social change. In proceeding in this direction we must be careful to balance between generalisable qualities and specific content. While this chapter affords insufficient space to describe in detail how to progress beyond postmaterialism in identifying the sources of environmentalism in particular societies, the following section sketches the contours of one useful way in which to proceed.

ROMANTIC AND RATIONAL ENVIRONMENTALISM

The pattern of clustering evident in Figure 7.4 suggests that two different types of environmentalism are emerging within advanced societies. These dual trajectories are depicted in Figure 7.5. On one hand, the ecological consciousness that has developed in most affluent nations – as exemplified by The Netherlands – can be seen as derivative of expanding postmaterialism. Underlying this trajectory is a growing tendency to question the utility of traditional commitments promoting economic growth and progress. This syndrome of values also includes preferences for participatory forms of democracy, especially with respect to the hazardous aspects of technology.

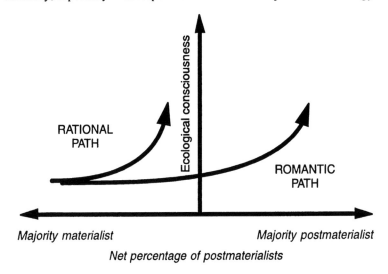

Figure 7.5 Alternative environmental trajectories

On the other hand, a small number of advanced nations appear to have adopted a trajectory involving a more pragmatic conception of nature that entails greater reliance on technology to resolve conflicts between economic accumulation and environmental protection. Interestingly, the countries notable for proceeding in this direction are Norway and Japan, the most materialistic societies (with the exception of Portugal) in our sample. Though this assessment is not intended to suggest that the environmental policy context in these two countries is identical, there are indications that both Norway and Japan, in their own ways, are pursuing paths that approximate a developmental process that has come to be known in recent years as 'ecological modernisation' (Huber, 1985; Jänicke, 1985; Simonis, 1988).

This view contends that certain societies have the capability to reorganise themselves for a third industrial revolution that will generate solutions for the design flaws of modernity. An important spur to this creative process is the imposition of strict environmental regulations that stimulate the development of ecologically enhanced technologies capable of overcoming the need for end-of-pipe treatment.

It is possible to trace the origins of these divergent paths back to the controversies between early romantic and rational expressions of environmentalism. Romantic environmentalism is comprised of several strands, each deriving from the unique political and cultural circumstances of different societies. For instance, in the United States this variety of environmentalism was given form in the writings of the nineteenth-century transcendentalists Ralph Waldo Emerson and Henry David Thoreau. These authors elevated nature from the realm of a resource to be used exclusively for economic exploitation and endowed it with sublime meaning. More contemporary writers such as Aldo Leopold, Barry Lopez, and Edward Abbey have married these values to a wilderness ethic and this philosophy has become the foundation for a distinct brand of radical environmental thought (Nash, 1974; Shabecoff, 1993).

In other societies different sources gave rise to similar sentiments. For instance, the German expression of romantic environmentalism is an outgrowth of the cultural romanticism that runs deep in the country's national identity (Bramwell, 1985; Dominick, 1992). In Britain, the first expressions of romantic environmentalism were presented in the writings of the community of late eighteenth-century authors that coalesced around William Wordsworth, and this thinking was later incorporated into the work of William Morris, Thomas Carlyle and John Ruskin (Bate, 1991; Wheeler, 1995).

Rational environmentalism is a contrasting approach that finds its origins in the functional specialisms of ecology, urban planning, economics and engineering. For practitioners in these fields the environment is not the backdrop for sentimental theorising about humanity's relationship with nature, but is rather a resource to be actively managed. This treatment of the environment is inherently anthropocentric, concentrating on how best to organise human activities in ways that minimise their disruptive interference with the natural world. Because of its reliance on instrumentality, heavy emphasis is placed on the role of technology in expanding human capabilities for interacting skilfully with nature. However, these professional managers recognise that current knowledge is limited and progress is achieved incrementally. Under such circumstances, today's pressing social and economic needs demand the making of difficult compromises with the environment.

Tension between romantic and rational environmentalism continues to be very much evident in most advanced nations. Though the degree of polarisation varies across this array of societies, environmental policy tends to be characterised by ambivalence and confusion as opposing constituencies struggle to determine the content of ecological interventions. In the United States, for instance, the Federal government has passed legislation since the 1960s calling for wilderness preservation, endangered species protection and zero-tolerance of carcinogenic chemicals in foodstuffs. Each of these initiatives embraces ardently romantic notions that privilege nature-enhancing values, often at considerable economic cost. Standing in ideological contrast to these deliberate actions to uphold nature are rational strategies towards the environment that sanction public endangerment from nuclear power, clear-cutting of public forests, and industrial emission of toxic chemicals. Rationalists, in justifying the continuation of these activities, typically emphasise three points: the appropriateness of technical analyses (for example, environmental impact statements, cost–benefit studies), the apolitical formulation of decisions and the technological improvements that will result over time.

While developing countries tend to give preference to rational environmentalism to preserve their potential for economic progress, affluent societies have room to manoeuvre in striving for some balance between romanticism and rationalism. Furthermore, those nations with political cultures conducive to postmaterialism will have publics with tendencies that favour romantic schemes for negotiating humanity's relationship with nature. For instance, the governments of strongly postmaterial countries have in recent years adopted environmental strategies with conspicuous romantic content. Perhaps the most striking example of this trend is taking place in The Netherlands where after more than 1000 years of steadfastly erecting human-engineered contrivances to hold back the sea, the Dutch are dismantling their dykes to permit the inundation of the country's lowlands (Bennett, 1991; Simons, 1993). Proposed in 1990 as part of 'The Netherlands' widely celebrated National Environmental Policy Plan, this unprecedented programme ultimately intends to return approximately 600 000 acres – in Europe's most densely populated country – to lakes, marshes and tidal lands.

Advanced nations with publics that forsake postmaterial commitments face much less intense pressure for romantic interventions to protect the environment and are subsequently able to maintain stridently instrumental postures with respect to its management. Understood in these terms, it is of little surprise that we find Norway and Japan promoting aggressive campaigns toward ecological modernisation. This strategy shares with its utilitarian predecessors a scientific understanding of nature and avoids interpreting human behaviours towards the environment in cumbersome ethical terms. Particularly illustrative of these countries' pursuit of a narrowly defined ecological agenda is the campaign they (along with Iceland) have led in recent years to overturn the commercial whaling moratorium established in 1986 by the International Whaling Commission (IWC). This coalition has asserted that certain whale populations have recovered sufficiently to permit carefully calculated harvests and that prevailing prohibitions actually contradict the tenets of sustainable development. Unsuccessful in their bid to roll back the ban, the Norwegians announced their intent in 1992 to resume limited harvests of minke whales regardless of the IWC's position on the acceptability of selective exploitation.

The whaling ban represents one of the romantic environmentalists' most notable accomplishments and whales, largely through the promotional efforts of influential advocacy organisations, have become a powerful symbol of ecological consciousness. The principal point of contention between the pro-whaling countries and the rest of the international community pivots on the conflicting roles of science and ethics in determining harvesting practices. There are some indications suggesting that global whale conservation programmes have been successful in enabling populations of some species to recover. Both Norway and Japan, displaying avowedly rational environmentalism, have used this evidence to justify the resumption of their whaling activities while other countries have based their position on ethical commitments that consider the slaughter of whales under any circumstances to be abhorrent. Norway's stated intentions to resume whaling elicited sharp opprobrium among nations with strong romantic leanings. For instance, several nations threatened to boycott the 1994 Winter Olympics in Lillehammer as an expression of their displeasure with this decision. However, the ideological gap between romantic and rational environmentalism was perhaps most graphically demonstrated when the United States House of Representatives passed by a vote of 347 to 0 a resolution to condemn Norway for its departure from international agreements (Darton, 1993).

CONCLUSION

Though caution is surely advisable when applying monocausal explanations to complex social phenomena, the preceding discussion suggests that postmaterialism provides a powerful rationale for the emergence of ecological consciousness in a broad cross-section of advanced nations. The plausibility of this interpretation rests in the fact that the world's advanced countries share relatively common institutional structures and are situated at roughly similar stages of economic development. As we have seen, however, this account is incomplete and a handful of critical anomalies uncovered by this comparative methodology cannot be readily reconciled by a strict application of this approach. While postmaterialism tends to facilitate the emergence of sentimental expressions of environmentalism, it is also apparent that a more pragmatic form of ecological consciousness can emerge in political cultures that do not promote this particular constellation of commitments.

As the operational milieu increasingly forces business concerns to confront ecological issues, managers invariably bring more pragmatic attitudes into the public arena. As this process has proceeded throughout much of Western Europe and North America since the early 1980s the formulation of policy has been marked by a distinct shift toward rational environmentalism, the form of ecological expression for which Japan (and to a lesser extent Norway) serve as the archetype. This desire to emulate Japan environmentally has been motivated largely by the business community's need to regain control of the debate over sustainable development and to advance a new interpretation that does not undermine the essence of free enterprise.

An indication that rational environmentalism is beginning to gain ground in countries where this ideological orientation previously faced formidable opposition is that even the most strident advocacy groups are making sweeping adjustments and stepping back from their romantic commitments. For example, several environmental organisations have in recent years entered the business consultancy field, a practice viewed by many campaigners as perverse. The United States-based Environmental Defense Fund has assisted McDonald's to design ways to reduce the waste stream produced by its restaurants. In Europe, Greenpeace, under an initiative known as Greenpeace Business, is currently offering corporate executives intensive environmental strategy seminars. Applied in such a manner, the Japanese corporatist model for improving ecological performance is likely to restrain the reassertion of more romantic sentiments and to modify the scope of environmental management so that it does not contravene economic objectives.

The most pronounced manifestation of this strategy has been the emergence of a new management philosophy referred to as 'eco-efficiency' that makes the counterintuitive claim that stricter environmental regulations can enhance the profitability of firms. Taking its lead from the 'quality revolution' spearheaded by Joseph Juran and W. Edward Deming, eco-efficiency stands conventional economic wisdom on its head, arguing that managers do not necessarily have to make trade-offs between their bottom line and environmental improvement. Proponents of this approach do not discount the fact that more responsible environmental behaviour may entail short-term costs as resources are devoted to the reengineering and marketing of new products. They contend, however, that strategies grounded in the principles of eco-efficiency can enable firms to acquire important competitive advantages that compensate for these initial outlays.

Although it remains to be seen whether eco-efficiency is capable of promoting appreciable environmental gains, as a rhetorical device it has enabled vanguard firms to express their commitment to ecological improvement in an economically practicable voice. Especially effective has been the use of this approach to neutralise calls for more radical reforms by environmentally concerned fiscal stakeholders and consumers. Furthermore, its promotion in influential corporate circles suggests that creative managers now recognise that changes in the operational milieu are forcing them to abandon their worn political tactics. The new environmental age requires firms to formulate strategies that at least acknowledge public demands for higher standards of accountability.

Notes

1. The Montreal Protocols, negotiated in 1987 to ban the further production of stratospheric ozone-depleting chlorofluorocarbons (CFCs), represent an important counter example, at least on their face. Despite this agreement's noteworthy accomplishments, enforcement difficulties have become apparent and an extensive illegal market for CFCs has developed in many parts of the world. According to reliable estimates, 22 000 tons of illicit CFCs are now smuggled annually into the United States (Wald, 1995).

2. Important initiatives, particularly in the United States, have resulted from these incidents. First, the 1979 accident at the Three Mile Island nuclear power facility effectively established a moratorium on the construction of new plants in the country that has lasted until the present day. Second, the 1984 Bhopal tragedy provided the stimulus for the passage of the Emergency Planning and Community Right-to-Know Act (EPCRA), legislation that created a national database on toxic chemical emissions and contributed to the growth of new grassroots environmental-protest constituencies. Finally, the *Exxon Valdez* oil spill in 1989 elevated concern regarding lax pollution control for oil transport and the Congress passed the Oil Pollution Act of 1990 that, among other regulatory objectives, mandates the gradual phasing-out of single-hull tankers.

3. It is worthwhile to note that firms that regularly confront barrages of proxy votes initiated by their institutional investors would appear not simply to suffer from a schism between owners and managers. Rather, such evidence would suggest that management is unable, or unwilling, to engage the

corporation's large shareholders in dialogue to resolve critical matters of policy or strategy.

4. Small investors, operating under the banner of 'corporate democracy', have been a long-standing, but largely ineffectual, source of protest. These groups of individual investors bring specific, often quirky, issues to proxy votes. However, owing to the limited resources behind these initiatives and the difficulties of communicating with dispersed shareholders, their sponsors have typically attracted only small numbers of supporters. Small-scale investor activism has recently been identified by advocates of more formidable social change and this tactic has taken on a more confrontational edge designed to mobilise direct-action protests at organisational gatherings. For example, several activist groups have begun encouraging their members to purchase small quantities of shares to gain the right to attend annual meetings.

5. Refer also to Bertsch (1991) for details regarding a similar code of conduct known as the MacBride Principles. Designed to promote fair employment practices in Northern Ireland, this code is named after Nobel laureate Sean MacBride.

6. In this case, one that ultimately had serious consequences for both international law and global trade agreements, environmentalists acting under the lead of the Earth Island Institute launched a campaign in 1988 to discourage the use of fishing techniques that captured dolphins as part of the tuna-harvesting process. This boycott initially targeted the Starkist brand (produced by Heinz), but effectively became commodity-wide due to the prevalence of dolphin-harming practices across the industry. After two years of vigorous campaigning, Heinz agreed to produce packaged tuna that was 'dolphin-safe' and most other domestic producers followed suit.

7. Corporate producers and their advertising consultants typically treat 'green marketing' as simply the most recent consumer fad and have responded accordingly. 'Ecologically conscious consumer behaviour' is the terminology generally employed to describe individuals with propensities to express their environmental preferences in consumption practices. Despite the limited scope of this approach, stricter product packaging requirements, especially those directives handed down by the European Commission, have contributed to a more expansive environmental consciousness among marketing professionals.

8. Mobil Chemical Company introduced a similar refuse bag that was advertised as being 'biodegradable', a term indicating the material would decompose under suitable environmental circumstances. However, these conditions rarely occurred with normal use of the product and Mobil was also forced to withdraw this claim (Davis, 1992).

9. Though an inchoate Green Party operates in the United States and has achieved some minor local successes, this form of political mobilisation has never been viable at the national level because of insurmountable barriers to entry. Rather, the American legal system, because of the country's propensity for litigious means of dispute resolution, has served as the principal channel to advance the environmental agenda.

10. Inglehart (1995) measures 'public support for environmental protection' as a composite index derived from four survey questions pertaining to willingness to pay for ecological improvements.

138   *The Trend towards Investor and Consumer Activism*

References

Bate, J. (1991) *Romantic Ecology: Wordsworth and the Environmental Tradition* (London: Routledge).

Bavaria, J. (1996) 'Strategic Response to Investor Activism (Letter)', *Sloan Management Review*, 37 (3), pp. 5–6.

Beck, U. (1992) *Risk Society: Towards a New Modernity* (London: Sage).

Bennett, G. (1991) 'The History of the Dutch National Environmental Policy Plan', *Environment*, 33 (7), p. 6.

Bertsch, K.A. (1991) *The MacBride Principles and U.S. Companies in Northern Ireland* (Washington, DC: Investor Responsibility Research Center).

Bramwell, A. (1985) *Blood and Soil: Richard Walter Darré and Hilter's Green Party* (Bourne End: Kensal Press).

Bramwell, A. (1994) *The Fading of the Greens: The Decline of Environmental Politics in the West* (New Haven, Conn.: Yale University Press).

Bullard, R.D. (ed.) (1994) *Unequal Protection: Environmental Justice and Communities of Color* (San Francisco: Sierra Club Books).

Cable, S. and Cable, C. (1995) *Environmental Problems: Grassroots Solutions* (New York: St Martin's Press).

Commoner, B. (1990) *Making Peace with the Planet* (London: Gollancz).

Darton, J. (1993) 'Norwegians Claim Their Whaling Rights', *New York Times*, 7 August, p. A1.

Davis, G.F. and Thompson, T.A. (1994) 'A Social Movement Perspective on Corporate Control', *Administrative Science Quarterly*, 39 (1), pp. 141–73.

Davis, J.J. (1992) 'Ethics and Environmental Marketing,' *Journal of Business Ethics*, 11 (1), pp. 1–87.

Davis, J.J. (1994) 'Environmental Advertising: Norms and Levels of Advertiser Trust', *Journalism Quarterly*, 71 (2), pp. 330–45.

Dominguez, J. and Robin, V. (1993) *Your Money or Your Life: Transforming Your Relationship with Money and Achieving Financial Independence* (New York: Penguin).

Dominick, R.H. (1992) *The Environmental Movement in Germany: Prophets and Pioneers* (Bloomington, Ind.: Indiana University Press).

Dowie, M. (1995) *Losing Ground: American Environmentalism at the Close of the Twentieth Century* (Cambridge, Mass.: MIT Press).

Elgin, D. (1993) *Voluntary Simplicity: Toward a Way of Life that is Outwardly Simple, Inwardly Rich*, Revised Edition (New York: William Morrow).

Friedman, M. (1995) 'On Promoting a Sustainable Future Through Consumer Activism', *Journal of Social Issues*, 51 (4), pp. 197–215.

Giddens, A. (1991) *Modernity and Self-Identity: Self and Society in the Late Modern Age* (Cambridge: Polity Press).

Goldberg, C. (1995) 'The Simple Life Lures Refugees from Stress', *New York Times*, 21 September, p. C1.

Goldblatt, D. (1996) *Social Theory and the Environment* (Cambridge: Polity Press).

Gottlieb, R. (1993) *Forcing the Spring: The Transformation of the American Environmental Movement* (Washington, DC: Island Press).

Gray, K.R. and Karp, R.E. (1993) 'An Experiment in Exporting U.S. Values Abroad: The Sullivan Principles and South Africa', *International Journal of Sociology and Social Policy*, 13 (7), pp. 1–14.

Hammitt, J.K. (1990) 'Risk Perceptions and Food Choice: An Exploratory Analysis of Organic Produce versus Conventional Produce Buyers', *Risk Analysis*, 10 (3), pp. 367–74.

Hawkins, K. (1984) *Environment and Enforcement: Regulation and the Social Definition of Pollution* (Oxford: Oxford University Press).

Hawley, J.P. (1995) 'Political Voice, Fiduciary Activism, and the Institutional Ownership of U.S. Corporations: The Role of Public and Noncorporate Pension Funds', *Sociological Perspectives*, 38 (3), pp. 415–35.

Hays, S.P. (1987) *Beauty, Health, and Permanence: Environmental Politics in the United States, 1955–1985* (Cambridge: Cambridge University Press).

Hirschman, A.O. (1970) *Exit, Voice, and Loyalty: Responses to Decline in Firms, Organizations, and State* (Cambridge, Mass: Harvard University Press).

Hoffman, A.J. (1996) 'A Strategic Response to Investor Activism', *Sloan Management Review*, 37 (2), pp. 51–64.

Huber, J. (1985) *Die Regenbogengesellschaft: Okologie and Sozialpolitik* (Frankfurt am Main: Fischer).

Inglehart, R. (1977) *The Silent Revolution: Changing Values and Political Style* (Princeton, NJ: Princeton University Press).

Inglehart, R. (1990) *Culture Shift in Advanced Industrial Society* (Princeton, NJ: Princeton University Press).

Inglehart, R. (1995) 'Public Support for Environmental Protection: Objective Problems and Subjective Values in 43 Societies', *PS: Political Science and Politics*, 28 (1), pp. 57–72.

Jahn, D. (1993) 'The Rise and Decline of New Politics and the Greens in Sweden and Germany: Resource Dependence and New Social Cleavages', *European Journal of Political Research*, 24 (2), pp. 177–94.

Jänicke, M. (1985) *Preventive Environmental Policy as Ecological Modernisation and Structural Policy* (Berlin: WZB).

Kangun, N., Carlson, L. and Grove, S.J. (1991) 'Environmental Advertising Claims: A Preliminary Investigation', *Journal of Public Policy and Marketing*, 10 (2), pp. 47–58.

Kazis, R. and Grossman, R. (1982) *Fear at Work: Job Blackmail, Labor, and the Environment* (New York: Pilgrim Press).

Lundqvist, L.F. (1980) *The Hare and the Tortoise: Clean Air Policies in the United States and Sweden* (Ann Arbor: University of Michigan Press).

Mayer, R.N., Scammon, D.L. and Zick, C.D. (1993) 'Poisoning the Well: Do Environmental Claims Strain Consumer Credulity', *Advances in Consumer Research*, 20, pp. 698–703.

Nash, R. (1974) *Wilderness and the American Mind* (New Haven, Conn.: Yale University Press).

Nelkin, D. and Brown, M.S. (1984) *Workers at Risk: Voices from the Workplace* (Chicago, Ill.: University of Chicago Press).

Paul, K. (1989) 'Corporate Social Monitoring in South Africa: A Decade of Achievement, an Uncertain Future', *Journal of Business Ethics*, 8 (6), pp. 463–9.

Pozen, R.C. (1994) 'Institutional Investors: The Reluctant Activists', *Harvard Business Review*, 72 (1), pp. 140–9.

Robinson, J. (1991) *Toil and Toxics: Workplace Struggles and Political Strategies for Occupational Health* (Berkeley: University of California Press).

Rosen, B.N., Sandler, D.M. and Shani, D. (1991) 'Social Issues and Socially Responsible Investment Behavior: A Preliminary Investigation', *Journal of Consumer Affairs*, 25 (2), pp. 221–34.

Salzhauer, A.L. (1991) 'Obstacles and Opportunities for a Consumer Eco-Label', *Environment*, 33 (8), p. 10.

Sanyal, R.N. and Neves, J.S. (1991) 'The Valdez Principles: Implications for Corporate Responsibility', *Journal of Business Ethics*, 10 (12), pp. 883–90.

Scammon, D.L. and Mayer, R.N. (1995) 'Agency Review of Environmental Marketing Claims: Case-by-Case Decomposition of the Issues', *Journal of Advertising*, 24 (2), pp. 33–43.

Schnaiberg, A. (1980) *The Environment: From Surplus to Scarcity* (Oxford: Oxford University Press).

Schor, J. (1996) 'Toward a Sustainable Consumption: Redefining the American Dream', unpublished manuscript, Harvard University.

Shabecoff, P. (1993) *A Fierce Green Fire: The American Environmental Movement* (New York: Hill & Wang).

Simonis, U.E. (1988) *Beyond Growth: Elements of Sustainable Development* (Berlin: Edition Sigma).

Simons, M. (1993) 'Dutch Do the Unthinkable: Sea is Let In', *New York Times*, 7 March, A1.

Smith, M.P. (1996) 'Shareholder Activism by Institutional Investors: Evidence from CalPERS', *Journal of Finance*, 51 (1), pp. 227–52.

Vogel, D. (1986) *National Styles of Regulation: Environmental Policy in Great Britain and the United States* (Ithaca, NY: Cornell University Press).

Wald, M.L. (1995) 'Group Sees Ozone Danger in Illicit Chemical Trade', *New York Times*, 17 September, A30.

Weale, A. (1992) *The New Politics of Pollution* (Manchester: Manchester University Press).

Welsh, D.F. (1993) 'Environmental Marketing and Federal Preemption of State Law: Eliminating the Gray Behind the Green', *California Law Review*, 81 (4), pp. 991–1027.

Wheeler, M. (1995) *Ruskin and Environment: The Storm Cloud of the Nineteenth Century* (Manchester: Manchester University Press).

8 The Challenge of Ethical Investment: Activism, Assets and Analysis

Russell Sparkes

ETHICAL INVESTMENT IS NOT THE SAME AS SHAREHOLDER ACTIVISM

The concept of a challenge implies something provoking a response, and such a title illustrates two widely held but misleading views of ethical investment: that it is confrontational and concerned with simple, negative, avoidance activity. The question of 'avoidance' will be dealt with later, but 'challenge' generates in the mind's eye a picture of people asking awkward questions at a company's annual general meeting, if not actually demonstrating outside it. However, that is *shareholder activism*, which needs to be carefully distinguished from *ethical investment*. The two grew up at the same time, and many of the people involved were the same, but over time they have diverged to such an extent that they can be classified as separate types of activities. The subtitle, *activism, assets and analysis*, refers to three aspects of the subject which seem particularly deserving of further consideration.

During a two-year period (1993–94) spent researching *The Ethical Investor* (Sparkes, 1995a), I found very little discussion of ethical investment in the British business ethics literature. Indeed, it was this paucity of information which was a factor in the decision to write the book. What little there was followed the approach of Craig Smith's work (1990) which calls ethical investment 'analogous to ethical purchase behaviour' (p. 175), which he sees as mostly in the form of consumer boycotts: 'ethical investors can operate by selling off investments or keeping them and using them to press for changes in the companies concerned' (p. 176). See also Cooper and Schegelmilch (1993). There is an update and review of ethical consumerism in Cohen's chapter in this volume.

Craig Smith's description is correct as far as it goes, but in the absence of deeper analysis it can result in the all-too-frequent confusion between shareholder activism and ethical investment. I must confess to pleading guilty to not addressing such issues in *The Ethical Investor*. The original manuscript did contain a final analytical chapter exploring these themes, but this was excised by the editor in order to make the book purely descriptive and easier to read.

The essence of shareholder activism is the usage of voting rights attached to ordinary shares to assert political or other objectives, normally in the form of critical resolutions at a company's annual general meeting. This is quite easy to do in the USA, but it is much harder in the UK where a stiff hurdle is set in terms of a minimum share capital requirement needed to insist on a resolution being considered. The difficulty British shareholder activists have in actually filing critical shareholder resolutions probably explains why they often resort to other activities which seem designed to embarrass a company's management in public.

One example which sticks in the mind is the pig (named 'Cedric' after British Gas's then Chief Executive) which was kept outside the British Gas annual general meeting (AGM) during the row over executive pay in that company. Such activists often seem to have a single-issue agenda which they perceive to be of overwhelming importance to the exclusion of all else. A typical example is given by Mackenzie, author of *The Shareholder Action Handbook* (1997) :

> Each year Partizans, a tiny but dogged London-based campaigning group, has launched a campaign on RTZ, the world's largest mining company. Partizans wants RTZ to act in a more environmentally responsible way, and to treat indigenous people with more respect. Partizans does not table resolutions, instead it asks difficult questions and seeks to attract press publicity for the causes it represents. *Occasionally it has stormed the podium in an effort to make the company and the press listen.* (p. 4; my emphasis)

Ethical investment and shareholder activism grew up at the same time and in the same place: the USA in the late 1960s. American universities queried investments in Dow Chemical, and that company's production of the chemical warfare substance, Agent Orange, in 1969, while a year later Ralph Nader's consumer activists put down nine critical resolutions at a General Motors shareholders' meeting alleging safety defects in its cars. These two activities may share the *same means*, that is, the use of ordinary shares, and there may well be overlapping *concerns* about social justice or the environment, but *the ends* are quite different. For shareholder activists maintaining the value of the shares they have bought, normally for only a small sum, is not a big issue. Their main aim is to be able to complain in a public forum about a company's activities in a particular field. Typical examples are the environment, animal rights, or indigenous peoples, although the privatised utilities have also generated significant demonstrations of public outrage. In contrast the first priority of ethical investment is the same as any other form of investment: to generate a return on capital subject to an appropriate level of risk regarding the security of that capital.

Investment means the allocation of capital for a productive use. When carried out in liquid financial assets there is a strong implication that the original capital is reasonably secure, and that a return will be generated upon it consisting of a mixture of income (interest or dividends) and capital appreciation. It is important to remember that 'investment' is a key element of ethical investment, since it is often overlooked by the media in favour of the 'social return'. Opinion polls indicate that about 35 per cent of the public are potential purchasers of ethical unit trusts on the basis that the financial return may be slightly below that of comparable conventional unit trusts. However, if it is stated that the return may be significantly lower, this proportion falls away rapidly. The definition of 'ethical investment' used in *The Ethical Investor* was: 'an investment strategy which combines financial and other goals' (p. 4). This definition seems quite robust, and enables a differentiation to be made between this and charitable donations where capital is freely given, and no financial return is expected from it.

(For completeness sake we should note that there is also a grey area between the two, known as *socially directed investment*. Typically savers give the use of their capital in the knowledge that it will be fully returned if they need it, while the interest charged is negligible. The zero-interest loan accounts offered by the Christian savings institution Shared Interest are a good example. Individuals have deposited £15m with Shared Interest to be lent on to the Third World at preferential terms. The loans made by community investment banks in the USA to rebuild poor inner city areas are another case in point.)

To conclude this section: the first priority of ethical investment is the same as any other form of investment – to generate a good return on capital. If people want their savings used in other ways where such considerations are not primary, that is not investment, but shareholder activism.

IS 'ETHICAL' THE RIGHT WORD?

The public face of ethical investment consists of the ethical unit trusts and investment trusts which increasingly advertise in the financial pages of our newspapers. Yet in terms of size their investment assets of £1.3bn under management are significantly less than the £5.0bn of ethically screened funds under the charge of the church investors. The reason why ethical unit trusts are so well-known is that they are marketed directly to the public; not only do they advertise, but they publicise themselves through newspaper articles and features. There is increasing scepticism, however, over whether the term 'ethical' should be applied to such funds which are run on a commercial basis.

The use of this terminology occurred in the UK as a historical accident. The first advocate of unit trusts 'combining conscience and capital' to be sold to the public was the former Investment Manager of the Central Finance Board of the Methodist Church (CFB), Charles Jacob. From 1972 to 1984 he was the major influence in persuading the initially sceptical authorities to allow such trusts, which they finally did in 1984. The first trust adopted his phrase 'Stewardship' and the growing industry naturally also adopted his generic term of 'ethical investment'.

It is also worth remembering that the oldest ethical investors in the UK are the church investment bodies, dating back to at least 1948 in the case of the Church Commissioners. Without getting involved in a theoretical debate about the meaning of the word 'ethics', we may assume its traditional meaning of a normative and systematic code of conduct. If any group in the modern Western world does have a justified claim to such a consistent code in what is generally regarded as a relativist world, the Christian churches would seem to be a leading candidate. There is a definitive statement of belief in the Bible. Questions of 'debt release' and the use of property are tackled in Leviticus and Deuteronomy, some of the very oldest books of the Old Testament, and such ideas were later developed by the prophets. Hence there is four thousand years' experience of interpreting that statement of belief, and in most churches there is a system of authority which enables disputed questions to be tackled. Not every church possesses the dogmatics to be able to say, '*Roma locuta est, causa finita*' ('Rome has spoken, the matter is closed'), but the principle is the same.

A brief mention of the Methodist tradition may be useful. This actually goes back to a sermon of John Wesley, *On The Right Use of Money*, published in 1760, and still one of the best theoretical justifications of ethical investment. In 1974 Derek Farrow, a Methodist minister, wrote: 'The plain fact of the matter is that there is no "clean" money because there is no one without sin . . . There are clearly degrees of "purity" but no "absolutes".' This continues to be the basic approach of the CFB. In the words of CFB Investment Manager Bill Seddon (1997):

> To me this seems the right Christian attitude. In our fallen world there is no such animal as a perfect human being, likewise there is no investment

which is ethically pure. Because all securities represent an underlying human activity, it is possible to criticise any investment on ethical grounds, whether it is a South African gold mine or a Bible publisher. However, it should be possible to find investments which constitute a workable compromise, and that is what we try and do. (p. 7)

Last year the CFB (1996) produced a two-page Mission Statement detailing its approach to ethical issues. It states a commitment:

- To provide a high quality investment service seeking above average financial returns for investors
- To follow a discipline in which the ethical dimension is an integral part of all investment decisions
- To construct investment portfolios which are consistent with the moral stance and teachings of the Christian faith
- To encourage strategic thinking on the ethics of investment
- To be a Christian witness in the investment community.

It seems logical that the three church investors – the Church Commissioners, the Central Board of Finance of the Church of England, and the Central Finance Board of the Methodist Church – have a justifiable claim to be known as 'ethical investors'. (Note that this is not meant to be an exclusive claim. Other charitable groups with a consistent theme would also fit the above criteria.)

There is however no consistent code shared between ethical unit and investment trusts purchased by the public, and their concerns and methods vary widely. Some focus mainly upon environmental issues, for example, while for others it is just one factor among many. The majority tend to use exclusion screens, normally provided by a specialist service called the Ethical Investment Research and Information Service (EIRIS), to weed out their definition of unacceptable companies. For some this appears to be the extent of their ethical concerns, and they then use normal investment techniques of maximising returns on the remaining portfolio. Others carry out in-depth ethical scrutiny of potential investments, while another group is more concerned to engage in dialogue with companies to alter their behaviour.

Critics have wondered whether the term 'ethical' should be applied to such funds, which are, after all, normally commercial enterprises. Investment management companies which run and promote such trusts could be accused of being more concerned with marketing certain simple concepts in order to attract new business than of pursuing moral goals. As Cowton (1994) writes:

At one level, ethical investment can be seen as just another product innovation that helps widen choice . . . The irony is that its occurrence can
be explained in pure, profit-seeking capitalistic terms, as financial
institutions seek to influence and exploit their environment in the interests of profitability. Thus individual investors, potentially at least,
have their values met or satisfied by institutions/people who do not
share these values at all, whose sole motive might be to make more
money. (p. 228)

It is also a fact that the charges on most ethical unit trusts are higher than
average, so they risk the charge of exploiting the goodwill of the ordinary
person in the street. The additional ethical research required necessitates
somewhat higher fees, but as this overhead is spread over the greater re-
venues of the larger funds it should become a relatively small-cost item. It is
certainly true that some of the larger ethical funds are believed to be highly
profitable.

A good example of such criticism was that published in March 1996 by
the Social Affairs Unit, a conservative 'think tank', and called *What has
'Ethical Investment' to do with Ethics?* (Anderson, 1996). It stated:

the criteria [used] reflect the criteria demanded by investors . . . the investment companies have indeed satisfied a customer demand. But that
does not mean what they are doing has a right to be labelled 'ethical' with
the at least occasional implication that other investments are unethical
. . . the overall objection to ethical investment codes is their aggressive
simplicity . . . a simplicity which ill fits them for their ethical work
. . . there is no reason why the various investment institutions should not
continue to serve [their customers] and their preferences. The only objection
this report makes is that they should not describe what they are doing as
ethical investment. (p. 20)

There seems considerable persuasive force in the above argument. It
would be resolved if we stopped using the term 'ethical investment' for
commercial unit trusts, and adopted the phrase generally used in America,
that of 'socially responsible investment', or SRI. However, in the UK the
genie seems out of the bottle, and we are stuck with 'ethical investment' as
the ordinary term in general use.

If ethical unit trusts do want to continue to use that term, one way forward,
which would bolster their moral authority, is the suggestion made in *The
Ethical Investor* that any unit trust which calls itself ethical should have an
independent advisory board. Such boards or committees of reference pro-

vide independent assurance to investors that the general aims of the trust are being pursued, while they can also encourage research into ethical issues and act as a means of solving difficult areas. The excellent work done in this field over many years by the advisory committees of the Friends Provident Stewardship Trust and the CIS Environ Fund deserves wider recognition.

One last thought on 'ethics'. Another criticism not infrequently voiced is that the ethical decisions of many funds seem to be made in a fairly arbitrary way. That is, once possible holdings have got through the exclusion sieve normally used, it seems to be up to the individual fund manager to decide how to apply such principles in practice. This criticism is probably neither fair nor valid, but it would help to answer such critics if ethical funds did make more information available about how they come to make their decisions. The CFB Mission Statement was described earlier, and the paper from the Jupiter Tyndall Group, *The Assessment Process for Green Investment* (1995), is a good example of environmental criteria being set out. Such information from market leaders in ethical unit trusts such as Friends Provident, CIS Environ or NPI Global Care would also be welcome.

A GROWING POOL OF ASSETS

It is now time to move on from 'activism' and semantics, and look at 'assets'. The extent to which more and more investment assets are being run on such constrained lines is striking. The £5bn of ethical funds run by the churches was described earlier. Investment assets of socially responsible unit trusts amounted to £1.3bn at the end of 1996. The latter are growing rapidly, up from £317m at the end of 1990, and £802m at the end of 1993. However, this is still small beer compared to the great weight of institutional investment funds – the £400bn invested in pension funds, or the £350bn in insurance funds. What is changing is that more and more ordinary investment institutions are starting to adopt ethical constraints and social/environmental screens.

The DEMOS report, 'The Money Game' (Sparkes, 1995b), which appeared in March 1995, argued that charitable investment funds were much larger than then commonly believed at around £45bn and that many of them had adopted, or were considering adopting, ethical investment strategies. Subsequent surveys have demonstrated the validity of these figures, and showed that some 12–15 per cent of charities were in fact already using ethical constraints, creating a pool of a further £7bn of ethical funds. Since charities are based on ethical principles – which are legally spelt out in their trust deeds – there is a strong incentive for them to consider the adoption of ethical constraints in their investment portfolios.

There is a complex body of case law regarding charity investment, but in essence ethical investment is permitted and even encouraged by the law, as long as it is in accordance with the ethical principles of the charity and not based upon the whims of the trustees. (For further information on this subject see Sparkes, 1997.) It seems likely that it is the traditional prudence of trustees, rather than the actual letter of the law, which is the main factor inhibiting many charities from introducing ethical constraints on their investment portfolios. The overall percentage is likely to rise significantly over the next few years, as the onerous requirements of the 1992/93 Charities Acts lead to a younger generation of trustees who are unlikely to be as cautious as their predecessors.

In January 1996 the Central Finance Board set up a new company called Epworth Investment Management Ltd as a vehicle to enable the CFB to offer its investment services to other churches and charities. (For legal reasons the CFB itself can only act for Methodist clients.) The investment policy of Epworth will be in line with the ethical approach of the CFB, and as far as I am aware, it is the first investment management company in the UK to offer ethical investment services, and nothing else. Another recognition of the growing interest of charities in this field was the launch, with great publicity, of a specialist unauthorised unit trust for gross funds using ethical screening by Friends Provident in September 1996, as was the guidance paper on ethical common investment funds issued by the Charity Commissioners in August 1996.

Last, pension funds have been investigating this field. Local authority pension funds have total investments of around £90bn. Between September 1995 and October 1996 eight different local authorities have put some of their assets into socially responsible investments. Typically, the sums have been fairly small, around £5–10m in each case, but there is a definite sense of their putting their toe in the water; many have indicated that significantly larger sums may be so invested after a three-year trial if investment performance is satisfactory. It is interesting that BZW Investment Management, who have no involvement in running ethical unit trusts, have recently borne the costs of setting up a three-person team to investigate corporate responsibility issues. This appears to suggest that they expect that in the future their large pension fund clients will require some expertise in this area.

ETHICAL INVESTORS AND THE CORPORATE SECTOR

Let us now move on from the investment institutions (the suppliers of capital) to the corporate sector (the users of capital). How do they feel about ethical investors? The experience of the Central Finance Board (CFB) suggests that informed ethical inquiry, as opposed to aggressive shareholder activism, works surprisingly well. For example, between the beginning of 1995 and October 1996 the CFB had meetings with Shell over its involvement in Nigeria, and with W.H. Smith about the distribution of pornographic magazines. It is worth stressing that these were not public, confrontational meetings. The prerogatives of share ownership were used to request a meeting with the management of these companies, normally at their offices. Significant research was done on the issues of concern before visiting the companies, and there was willingness to learn from the company's experience. In all of these meetings the CFB found what you might consider to be a surprising amount of common ground with company executives, and it is still a shareholder in both.

A fair criticism which is often thrown at the ethical investment movement is the question of whether it makes any difference to corporate behaviour. In fact there appears abundant evidence indicating that it does. For example, in the case of Nigeria CFB believe Shell to have become more open and receptive to outside comment, more sensitive about conditions in Ogoniland, and CFB understand that they have begun fruitful dialogue with the local churches in Nigeria. W.H. Smith recently announced that it was withdrawing the sale of some 'top shelf' magazines. The company stated that the main reason was financial, a response to declining circulations, but that negative comments from investors had also been a factor behind this decision. A further example is the pressure put upon Fisons in the early 1990s by green investors to withdraw from the peat extraction business. The corporate governance agency, Pensions and Investment Research (PIRC), observed at the time: 'The Fisons case shows it is practical for investors to get companies to respond. In fact investors provided the only effective form of pressure in this case' (Coyle, 1991, p. 12).

Now this is very different from the popular image of ethical investment which, as argued earlier, owes more to shareholder activism. You can well imagine that if people buy a few shares in Shell or Bass to attack the board publicly, they will not be well-received. Indeed, company managements may at times feel that this is an attempt to hijack the democratic process by which directors report to shareholders. People who buy a few shares in such companies to attack their core business are also unlikely to be well-received.

Ethical unit trusts probably fall somewhere in the middle of these two extremes. The fact that they are mass-marketed to the public inevitably makes their ethical policies fairly simple, which in turn tends to make them focus on a policy of exclusion and exit, rather than dialogue and engagement. For many such trusts the majority of their 'ethical' effort lies in devising exclusion screens to weed out undesirable areas, and the usual response to a problem is to sell the shares. (This is less true for the largest funds such as Friends Provident, CIS Environ or NPI Global Care which do engage in dialogue with management about difficult areas.)

A church or charity investor does not have to sell its products to the public, and therefore it is arguable that it can evolve a more complex ethical strategy and establish the internal means to enforce it. For example, the CFB has a threefold line of attack on these issues. All fund managers are expected to look constantly for possible ethical issues in their work at the same time as they examine financial items. Ethical issues are discussed both in informal internal meetings, and at the monthly Investment Committee where the investment performance of CFB's various funds is formally reviewed. Last, there is the Advisory Joint Committee on the Ethics of Investment which meets four times a year and which is accountable to the Methodist Conference. Its membership is evenly divided between representatives of the Central Finance Board and those from other areas of the church concerned with its social mission. In sum, 'ethics is always on the agenda'.

Many years' experience of coping with ethical issues has enabled the CFB to develop a structured and disciplined approach to such problems. A good example might be the question of the apparent arbitrariness of ethical decisions mentioned earlier. I would argue that this approach is actually very similar to the way case law develops. There are certain core principles, but it is the application of these principles to practical cases which develops, deepens and expands understanding.

Perhaps a practical example may illustrate the point. The question of the involvement of companies in the defence industry has always been an important issue for the CFB. In the early 1980s the CFB's approach to companies involved in some way in defence was fairly clear-cut. Companies producing weapons were not acceptable, whereas little problem was seen with suppliers of food or clothing to the military. Other factors taken into account were the proportion of sales to the military for an individual company and the type of products manufactured, some being more offensive than others.

In 1988 an internal paper was produced stating that the issue was becoming more complicated as an increasing proportion of modern military equipment contained electronic circuits. In most cases, though not all, these were designed for commercial use but they could be used, or adapted, for military applications. The paper argued for two general principles:

- That the CFB should continue to avoid companies which had a high level of exposure to the defence industry

- That there were certain defence products whose manufacture was judged to be totally unacceptable. (Anti-personnel mines might be a case of the latter.)

However, it was noted that there were many electronics companies which did supply components to defence contractors, but which did not fall into the above categories. It was argued that just as the CFB did not exclude certain food or paper companies from the portfolio on the grounds that their products *could* be used by the brewing or tobacco industries, so it should not exclude electronics companies just because their integrated circuits or screens could be used militarily. The conclusion was to:

- Exclude suppliers of electrical components to the defence industry on ethical grounds only when the defence proportion was thought to be too large. Account would be taken of the extent to which the end use was offensive weapons, defensive (anti-missile missiles), or other (communications)
- Monitor the extent to which electronics companies' products and services were sold exclusively to the defence industry and exclude them if this proportion became too high
- Take account of the non-defence business and how it affected the community

This approach, with its emphasis on dialogue, research and engagement, is clearly distinct from the confrontation typical of shareholder activism. Assuming that an increasing proportion of charity and pension funds will be managed in the future on ethical lines, it seems likely that they will adopt the engagement route rather than that of confrontation. If so, it seems probable that there will be much more scope for dialogue between ethical investors and the business ethics profession than has hitherto been the case.

A THEORETICAL OBSTACLE

Let us now consider a theoretical obstacle. There are those who reject the whole concept of corporate responsibility, that is, the concept of business as anything more than *a priori* a profit-maximiser within a competitive framework; but does not this merely illustrate the restricted conceptual framework of some analysts? To give some examples: Brittan (1993), 'Corporate responsibility lacks the legitimacy of either the market or the political system' (1993, p. 10); or Sternberg (1994), who states that 'the defining purpose of business is to maximise owner value over the longer term by selling goods or services' (1994, p. 32). I must confess that I do not find the latter's argument particularly convincing. Taking Sternberg's definition of business, for example, she concludes that: 'using business resources for non-business purposes is theft – an unjustified appropriation of the owners' property' (1994, p. 41). But this is surely a truism given the initial definition of business as nothing more than a mechanism for generating owner value.

The most famous counterblast against business ethics was Friedman's 1970 article. He starts off by declaiming that anyone advocating social responsibility for business is 'preaching pure and unadulterated socialism', and that they 'are notable for their analytical looseness and lack of rigour' (p. 9). In fact, it is Friedman's thoughts which might be considered superficial and casual. He has essentially one philosophical and one economic argument, but the philosophical argument, that only people can have responsibilities and that business as a whole cannot be said to have responsibilities, is briefly stated and never justified. Thus businesspeople are seen only as agents of the shareholders who ultimately employ them, and in Friedman's view as businesspeople their only duty is to these owners. The economic argument is that any action by a businessperson that does not aim to maximise profits amounts to a tax on that business, which should be left to government alone. He concludes:

the doctrine of social responsibility . . . is fundamentally subversive . . . there is one and only one social responsibility of business – to use its resources and engage in activities designed to increase its profits so long as it . . . engages in open and free competition without deception and fraud. (1970, p. 12)

Robert Solomon, Professor of Philosophy at the University of Austin, Texas, takes a different view, and brings his professional expertise in conceptual analysis to areas of confusion or misunderstanding. Solomon (1992) points out that:

business activity is misconceived in an amoral way, subsumed (or hidden) under the all-purpose imagery of 'competitiveness'. But 'competition' is but one of a large number of relationships that companies have with one another and with other members of the community, and an overemphasis on competition can be disastrous for the sense of community, and for the underlying co-operation that is necessary for any business activity. (p. 41)

Some might say that recent scandals in the City of London, where the stress is very much on individual performance, demonstrate Solomon's point.

Of course, Friedman cannot answer the question which lies at the heart of business ethics: what if there are activities which benefit shareholders to the detriment of society at large or vice versa? His basic *a priori* assumption is that this cannot occur. Solomon is fairly dismissive of Friedman's article:

> its nonsensically one-sided assumption of responsibility to his pathetic understanding of stockholder personality as 'homo economicus' . . . such talk about the primacy of profits and the obligation to provide them is not only vacuous and misleading, it eclipses the larger picture and all the other purposes that business is designed and managers are hired to serve. (1992, p. 45)

If the traditional agency model of the company has weak philosophical foundations, it is also true that it is under increasing attack as a descriptive model of how companies actually operate in practice. There seems little point in the recent growth of corporate governance as a subject if companies actually do work in textbook fashion. The beginning of corporate governance as a distinct entity is normally dated to Berle and Means' famous book first published in 1932, although there is a clear reference to it by Adam Smith dating from 1776:

> The directors of such companies, however, being the managers rather of other people's money than of their own, it cannot be well expected that they should watch over it with the same anxious vigilance with which the partners in a private copartnery [partnership] frequently watch over their own. (1977, p. 229)

One of the most vigorous attacks on the traditional view was that of Kay and Silberston in 1995:

> Much of the concern with corporate governance – a concern which is largely Anglo-American – arises from the tension between the Anglo-American model and the practical reality of how large corporations operate everywhere. We believe that the organic model of corporate behaviour – which gives to the corporation life independent from its shareholders or stakeholders – describes the actual behaviour of large companies and their managers far better than does the principal–agent perspective, and that this is as true in Britain and the United States as it is in Japan. (p. 86)

Kay and Silberston go on to advocate the abandonment of the traditional 'shareholder agency' model of corporate responsibility and its replacement with the concept of trusteeship:

The notion that boards of directors are the trustees of the tangible and intangible assets of the corporation, rather than the agents of the shareholders, is one which the executives of . . . many British firms would immediately recognise. The duty of the trustee is to preserve and enhance the value of the assets under his control, and to balance fairly the various claims to the returns which these assets generate . . . The responsibility of the trustees is to sustain the corporation's assets. This differs from the value of the corporation's shares . . . [which] arises because the assets of the corporation include the skills of its employees, the expectations of customers and suppliers, and the company's reputation in the community. (p. 91)

Discussions of corporate governance and business ethics often seem to forget that the creation of the legal status of limited liability for the company is fairly recent – it dates from the 1840s. This had two corollaries: first that in law the company is a separate entity from the interests of the shareholders, unlike the earlier unlimited company which was viewed as effectively no more than a glorified partnership of equals. In the famous words of Lord Justice Evershed in the Short Brothers judgment of 1947: 'shareholders are not in the eye of the law part-owners of the undertaking. The undertaking is something different from the totality of its shareholdings' (see Goyder, 1993, p. 18).

Second, and developing Kay and Silberston's point about trusteeship, it is curious how this legal privilege of limited liability is taken for granted, and never questioned. The legal duties of charity trustees have been developed and expanded over the centuries both by case law and by statute, the last significant change being the Charities Acts of 1992–93. In fact the law places quite a considerable burden upon charities, which makes a curious contrast with the fairly limited requirements placed upon company directors which have changed little since the 1948 Companies Act.

DOES ETHICS MAKE ECONOMIC SENSE?

In December 1992 the Report of the Committee on the Financial Aspects of Corporate Governance (see Cadbury, this volume) sent shock waves through the boardrooms of the UK, with its explicit criticisms of the way some companies were being run. It advocated a code of good practice to improve corporate governance, including business ethics, and stressed the need for non-executive directors to ensure this: 'Non-executive directors should bring an independent judgement to bear on issues of strategy, performance, resources – including key appointments – *and standards of conduct*' (para. 2.1, p. 6, my emphasis).

Shortly after Cadbury, Drummond and Wilson sent survey questions to non-executive directors of Britain's largest 500 companies, of which 118 gave usable replies. The results were published in their book, *The Importance of Being Ethical* (1992). All of them felt that business ethics was a very important issue, and 56 per cent of the companies had discussed business ethics at board level in the previous six months. The main conclusions of the report were that for most companies it was the chief executive who determined what the business ethics of the company should be, if any. Although 43 per cent had ethics codes, only 8 per cent carried out an ethics audit, while 61 per cent put their faith in old-fashioned disciplinary measures.

In a recent paper Jones and Pollitt (1996) examined 'the economics of corporate integrity'. They assert two arguments why business integrity could be a successful strategy in purely economic terms. The first is the theory of reputation, that in any business which aims for long-term success, its reputation for quality is a significant competitive asset, 'goodwill', which can be significantly damaged by exposure of unethical behaviour. In other words, the short-term benefits of cheating are outweighed by the long-term costs. Drummond agrees:

If you take the view, as I do, that a company's reputation is its most valuable asset, (I call it a 'meta brand'), then companies need to be aware where they could be vulnerable to problems in such areas, before the problems and associated bad publicity emerge. But note that the aim is not the negative one of punishing poor performers, but the positive one of building corporate values based on integrity and reliability. (See Drummond in Sparkes, 1995, p. 224)

Given the information age we live in, poor ethics will be noticed, and sales will suffer. However, as will be argued later, it is the *use of non-financial techniques* to assess the performance of companies, devised by ethical investors but increasingly used by standard investment institutions, which is and will become an *increasingly important feedback mechanism*. Companies which fail ethically will not just see their sales suffer, they will see their access to capital restricted and its cost increase.

The growth of ethical unit trusts is merely one aspect of the way values are increasingly being used as part of the package being offered to customers. Affinity cards are another good example of an idea which started in the charity sector and which has crossed over to the mainstream economy. A sign of their popularity is that they are the only area of credit card usage which is growing steadily – at the end of 1995 the total of credit cards in issue was lower than its peak of 1989. A typical example is that offered by the Cooperative Bank in October 1993 when it added Amnesty International to its affinity card list. Amnesty gets £5 for every new account opened and 20p for every £100 spent. Affinity cards have worked very well for some charities, as well as generating substantial and profitable new business for the issuing banks. The Leeds Permanent's card has raised £4m for its group of three charities, while the largest amount received by a single charity card was over £1m for the card issued by the Co-operative Bank for the Royal Society for the Protection of Birds.

A more tangible example is the UK coffee market, one of the most competitive in the country. Despite this the 'fairtrade' brand Cafédirect became one of the leading brands of ground coffee in the UK by the end of 1994 with annual sales of two million packets. It was stocked by all the major supermarket chains. A number of consumer surveys – the latest was by Mintel in December 1994 – show that the public is increasingly concerned about ethical and environmental issues, and around 35–40 per cent use these factors in their purchasing decisions.

In September 1993 the National Children's Home (now NCH Action for Children) published a report called *Business and Charities – the Win–Win Situation*. This argued that cause-related marketing offered great benefits to companies, and that such corporate fundraising had grown to reach 15 per cent of NCH's total voluntary income. Despite this, the report found that 72 of the top 100 UK companies had no company policy about charity links, although most companies believed cause-related marketing was growing in importance and would continue to do so. The Kingfisher group, parent company of Woolworth, Comet and B&Q, had found that: 'Cause-related marketing does provide the key at no great cost to permanent customer loyalty. It has an emotional pull which any mere price promotion isn't going to provide.' Most managers in business will tell you that sustaining repeat business is usually a much more profitable strategy than trying to generate new custom.

The second argument is a broader economic argument of transaction costs, that the ethical firm can, according to Jones and Pollitt (1996, p. 38), 'undertake many economic transactions at much lower cost than an equivalent transaction organised via the price mechanism because of the bounded rationality of individuals and the problems of monitoring and avoiding opportunism in contracts with those outside the firm'. The City of London provides a good example of how this might work from a macro-economic viewpoint. For many years it was organised on the informal basis of 'my word is my bond', and voluntary self-regulation was the rule. In the 1980s, as Jones and Pollitt note, a number of financial scandals undermined the credibility of this system. The result was the imposition by the

Financial Services Act of a cumbersome and bureaucratic 'compliance' procedure which was not necessary before.

Signs that the debate had reached the political arena were given by the publication by the radical think tank DEMOS in September 1995 of Carmichael's *Business Ethics: The New Bottom Line*, an act which would have been inconceivable even a couple of years before. This argues for a third economic benefit from good business ethics – as a feedback mechanism ensuring that the company is open to the environment facing it. Rather like the philosopher Karl Popper's critique of Marxism, the company dominated by a tyrannical chief executive will tend to tell him or her what he or she wants to hear, rather than what problems do actually exist. In Popperian terms it will be a closed rather than a open society:

> In this sense, the collapse of Barings Bank is a classic case of the failure of ethical controls, not just of managerial or financial ones. It is invariably the case that before a major disaster – be it the Space Shuttle Challenger, BCCI or Barings – there are people within the organisation who are warning of the problem. Disasters of this magnitude strike rarely, but when they do they can destroy a company. Indeed, even apart from its other benefits, the cost of an ethical process can be seen as disaster insurance, as a crucial part of risk management. (Carmichael, 1995, p. 12)

Kay and Silberston (1995) push the analogy with Communism even further:

> There are obvious resemblances between the system of corporate governance we have and entrenched authoritarian political systems, such as those which prevailed in Eastern Europe before the fall of the Berlin wall. The governing elite is self-perpetuating, in the sense that it appoints its own members by reference to its own criteria . . . There is a nominal process of accountability through election of directors, but in practice it is as defunct as the meaningless elections which routinely returned Mr Brezhnev and Herr Honecker to power. (p. 86)

One way round this 'agency' problem is for more active involvement by institutional shareholders. Clearly shareholder voting is one aspect of this, although there is a real risk that this can degenerate into automatic 'box-ticking'. Regular and informed discussion between institutional shareholders and corporate managements seems a better way. Given the assumption that ethical investors have their attention focused on social and environmental concerns which in certain cases later become the subject of legal penalty, their actions may make senior management more aware of potential problems than they otherwise would be. In Oxford Analytica's (1992) terms:

> Given the very limited role of most boards in actually determining the direction of their companies, their ability to oversee management's direction and to call it to account for its actions – preferably before a crisis point is reached – is a critical element of effective governance. Oversight is far easier to exercise when the board includes a number of outside directors who are backed by major shareholders. (p. 146)

Since the late 1980s this point has been forcefully made in the USA by the largest institutional investor, the $100bn Californian state pension fund normally known as CalPERS, which stated:

> Our entire investment philosophy is based on the premise that we are long-term investors. Our average holding period is between eight and ten years . . . we seek a return to corporations being accountable to their shareholders. If accountability exists, we are confident that corporate performance will follow. (Hanson, 1993, p. 32)

Of course CalPERS' activity was not based on any claims of being ethical, but simply in the belief that *relational investing*, where investment institutions maintain close links with companies in which they have shareholdings, increases financial returns. Wilshire Associates analysed 42 US companies where CalPERS had taken increasing involvement between 1987 and 1992. This group had significantly underperformed the US benchmark, the S&P 500 index, in the previous five years. Wilshire found that in the subsequent five years after CalPERS had contacted them they outperformed the S&P 500 by 41 per cent. The study also found that increasing input from shareholders had the most financial benefit when it focused on corporate strategy in a dialogue with management. These results were confirmed in a recent study of CalPERS' relationship investing by Smith (1996).

Outside the world of theory, most businesses know that it makes good sense to protect and sustain the community in which they operate. A letter published in the *Financial Times* in September 1993 under the corporate banner of the charity Business in the Community provides a good illustration: (Shaw *et al.*, 1993)

> Business in the Community has always agreed that the primary role of business is to create sustainable wealth by meeting customers' needs

. . . [but] business can help to build the social environment it needs for long-term wealth creation . . . There is clear evidence that customers increasingly expect businesses to play their part in tackling social issues; in 1992 Mori research found that 73% of adults are more inclined to buy products from companies that support the community and society . . . A survey by MSS of the UK's top 1000 companies found that 75% believe that employee involvement in the community improves morale, 71% that it builds teams, and 65% that it offers training opportunities. Employees are even more enthusiastic – 84% told Mori that a company that supports society and the community is probably a good company to work for. (p. 11)

NEW MEASURES OF BUSINESS SUCCESS

Finally let us consider the last of the three themes in the subtitle – *analysis*. The thesis is simple: that we live in a world of such complexity and rapid change that traditional measurement systems of financial success are of diminishing utility. To quote from Professor Charles Handy of the London Business School in his 1994 book *The Empty Raincoat*:

It will be increasingly difficult for shareholders to know what they are buying into, or to what sort of risks they are exposed. It will be all the more difficult because the real assets of the business, the intellectual assets, will still be largely unquantifiable, *unless accountancy groups come up with new measures*. In the best business today the market value of the business is three or four times the tangible assets, and in a good manufacturing company, labour costs should not be more than 10% of the product price. *That leaves a lot of unmeasured space*. (my emphasis; quoted in Sparkes, 1995a, p. 227)

To those sceptical of Handy's theoretical argument, consider a practical example. The US equity market is currently trading (March 1997) at record levels, and looks overvalued on most traditional criteria. One measurement on which it appears particularly overvalued is Tobin's Q Ratio, the relationship between the value placed on US industry by the stock market and its replacement cost in real terms. Since this ratio now stands at a higher level than it did in the great bull markets of 1929 or 1968, it is receiving a lot of attention in the financial press. One of the largest companies in the USA is the software giant Microsoft, valued at over $90bn. Since it has relatively small capital investment in plant and machinery, its fixed assets, and therefore its book replacement value, are a small fraction of its stock market capitalisation. Its real assets are the skills of the people who work for it, and the potential earning power of the software it develops.

In December 1990 Handy gave a lecture at the Royal Society of Arts entitled 'What is a Company For?'. He concluded by reviving the notion of stakeholders:

> I see the company as operating in a bounded space, a sort of hexagonal ring, surrounded by competing pressures from financiers, the employees, the customers, the suppliers, the environment, and the community – the so-called 'stakeholders'. With that ring of forces I want to see the development of the 'existential corporation', the corporation whose principal purpose is to fulfil itself, to grow and develop the best that it can be . . . it is not a piece of property, inhabited by humans, it is a community which itself has property. (p. 22)

This lecture led to the formal establishment of the RSA Inquiry in January 1993. Called *Tomorrow's Company: The Role of Business in a Changing World*, it brought together the heads of 25 of the UK's top companies under the leadership of Sir Anthony Cleaver, Chairman of IBM UK. The declared aim was practical – to stimulate competitive performance by provoking business leaders to think about the sources of sustainable business success. Sir Anthony Cleaver (1994) had no doubts of the *practical nature* of the Inquiry:

> Of course financial figures are important, we're a group of businessmen, we are very conscious that the bottom line does matter, but, if you think about it, it's really a historic measure. It tells you where you've been. If you want to know where you're going, the questions are about your people, about your suppliers, about your customer relationships, is the community going to inhibit you because it does not like the way you do business. And they are, I think, much more capable of being predictive measures.

There was a striking postscript to the RSA Inquiry, which reported in the spring of 1995. In September 1996 the investment bank Kleinwort Benson announced that it had analysed the stock market performance of companies under the RSA's inclusive approach to business, that is, which demonstrated quality relationships with customers, employees, suppliers and the community. The bank then stated that it was creating an investment fund to invest specifically in these companies. Not that Kleinwort Benson was claiming that this new fund was 'ethical' in any way – it merely thought that it had discovered new measures of corporate and hence financial success. In the words of one director:

> The Tomorrow's Company fund is *not an ethical fund*, but it is *a fund which has ethics*. We think that the RSA Inquiry has isolated an extra layer of corporate analysis which enables us to identify companies which will be successful over the long term. We use it in addition to traditional financial analysis, as part of our investment process. In our view we live in a world where global competition means low inflation but also makes it very difficult for British companies to compete successfully simply on the basis of price alone. Sustained success comes from generating added value in a number of ways: through continuous innovation for example, or by constantly upgrading service through staff training, or by working with suppliers to jointly solve problems. Think of Unipart's success in the automotive parts business, or of Marks & Spencer's close attention to customer needs and product quality. To repeat, this is not an 'ethical screen', but a vehicle for identifying companies with a corporate success model which will deliver long-term growth in shareholder value. (Author's notes from presentation by Brennan Hiorns, Investment Director of Kleinwort Benson Investment Management; emphasis added)

Kleinwort Benson claimed that its research offered objective criteria by which such 'social variables' could be independently assessed. This is in the form of a 'scorecard' of seven key factors: leadership, basic process, employees, investors, customers, suppliers, society. The top three items are given a weighting of 50 per cent. The model is stated to have predictive value – for example, consumer surveys showed increasing disaffection with the supermarkets *before* this showed up in sluggish sales and profits growth, and hence before it was reflected in poor stockmarket performance. The bank added: 'We researched companies showing Tomorrow's Company characteristics and found that between December 1992 and June 1996 a portfolio of 32 of these had risen 90%, against a gain of 38% in the FT All-Share index' (in Jamieson, 1996).

Handy's assertion of the need for accountancy groups to come up with new measures of success may be satisfied by something now in its infancy – a 'social audit'. This has been around as a theoretical concept for years, but no one had tried it out in practice, until a small charity called Traidcraft did so in 1993 (see Sparkes, 1995a, pp. 244–7). In isolation this has no more than curiosity value, but when in late 1994 Body Shop came under attack from allegations that the company did not live up to the image it had created of itself, its response was to commission a detailed social audit, published in June 1996 under the title of *Values Report*. This consisted of three sections, looking at social aspects, environmental aspects and animal protection issues. The report is not just anecdotal, but attempts to supply quantifiable answers.

If companies do carry out internal 'ethical audits', it would seem only a matter of time before this overlaps with the demands of ethical fund managers for more social information on a potential company investment. It is arguable that the market-place is just beginning to wake up to the comparative advantage that the best ethical investors have over other more traditional fund managers in some of these areas. The fact that Kleinwort Benson is launching a Tomorrow's Company fund suggests that the general fund management community is becoming aware of this, as does the creation of a similar unit at BZW Investment Management.

To conclude this section is another quotation from Sir Anthony Cleaver discussing the RSA Inquiry:

> I do believe that in the future we may see a standardised approach to a whole range of measures, but that I think should come because it evolves, because if we do our job properly in the companies, we will persuade the [City] analysts that's what they ought to look at, and then they will start to demand the same from other companies. Let me give you one example – the question of the environment. If I take you back just ten years ago, the average company report had no reference to the environment at all, then what happened, the pressure built up from the community, from employees, from customers. First the Chairman stood up and said that his company had a responsible policy with regard to the environment, then a couple of years later it became a paragraph, or even a page, in the annual review with a few pretty pictures and some more pious statements. That's all moved on, most of the leading companies now produce figures, they actually say 'we measured our impact on the environment last year, and we're setting targets, we're moving forward'. Ten years ago, you would have bet me that wouldn't happen.

THE REWARDS OF VIRTUE AND NEW MEASURES OF INVESTMENT ANALYSIS

The other key question regarding ethical investment is what it costs the investor. Does it, as many commentators suggest, result in lower financial returns relative to comparable non-ethical investments? Theoretically, of course, there is no reason why excluding certain types of investment on non-financial grounds should necessarily lower financial returns – it might increase them. All financial theory can say is that, in the absence of compensating factors, such exclusion will increase volatility or result in lower risk-adjusted returns. *The Ethical Investor* (Sparkes, 1995a, ch. 6) identifies four possible positive effects which could overcome the negative impact of reduced diversification and perhaps even lead to higher risk-adjusted returns:

- That exclusion of certain companies on grounds of moral or environmental repugnance anticipates later legal action and financial problems – the *anticipation effect*
- That responsible investors are forced to avoid large conglomerates, and concentrate on smaller companies which over time grow faster – the *small companies effect*
- That properly done ethical/green investment needs a higher level of knowledge about the companies invested in than ordinary investment managers possess – the *information effect*
- That the positive criteria used by such funds help them target well-run companies – a *positive selection effect*

Early advocates of ethical investment tended to focus on the anticipation effect, the argument being that such investors avoid companies involved in activities increasingly regarded as socially unacceptable. Such companies could either find demand collapsing, as in the fur trade, or be subject to increasing legal and financial cost, such as tobacco or certain heavily polluting industries. This argument works well for the above industries, but is less convincing for alcohol, pornography in general, or defence.

Attempts to demonstrate such effects by reconstructing stock market indices such as the Financial Times Actuaries classifications to develop 'ethical indices' have proved less than convincing. The consistent answer seems to come back that there is no statistically meaningful difference between ethical and conventional indices. A typical set of results was produced by BARRA Associates (1989) looking at imposing ethical constraints on certain sections of the FT All-Share index over the previous five years. BARRA found that the overall effect of imposing all the usual exclusions on a theoretical portfolio was to increase the annual return by 0.06 per cent p.a. compared to the index – statistically insignificant.

Part of the explanation for these results is that most stock market classifications of large companies are necessarily imprecise. So-called tobacco companies may derive much of their income from financial services or food manufacturing, while luxury goods companies manufacture cigarettes. Simpson (1991) quotes Congdon who reported internal analysis by Friends Provident showing little evidence that sector exclusion on its own has a clear impact: 'the distribution is about what you would expect from any random sample of fully discretionary funds. So far, therefore, it would appear that an ethical bias is not in itself instrumental in performance one way or the other' (p. 94).

It is partly because most large companies have a variety of activities that many ethical funds have sought 'pure plays' in the smaller capitalisation area. This is often claimed to be the foundation of good relative performance from ethical funds and was conventional wisdom at the end of the 1980s. As Congdon (in Simpson, 1991) put it:

> It may be cynically argued that much of the good performance was achieved courtesy of the 'smaller companies' effect; that ethical criteria forced funds willy-nilly into smaller companies, a sector which coincidentally produced strong outperformance in the late 1980s . . . There is only limited truth in this. Certainly most ethical funds will tend to have a bias towards smaller companies . . . The performance of the smaller companies sector is an important issue, however, because it does not correlate exactly with that of the total index. Over the long term, smaller companies as a species will tend to outperform their larger counterparts. (p. 89)

It is 'Goodhart's Law' which states that once the authorities target a financial variable such as the money supply it loses its predictive capacity. The same is often true in the stock market. Small companies performed very well in the 'Lawson boom' of the late 1980s, and the 'small cap' effect was widely proclaimed at that time as a winning stock market formula – just in time for the recession of 1990–92, and significant relative underperformance by the small company sector compared to the benchmark FT All-Share index. Over the same period most ethical unit trusts produced good investment performance relative to comparable non-ethical trusts, thus showing little correlation with the negative effects of small company investment.

The real test of any investment formula is over the long term, at least five years. In 1990 the WM Company of consulting actuaries produced a research paper, *The Implications of Ethical Constraints on Investment Returns*. This examined the investment performance of 126 charity funds for the five years ending in 1989, of which 44 were restricted by ethical constraints from investing in companies active in South Africa, tobacco, alcohol or gambling. The results, as shown in Table 8.1, were interesting.

Table 8.1 Historical performance of charitable investment funds

UK equity investment	1989	5 years to 1989
All charities	+35.0%	+19.5%
Ethical charities	+36.5%	+19.9%

Source: WM Company (1990).

Clearly, the ethical investment restrictions had no negative impact, in fact they appeared to give a positive boost to investment performance. The WM Company: 'In general the message seems to be that [ethical] constraints do not damage your wealth.' WM revisited the subject in February 1997 with similar results. A critic might argue that these charity funds were very small, and a tiny, specialised part of the market. The obvious next step was to analyse the performance of ethical unit trusts given the intense competition of that sector of the market.

Ethical investment is such a young and rapidly growing field that the data to achieve a statistically valid analysis simply were not available until recently. To the best of my knowledge it appears that the first attempt to do so was by the author of this chapter and published in *Professional Investor*, the journal of the Institute of Investment Management and Research, in March 1994 under the title of 'The Rewards of Virtue'. This found that an investor who had invested on a weighted basis at the beginning of 1991 in the nine funds with a minimum track record of three years would have seen the value of his portfolio increase in value by 66.2 per cent by the end of 1993. This compared with a 62.4 per cent increase in the average UK growth trust over the period. There was also a positive risk-adjusted effect. Table 8.2 shows some of the data. (In accordance with normal practice, each trust is ranked against its peer group of UK growth trusts on both an annual and three-year basis. There were insufficient data to do the same exercise for international ethical funds, which is why well-known funds such as CIS Environ and Jupiter Ecology were not analysed.)

It is interesting that many of the above funds showed evidence of a deterioration in relative investment performance as the period progressed. This may well indicate that for many of them the poor performance of small companies at that time *was* a negative factor. However, for the sector as a whole this was not the case, suggesting that some positive factor was overcoming this negative effect. The article concluded that this positive factor was *an extra layer of analysis*. The evidence seemed to indicate that the best financial performance came from funds carrying out significant ethical research on their own account (see Sparkes 1995a, pp. 110–11):

Table 8.2   Historical performance of ethical investment funds
(quartile rankings)

	1993 Size £m	1991	1992	1993	3 years	Agg. score
Abbey Ethical	20.6	1st	3rd	2nd	1st	0.337
Allchurches Amity	17.6	3rd	2nd	4th	4th	0.426
Eagle Star						
Environmental						
Oppurtunities	12.4	1st	1st	4th	1st	0.375
Fidelity UK Growth	75.5	2nd	1st	1st	1st	0.181
Friends Provident						
Stewardship	154.4	2nd	3rd	2nd	2nd	0.309
NM Conscience	12.3	1st	3rd	4th	2nd	0.422
Scottish Equitable	12.6	2nd	3rd	4th	3rd	0.403
Sovereign Ethical	8.3	2nd	4th	3rd	4th	0.433
TSB Environmental	21.4	1st	3rd	4th	2nd	0.386
Sector ave. % change		+7.4	+10.0	+20.7	+62.4	
No. of funds		146	144	132		

Source: Data derived from that published in Money Management magazine.
The aggregate score is a measure of the mean percentile ranking
adjusted for the standard deviation.

Ethical investment is becoming more complex and difficult to do. It is
becoming an asset class in its own right, and one that requires the allocation of adequate resources to do well. In sum, this would appear to indicate that there is indeed a very clear positive selection effect. Indeed, the
evidence suggests that it is the actual process of selection, if carried out
thoroughly, which is the real reason why ethical investment has produced
superior investment, rather than a concentration on the products excluded, as the Press has tended to think. Ethical and ecological screening
is an essential part of any ethical fund manager's life, and one that is very
time-consuming and becoming more so. A sign that the thesis of superior
returns is due to the intensive research required, rather than to exclusions,
was given by Peter Sylvester of Friends Provident when he described the
good performance of the Stewardship funds in December 1993, 'We get
the performance because we've had to spend more time researching than
most people do nowadays. We have to look at companies in much greater
detail to get to know them' (Sparkes 1995a, p. 111).

It was encouraging to see these positive conclusions replicated in
a paper entitled   'The Financial Performance of Ethical Investment
Funds' (Mallin et al., 1995). The authors found that on a risk-adjusted

basis, and using three different measures of excess returns (Jensen, Treynor and Sharpe), the ethical funds outperformed the non-ethical ones.

Conventional investment analysis has perhaps two main aims: to enable the potential investor to track the performance of a company over time, or to be able to make comparisons between similar companies in the same industry. In either case, the ultimate purpose of such *fundamental analysis* is to identify companies whose long-term profits' growth are likely to generate long-term share price outperformance. Economists may not realise how relatively young investment analysis is as a subject in the UK. It was not until 1968 that the Companies Act obliged companies to reveal turnover, and comparable accounting practices between companies were not instituted until 1970 with the introduction of Statements of Standard of Accounting Practice (SSAPs). (Ethics and scandal played a role in this. The financial world was shocked in 1968 when the stated profits of a publisher called Pergamon Press were found in practice to be a large loss – the owner being a certain Robert Maxwell.) The first book on investment analysis specifically designed for professional institutional investors was Weaver's *Investment Analysis*, sponsored by the Society of Investment Analysis. It did not appear until 1971.

Hence the analysis of companies on non-standard financial criteria may be at a similar stage now as traditional investment analysis was in the early 1970s. Let me give you a practical example of something we are starting to do at the CFB. It is in its early stages, and the conclusions may only be described as tentative, but it illustrates the point. At the CFB we subscribe to the ethical database and screening service of EIRIS, as do the majority of ethical investors. What we have tried to do is weight a number of areas, both positive and negative, and track how they change over certain time periods. Just like a normal financial analyst, we can monitor a company in relation to its peers, and assess how its performance in these so-called 'soft areas' changes dynamically across time. This is something which we have only been doing for a little while, but this ethical 'credit scoring' has thrown up some interesting and useful data. For example, two companies which both received medium concern scores were BP and a certain conglomerate. BP's negative scores were all in the environmental area and related to fossil fuels, in other words, purely in relation to its functions as an oil company; but it was felt to be a well-run company which attempted to minimise the negative impact of those activities. In contrast the conglomerate's operations do not fall into the traditional prohibited categories, but the negative scores in separate areas such as health and safety, pollution and so on all gave the opposite impression.

CONCLUSION

In this chapter I have attempted to show that ethical investment does indeed have a key role to play within the overall business ethics sector and in the way that values impact upon economic performance. It is important that ethical investment is distinguished from shareholder activism, for the aims and approach are ultimately different.

It also seems likely that ethical investment is 'coming of age'. It is no longer just a minority pursuit of a few small unit trusts. Rather it is increasingly being embraced by large charity investors and local authority pension funds. Over time the current media-inspired image of ethical investment as concerned with a mechanistic avoidance approach will change to reflect the wider reality. A world in which large institutional investors take the responsibilities of share ownership seriously is one in which the subject has much to offer to, but also to learn from, business ethics. In particular, ethical investors can contribute their practical experience of researching social data on companies and of analysing and quantifying that data.

In conclusion, I want to highlight and repeat a remark of John Drummond: 'But note that the aim is not the negative one of punishing poor performers, but the positive one of building corporate values based on integrity and reliability.' For me that is exactly what ethical investment is all about. As such, it indicates common ground where economists, business ethicists and ethical investors can pursue a dialogue which has been lacking in the past.

Ethical investment fulfils various objectives, not least of which is the maintenance of the importance of ethical values in the sometimes ruthless world of finance. But ethical investment also has a real and distinct contribution to the interplay of ethics and economic performance. I want to put forward what I believe to be a new thesis: *that ethical investors are playing the unexpected role of pioneers who look at business in new ways.* And that, I submit, is its real challenge to economists, business ethicists, and also to those who are labourers in the field.

References

Anderson, D. (ed.) (1996) *What has 'Ethical Investment' to do with Ethics?* (London: Social Affairs Unit).
BARRA Associates (1989) *Survey of Ethical Investment 1983–1988*, available from EIRIS, London.
Berle, A.A. and Means, G.C. (1932) *The Modern Corporation and Private Company* (New York: Macmillan).

Brittan, S. (1997) 'How Economics is Linked to Ethics', *Financial Times*, 2 September, p. 17.

Carmichael, S. (1995) *Business Ethics: The New Bottom Line* (London: DEMOS).

Central Board of Finance Board of the Methodist Church (1996) *The 1996 Annual Report of the Central Finance Board of the Methodist Church* (London: CFB).

Cleaver, Anthony (1994) *BBC Radio – In Business*.

Committee on the Financial Aspects of Corporate Governance [Cadbury Report] (1992) *Code of Best Practice* (London: Gee Publishing).

Cooper, C. and Schlegelmilch, B. (1993) 'Key Issues in Ethical investment', *Business Ethics: A European Review*, 2(4), pp. 213–27.

Cowton, C. (1994) 'The Development of Ethical Investment Products', in *ACT Guide to Ethical Conflicts in Finance* (Oxford: Blackwell).

Coyle, D. (1995) Investing in the Future, *Investors Chronicle*, Business and the Environment Survey, p. 12, 20 September.

Drummond, J. and Wilson, A. (1992) *The Importance of Being Ethical* (Ashridge: Ashridge Management College).

Farrow, D. (1974) 'The Ethics of Investment', *The Epworth Review*, February.

Friedman, M. (1970) 'The Social Responsibility of Business is to Increase its Profits', *New York Times*, reprinted in Desjardins, J.R. and McCall, J.J., *Contemporary Issues in Business Ethics* (Belmont, CA. Wordsworth Publishing) 1990.

Goyder, G. (1993) *The Just Enterprise* (London: Adamantine Press).

Handy, C. (1991) 'What is a Company For?', *RSA Journal*, vol. 89, no. 5416, March pp. 231–9.

Handy, C. (1994) *The Empty Raincoat* (London: Hutchinson).

Hanson, D. (CalPERS Chief Executive) (1993) 'Putting Investors Back in Power', *Professional Investor*, April, vol. 4, no. 4, pp. 32–3.

Jamieson, B. (1996) 'Kleinwort Launching New Fund for Tomorrow', *Sunday Telegraph*, 8 September, p. 24.

Jones, I.W. and Pollitt, M.G. (1996) 'Economics, Ethics and Integrity in Business', *Journal of General Management*, 21 (3), pp. 30–47.

Jupiter Environmental Research Unit (1995) *The Assessment Process for Green Investment*, June (London: Jupiter Tyndall Group).

Kay, J. and Silberston, A. (1995) 'Corporate Governance', *National Institute Economic Review*, 153 (3), p. 84–95.

Mackenzie, C. (1997) 'Shareholder Action', *The Christian Democrat*, February, no. 39, p. 11.

Mallin, C., Saadouni, B. and Briston, R. (1995) 'The Financial Performance of Ethical Investment Funds', *Journal of Business Finance and Accounting*, June, 22 (4), pp. 483–96.

NCH Action for Children (1993) *Business and Charities – the Win–Win Situation* (London: NCH Action for Children).

Oxford Analytica (1992) *Board Directors and Corporate Governance trends in the G7 Countries* (Oxford: Oxford Analytica).

Seddon, W. (1997) 'Salt and Light', *Full Measure – The Journal of Anglican Stewardship*, issue no. 8, April, pp. 2–3, 7.

Shaw, N. *et al.* (1997) 'Letter to the Editor From M.N. Shaw and Others' *Financial Times*, 14 September, p. 11.

Simpson, A. (1991) *The Greening of Global Investment* (London: Economist Books).

170   *The Challenge of Ethical Investment*

Smith, A. (1977) *The Wealth of Nations* (London: Pelican). First published 1776.

Smith, C.N. (1990) *Morality and the Market, Consumer Pressure for Corporate Accountability* (London: Routledge).

Smith, M.P. (1996) 'Shareholder Activism by Institutional Investors: Evidence From CalPERS', *Journal of Finance*, 51 (1), pp. 227–52.

Solomon, R.C. (1992) *Ethics and Excellence – Co-operation and Integrity in Business* (Oxford: Oxford University Press).

Sparkes, R.K. (1994) 'The Rewards of Virtue', *Professional Investor*, March, vol. 5, no. 2, pp. 23–5.

Sparkes R.K. (1995a) *The Ethical Investor* (London: HarperCollins).

Sparkes R.K. (1995b) *The Money Game* (London: *DEMOS*).

Sparkes R.K. (1997) 'Putting the Ethics into Investment', *NCVO News*, February, no. 81, pp. 18–19.

Sternberg, E. (1994) *Just Business* (London: Little, Brown).

Weaver, D. (1971) *Investment Analysis* (London: Longman in association with the Society of Investment Analysis).

WM Company (1990) *The Implications of Ethical Constraints on Investment Returns* (London: WM Company).

WM Company (1997) *You Can Have Your Ethical Cake and Eat It* (London: WM Company).

9 Business Ethics and Corporate Culture

Clive Wright

INTRODUCTION

I well remember what was probably my initiation into considering the subject of business ethics. In the mid-1970s I was asked by my employers at the time – Esso – to sign a statement regarding conflicts of interest. My reaction was not a favourable one: I felt rather as though my integrity was impugned by the suggestion that I would deliberately pursue interests that conflicted with those of my employer. It seemed obvious and natural to me (and, I think, to most other employees) that one would not carry on personal activities that were in conflict with the interests of one's employer. Even at the end of the liberating 1960s, it was still reasonable to assume shared common values in our society and within the community represented by the company. Today I would feel uneasy at making that assumption. It would seem to me now eminently sensible for an employer to reduce the chances of confusion by spelling out clearly the principles to be followed in the company. Postmodern thinking and the logical positivists have indicated relativism where once we assumed a great degree of concurrence.

From those comments it is reasonable to assume that there has been a 180-degree change of direction since the 1960s. From feeling affronted and upset when asked to indicate formal acceptance of a written code of ethics, many people have moved to strong advocacy and support of such codes. This changed viewpoint reflects a society which is reluctant to articulate precise, rigid principles. This in turn means that many citizens may be ambivalent about the basis for agreed rules of conduct and consequently inconsistent in identifying or applying such rules in their own conduct.

The intellectual basis for this relativism or wholly subjective basis for morality is well-known and it is not the purpose of this chapter to explore that subject. The situation is well-summarised by Lord Hailsham in a short book published in 1995: *Values: Collapse and Cure*. The book is remarkable in two respects: it is a very lucid analysis written by a nonogenarian; it is also printed in the author's own manuscript, with hardly any corrections and no trace of illegibility.

The seeds of intellectual doubt have been accompanied by a readiness to relativise ethical considerations at the more mundane levels of daily life. Take an example. When one of the notorious criminal Kray twins died recently, some of his friends decided to give him a traditional East End funeral – with black horses, top hats and black crepe and so on. This, of course, attracted media attention. On the evening of the funeral a radio reporter described the occasion and interviewed mourners, including a lady who had known the twins as small children. She described at length what simplehearted, kind, generous and thoughtful lads they were and how good they had been to family and friends. The interviewer interrupted the eulogy to point out that the dead man was a convicted murderer and had been involved in several nasty killings. The lady readily agreed but explained that the victims were themselves all thugs and criminals. This, she said, justified and excused the murders. The new climate had reached a significant point: even murder was now relativised.

Anecdotal evidence is not, of course, sufficient but there is a respectable canon of survey data which indicates that whilst broad societal consensus on moral issues can be found, there is great reluctance to translate this into hard and fast precepts or to offer some kind of vade-mecum to cover all eventualities.

Paradoxically, accompanying this weakening of the perceived rights and wrongs of conduct, we can recognise a readiness in society to condemn and punish those who are perceived to fall short in their behaviour. This applies particularly to public figures: politicians and members of the royal family are castigated for sexual misbehaviour; fat-cat executives are execrated for greed and selfishness. We must, of course, be wary of our perceptions in these areas, since they are often conditioned by what we read, learn and see through the filter of the popular media. Nevertheless, such perceptions are real.

In the case of companies, this paradox should be taken very seriously. We now recognise that perceived integrity and acceptable public behaviour are very important components of corporate reputation. And corporate reputation is, for many companies, an essential element in business success. A good reputation is a prerequisite for a successful company. Opinion surveys regularly show the high esteem in which Marks & Spencer is held. That esteem includes a public perception of the decency of the company's behaviour. That, in turn, contributes to our decision to buy Marks & Spencer's good-value, attractive merchandise.

These comments are by way of introduction: an overly simplified account of how many have come to a recognition of the need for codes of ethics for any company that may have serious concerns about the impact on its business of a reputation for unacceptable behaviour.

SOME GENERAL CONSIDERATIONS

Other chapters in this book consider codes of ethics and their role. Such codes can be global – as for example, the CERES Principles on environmental practice; professional – as in the case of industrial hygienists or bankers; covering an industry – as in the case of the chemical industry's Responsible Care commitment; or specific to a particular company. This chapter is concerned only with statements of principle and codes of ethics within individual companies.

There is a wide academic interest in business ethics but this chapter is written from the perspective of the practitioner businessperson. A robust intellectual basis and coherence is a necessary prerequisite for our discussion, but the emphasis here lies more in the practical application and consequences of codes of ethics.

It is still the case that practitioners like myself do not perceive there to be an extensive canon of study in the field of business ethics and corporate culture. There are no schools of thought or widely discussed themes in this area. If we put aside those who might uncharitably describe corporate culture as an oxymoron, it is difficult to identify much in the literature about business ethics which examines ethical considerations as part of the business process. The United States, where the introduction and use of codes has been taken up far in advance of Europe, may offer more to the diligent researcher. It is to be hoped that this chapter may stimulate more research into the subject.

There is in the United Kingdom an organisation which seeks to promote the use of codes of business ethics. In 1986 a group of practising business executives founded the Institute of Business Ethics and I am very pleased to have been one of them. The Institute was launched and has been run by a group of senior, active business executives. One of its primary aims has been to encourage companies to produce, adopt and implement codes of business principles and ethics. To this end, the Institute has issued several publications which explain why codes are desirable, give guidance on producing a code and examine good practice in applying codes.[1] These publications have been successful and sales have been encouraging. It may well be that they have contributed to the growing practice of companies adopting such codes. Surveys conducted by the Institute (since 1986) show a steady increase in their use amongst the larger companies in the UK, nearly half of whom now have a statement or code of some kind. No member of the Institute would seek to read too much into this trend but it does provide evidence of growing awareness by the corporate sector that the ethics of how business is conducted should not be ignored.

It was pointed out above that there is not an extensive canon of study in the field of business ethics and corporate culture. This perhaps requires some elaboration. There is an extensive growing literature on business ethics but the overall quality is uneven. Likewise much has been written on corporate culture, examining what makes for success, employee commitment, innovative attitudes and so on. What seems to be rare is an examination of how business ethics can be developed as part of the corporate culture.

However, we should recognise that whilst this link is not explicitly explored in much of the current debate about corporate governance, it is clearly an integral element of that debate. In her book *Just Business* (1994), Elaine Sternberg says, 'The specifically ethical task of corporate governance is that of holding shareholders to their proper corporate purposes' (p. 200). She goes on to point out that determining corporate ends is one of the fundamental ways in which ethical values can be imparted to what is otherwise a morally neutral form. It is to be hoped that not too many people would disagree with the proposition that it would be difficult to conduct an inherently unethical activity, such as manufacturing instruments of torture, in an ethical way. This of course begs a very large question on which very different views will be expressed. To mention armaments, tobacco or alcohol can provoke debate about the ethical nature of the very business activity itself. It is not the intention in this chapter to wander into this field. Rather, it concentrates upon how ethical considerations are brought into the daily activities of business. Corporate culture refers to that common understanding, purpose and way of doing things that characterise one company and make it distinct from another.

It is also appropriate to address one other area that might be considered reasonably to fall within the scope suggested by the title of this chapter. This is the whole area of business methods – that is to say what we frequently refer to today as 'the market'. 'The market' is, of course a convenient shorthand for a whole range of activity in the commercial field. It embraces competition, consumer choice, advertising and promotion, marketing and selling and so forth. We largely accept that some form of free-market, capitalist, free-enterprise system operates in most Western and industrialised countries. There remain, of course, many who dislike this model and would wish to see it either significantly or totally changed. And some of their objections would, in their view, be on ethical grounds.

This is clearly not the occasion on which to debate this fundamental issue. The chapter avoids doing so, not for reasons of cowardice or lack of conviction, but because, as previously stated, our interest lies in the practical issues. For practical purposes, it is assumed that the present system of the market economy is a basic given. We are here concerned with what occurs in daily practice and the ethical considerations that may arise in that context. We shall not deal with macro socio-political issues or debate whether our current free-market model or some more dirigiste system occupies the moral high ground. The distinction that is drawn – between the ethical concerns arising in daily practice and those which relate to the economic system itself – is neither totally clear nor easy to sustain. But let us assume for practical purposes that we are here concerned with the ethical dimensions of generally accepted activities and that these activities would not and do not constitute an affront to ordinary decency. In assuming a degree of moral neutrality on the macro issues, we will do so recognising that many, such as Marxists, would attack the moral basis of what goes on in business, whilst others will argue for the moral high ground occupied by market and entrepreneurial activity (see Novak, 1996).

CORPORATE CULTURE: THE INTERNATIONAL DIMENSION

Corporate culture was described above as that common understanding, purpose and way of doing things that may characterise a company and differentiate it from another. These qualities have been widely analysed in business literature, frequently with a view to assessing the effect of corporate style and culture upon the company's success or failure. As already stated, there appears to be no significant body of research into the part played by ethical considerations in corporate culture. We shall, however, look at some recent studies into benchmarking and best practice on how to bring ethical considerations into the business process.

There is one aspect of corporate culture which merits our attention before we turn to these studies. It is those differences of corporate culture which derive from regional characteristics. Recently a talk given by Jan Timmer, the head of Philips, provocatively identified and characterised the value systems of three groupings: Anglo/American; Rhineland/mainland European; Eastern/Asian. The characteristics that he attributed to each of these groupings were, he admitted, very general and open to a great deal of discussion. He nevertheless thought them significant in support of the thesis he was proposing. Timmer believes that European business is too analytical, not sufficiently good at seizing opportunities and too slow in reaching decisions. He attributed these weaknesses to the underlying value system of Rhineland business. It is interesting to recapitulate Timmer's broad characteristics:

- *Anglo/American value systems*
  Labour relations: Hire/fire
  Objectives of firm: Maximisation of shareholder value
  Emphasis on the bottom-line (concentration upon the short-term)
  Attitude to trade: Support for free trade
  General cultural traits: Emphasis on the individual
  'Work, jog, relax'
- *Rhineland/mainland European value systems*
  Labour relations: Rigid labour regulations/good social benefits
  Objectives of firm: Balance stakeholder interests
  Continuity-orientated (profit is necessary for continuity)
  Attitude to trade: Free and managed trade
  General cultural traits: Solidarity/emphasis on the social structure of society
  'Work to live'
- *Eastern/Asian value systems*
  Labour relations: Lifetime employment
  Keiretsu – linked relations between people/groups
  Objectives of firm: Market-share orientated (long-term goals)
  Attitude to trade: Protectionist
  General cultural traits: Domination of the group
  'Live to work'

Someone once said, 'All generalisations are wrong – including this one.' It is unlikely that Mr Timmer would deny a degree of simplistic generalisation in his characterisations. But neither would most of us deny a great deal of significance and validity in them, even if we wished to dispute some of them or probe more deeply into meaning and definition. For our purposes, the general recognition of some of these differences in value systems must be important in addressing business ethics and corporate culture.

If there is any validity, for example, in the perceived regional differences with regard to employment philosophy, balancing of stakeholder interests or attitudes towards individuals, then there will be potential for tension in the value system of an international company which operates across all three of the geographical regions concerned. This is a rather different consideration from making all values relative or subjective – to which we referred at the outset. A set of guidelines or principles, incorporated into a code of business ethics, need not stub its toe on any fundamental inconsistency in encountering such differences. But there will be an undoubted challenge in integrating these principles into different cultures. The problems of terminology, interpretation, sensitivity – not to mention language – will be numerous. And these matters cannot be overlooked or dismissed.

Indeed, it is now clear to those working in an international business environment that the so-called global dimension of business presents a major area to be explored as companies seek to establish and build their ethical performance and credentials. It is a commonplace that companies encounter difficulties in handling the day-to-day differences in business practices when frontiers are crossed. These same challenges arise in the field of business ethics. The positioning of business ethics within the corporate culture becomes a very important factor as a company diversifies its geographical and cultural spread. We, in the West, have long been familiar with the charges of economic imperialism. Special care is needed to avoid the charge of moral imperialism. Other countries and cultures will not accept a Western set of values imposed from outside.

This subject is developed by Neil Hood in his chapter on 'Business Ethics and Transnational Corporations'. He points out that different weights are placed upon specific ethical standards in different environments and that the task of a transnational corporation in communicating its fundamental values to all stakeholders is a large one. It is clear that this international dimension will be of growing importance in the field of business ethics.

BENCHMARKING AND GOOD PRACTICE IN BUSINESS ETHICS

One can often identify two points of departure when a company embarks upon defining its principles and establishing a code of ethics. The *external* imperative may be to meet the standards and expectations of society. Regrettably, this imperative often arises as the result of some scandal or misbehaviour which occurs within an industry or a company. The 1970s Lockheed scandals were an example. As already explained, it may also arise from a legitimate concern with reputation, of which perceived ethical standards will be an important part. The *internal* imperative will derive from a strong sense within a company that it wishes to make a clear commitment to its own principles and beliefs. This will usually arise because the owner of the company, the chief executive officer (CEO) or a small group of senior executives wishes to articulate these values.

Companies rarely govern their behaviour by only one of these imperatives. A company decision to define and establish a code of business ethics will usually be brought about both by a recognition of external expectations and by a desire to set the company's own standards. However, the internal imperative will clearly be more significant when we relate business ethics to corporate culture.

The externally driven imperative for a company to consider its ethical standards may be specific to the company. The recent accusations against British Airways (BA), about alleged dirty tricks used to hurt a competitor, brought about widespread public concern. Shortly afterwards BA introduced a code of conduct which was instigated by top management, with little involvement of the whole workforce at that stage. In such circumstances it is important for the company to ensure that an internal drive and motivation is nurtured if the code is to become effective.

The external imperative may also be a general one, reflecting either a change in public expectation or public disquiet about a particular industry or activity. Public expectation can shift quite quickly and sharply, of course. It is not so long ago that insider dealing was a widely accepted practice; now it is prohibited by law. If a shift in public opinion is broad in its scope, it may allow a company to respond in a more institutional fashion. Both the banking and chemical industries are examples where adverse public attitudes have emerged, based on negative perceptions of behaviour by companies in those sectors. The company-wide consultation and procedures that characterise the ethics programme in the NatWest Bank, and the broad extent of the chemical industry's Responsible Care initiative both demonstrate that a knee-jerk, top-down reaction need not be the only response to external pressures.

The internal imperative within a company to emphasise certain values and commitments can never be indifferent to external pressures and perceptions. A code or statement of principles will be a public document, even if primarily intended for internal audiences. For this reason, if for no other, it is unlikely that a company would articulate inappropriate values.

However, it must be recognised that value systems may exist within an organisation that are not formulated in a code. There have been many examples of a widespread internal culture of ethnic discrimination or sexual harassment within a company. The existence of such inappropriate value systems represents an argument in favour of adopting formal codes. A clear public commitment to a set of values articulated in a code will make the perpetuation of inappropriate values increasingly difficult. In a democratic society, it is barely conceivable that such a code could embody concepts that affront common decency.

Business ethics and a company code will only be effective in a company if they are made to be part of the 'bloodstream' of the company. Put another way, business ethics should not be an add-on, a kind of afterthought. If a code is developed in response to some misdemeanour or public scandal it may well start as an add-on. This is not, of course, necessarily bad. Repentance and redemption are available to all. But if a company's approach to business ethics has its genesis solely or largely in response to some external factor, the temptation for window dressing or – put simply – cosmetics or humbug must be recognised. If the criterion of bloodstream is to be met, then the internal desire and intention must be strong.

Business is no different from any other aspect of human activity. There will be frequent falling short and misbehaviour. Lapses by the business community often have a high profile. Very frequently the misdemeanour is something that affects many people and may well be something that everyone can understand and deplore. Misappropriation of large sums of money, a serious accident or an environmental catastrophe will all bring notoriety. It is not surprising, therefore, that the early moves to adopt principles and company codes were very often a response to such incidents and the attendant high-profile public disquiet.

It is for this reason, perhaps, that it is only comparatively recently that attention has begun to turn to best practice in the application of codes of ethics. One very straightforward way to do this is by benchmarking and by examination of case studies. The gradually emerging study of this area gives us some information on business ethics and corporate culture. It is relevant to refer to some studies that have been conducted in recent years.

In 1993 Ashridge College surveyed the views of non-executive directors of 500 leading companies. The report by Wilson and Drummond was published under the title *The Importance of Being Ethical* (1993). Amongst the survey findings, it established that over half of the respondents believed the task of ensuring effective application of the ethics process rested with one person, usually the CEO. Other respondents considered the job to be shared between two people: the CEO and the chairman. Turning to effectiveness in ensuring high standards, respondents emphasised three methods: ethics training, use and dissemination of a code and disciplinary procedures. However, the practice of ethics training was not widespread and the validity of this particular finding remained largely untested.

This study also identified uncertainty amongst respondents about monitoring and enforcing ethical processes. This seemed to point to a lack of sense of company-wide standards of ethical behaviour.

Also in 1993 the Institute of Management and the School of Management at the University of Bath carried out a joint research project into ethical awareness and the relationship between individuals' own ethics and those within their organisation (Brigley, 1994). The views of 712 managers were obtained.

Ninety per cent of respondents claimed to adopt an ethical perspective to management and about 70 per cent saw congruence between their own views and those of their company. However, 30 per cent identified senior management as the main obstacle to ethical management in their organisations. Company codes and other internal factors were seen as conditioning the respondents' outlook on ethics rather than, say, wider professional affiliations. Ninety-six per cent of respondents saw it as a managerial responsibility to provide ethical leadership.

A survey in 1995 conducted by the Institute of Internal Auditors amongst 500 UK CEOs sought to determine what controls were available to monitor and maintain ethical business standards. The study confirmed the view that the CEO must be responsible for the whole ethics process. Company secretaries and auditors were seen to have important roles with regard to investigations.

In the USA the Ethics Resource Centre issued a report in 1994 based on a sample of 4035 employees and managers. Some two-thirds of respondents said they relied on the company code with one-third saying it was consulted frequently. Greater awareness and knowledge of the code seemed to exist where ethics training was given. Of special interest, nearly one-third of respondents felt pressurised to engage in misconduct to meet business objectives. It would, of course, be interesting to know more about these pressures.

In 1995 the Institute of Business Ethics surveyed 75 companies to find out about the use of and experience with codes of ethics (Webley, 1995). The report revealed some interesting facts, especially with regard to business ethics and corporate culture. A third of companies did not give copies of their code to all employees and the same proportion of companies surveyed had no procedure for reviewing and updating the code. These findings are somewhat disturbing. Less than half of the companies made conformity to the code a part of the employment contract.

Half the companies identified the CEO as the person responsible for producing and implementing the code, and the company secretary as important in ensuring compliance.

The most recent publication that we looked at was produced by the Industrial Society, as part of its Managing Best Practice series. The report surveyed 313 managers on managing ethics and also provided five case studies together with a consultancy section. The report attracted some media attention because one of the findings was that 80 per cent of respondents identified a gap between the theory and practice of ethical management. *The Independent* cited this as proof that senior executives are hypocrites. (It would be astonishing if every company claimed total compliance with its ethical standards. To do so would suggest blind ignorance, hubris or lack of contact with reality.)

More interesting was the finding that 90 per cent of respondents recognised that ethical standards were important and that over 60 per cent of companies produce general principles to guide employee conduct. About 40 per cent had codes.

It was also noteworthy that two-fifths of respondents reported that employees had never been consulted on ethics and less than 20 per cent used team briefings, focus groups or consultation with unions for this purpose. The most common methods of informing employees are handbooks, induction training and the example of senior managers.

An interesting point to emerge from the Industrial Society survey was that three-quarters of respondents believe that maintaining ethical standards would have a positive effect on financial performance, with 20 per cent saying that it would have a very positive effect. Only 1 per cent said the effect would be negative.

The relationship between ethical behaviour and financial performance is, of course, crucial and it is encouraging that the Industrial Society survey was so positive. This is an area that merits more consideration. In the mid-1980s Mark Pastin conducted a two-year study into the relationship between organisational performance and ethics. Whilst business performance was relatively straight forward to track, measurement of ethical performance was, of course, difficult. It seems that despite this difficulty the study concluded that although ethics is an intangible factor it yields tangible results and that there was a consistent relationship between ethics and performance. The author stopped short of concluding that ethical thinking guarantees high performance but stated that a solid ethical framework assisted managers in coping with complex business issues and intense scrutiny.

With the emergence of ethical investment funds, a wider body of data will gradually become available. This may in time enable more analysis to be carried out examining the relationship of principles – for example, on equal opportunity – and relative performance. Nevertheless, given the complexity of variables that may have an impact upon a company's performance, isolating the effect of ethical performance is likely to remain difficult.

THE INTEGRATION OF BUSINESS ETHICS INTO CORPORATE CULTURE

A number of important points emerge from these studies and it is worth briefly summarising some of those most relevant to our consideration of the process by which ethical cultures within firms are set:

- The commitment and visible involvement of senior management is seen as vital. The CEO and perhaps the chairman are considered to have prime personal responsibility. But there is a danger that if senior management does not follow its own ethical prescriptions then there will be a perception of double standards. In its most acute form this would identify senior management as a barrier to ethical behaviour.
- The use of codes, disseminated in a written document, is seen to be helpful, describing the mission and principles that should govern conduct. The code should be in the possession of every employee.
- Ethics training for employees can help to improve awareness and understanding.
- An emphasis upon ethical standards can generate a positive employee response. This can be strengthened if employees are involved in a consultative process about the code of ethics.
- Whilst ethical standards do not guarantee profitable performance, there is certainly no evidence that they damage it. And since reputation and performance are closely linked, the contribution of ethical standards to reputation can be an important factor in business performance.

The articulation of a company's ethical standards is not in itself sufficient. There must be follow-up, monitoring, audit and sanctions to be applied when the standards are breached.

The publication by the Institute of Business Ethics (IBE), *Applying Codes of Business Ethics* (Webley, 1995), identifies twelve steps for implementing a code of business ethics. These steps are:

integration of the code into the running of the business
endorsement by the chairman and CEO
distribution to all employees
breaches – what to do when faced with a potential breach
personal response by employees
affirmation of the code as a regular procedure
regular review
contractual adherence

training in issues raised by the code
translation into relevant languages
distribution to business partners
Annual Report to include the code.

These twelve steps provide an excellent checklist which, if followed, will go a long way towards ensuring that a company's code of ethics will be effectively integrated. They constitute, as IBE claims, a programme of best practice. In the same publication IBE looks at case studies in which five different companies set out their experience and demonstrated features that were specific to their organisation.

The points which emerged from the studies, together with the twelve steps identified by IBE, constitute a comprehensive array of actions that will materially assist the integration of the codes of ethics into a company's business. In endorsing these points it is helpful to take our examination a little further.

As stated earlier, one of this chapter's primary theses is that business ethics, to be effective and to be genuine, must be part of the bloodstream of a corporation. This suggests that while the external imperatives that are considered may provide an impetus for the corporation to look at its ethical performance, the key factor will be its own internal standards and commitment to these standards for the values that they represent. The code of business ethics, when viewed in this light, becomes an integral element of company policies.

There is perhaps an analogy with quality. Most mission statements drawn up by corporations will contain a reference to quality. (This may not be expressed specifically as a commitment to quality. For example, a mission statement such as a commitment to the highest standards of performance or service or goods would effectively be a stake in the ground for quality.) The company which seriously intends to introduce and make effective the concept of quality will work to a quality programme. It will identify goals and objectives that are set out in a programme to obtain an appropriate certification, such as ISO 9000. To achieve this, a quality management process must be established. Likewise for business ethics to be fully and successfully integrated into the company corporate culture a similar approach should be adopted. To any thesis that business ethics should be bloodstream we should therefore add the thesis that it should be a management discipline. In this it is similar to quality or safety or concern for environmental conservation: something which becomes an attitude of mind throughout the organisation.

In a company like Dupont, the commitment to safety is total. Safety considerations are paramount throughout its operations, both manufacturing and ancillary. Safety consciousness is encouraged everywhere – in the factory, the offices, the home and the garden. As a result the company's safety performance becomes a quality standard in which continuous improvement is the norm.

In another company where I worked, with a major commitment to safety, the incidence of accidents reached such a low point that measurement of further improvement became difficult. Sites were striving to reduce a derisory number of first-aid incidents. To maintain the climate of continuous improvement the company introduced a system of 'near-miss' reporting. Employees were expected to report every time an accident nearly happened or where they saw a potential accident, even if there had been no 'near-miss'. On the basis of this system a profile was constructed of those activities or jobs or locations where the risk was higher, thus meriting anticipatory scrutiny and attention. This prevention programme addressed the accident before it happened.

It would be inappropriate to push these analogies too far. Lapses in quality or accidents are measurable events and statistical analysis of quantified data is a management tool for achieving better performance. The field of ethical consideration is not susceptible to the same quantification and analysis.

There is an adage which says 'if you cannot measure it, you cannot manage it' and for practical purposes that is a useful approach. Because the problem of measurement in the business ethics area is a very real one, there will be a temptation to say that the process cannot be managed. But this is not the case. Just as it is possible – indeed essential – to create a state of mind on quality, so the same management approach and disciplines should be brought to bear on business ethics. As we have already seen, we would be unwise to expect all employees within a company to know what that company expects in the field of ethics. We must therefore institutionalise ethics in the organisation so that we internalise the imperative and establish and reinforce an appropriate attitude of mind.

In accordance with the bloodstream principle, the integration of business ethics should be a seamless continuum throughout the organisation. This can be illustrated by a pyramid – see Figure 9.1.

Every pyramid demonstrates that higher levels are sustained by lower levels. And so, in practice, it is with this pyramid which represents the conceptual hierarchy within a corporation. There is, however, an important difference. In our conceptual pyramid, the construction process begins at the top, by articulating in simple, broad terms the mission of the company. We all know lots of mission statements from the very simple statements like 'we aim to make the best widgets' to more complex and sophisticated statements which often reflect a more complicated or mature business. By itself a mission statement has little meaning. To begin the process of making the mission a reality we need to establish the principles upon which that mission is based. Typically principles refer to generalised concepts such as integrity, respect for people, commitments to safety and environmental conservation. These are the underlying principles, the absence of which would prejudice the mission.

Figure 9.1 The conceptual hierarchy within a corporation

Again, a statement of principle, such as respect for people or minimising damage to the environment, remains by itself a pious hope, an aspiration. To have real effect it requires elaboration and explanation. Thus a principle of minimising environmental damage must address matters such as the treatment of waste, product stewardship, pollution prevention and so on. The principle must be translated into a code of practice embodying the broad ways in which different aspects of that principle are to be addressed and adhered to. Nevertheless, even a code of practice still remains generalised. Codes of practice such as those contained within the chemical industry's

Responsible Care initiative or that developed by the International Chamber of Commerce on environmental conservation can be subscribed to by hundreds of different companies with widely differing activities and fields of operation. To the cynic, a code of practice remains too imprecise and too general to guarantee performance at any particular level.

It is at the next level down the pyramid that a company starts to translate good intentions into good practice: by formulation of policies. There is, of course, a big gulf between subscribing to a code of practice which is usually too generalised to ensure strict enforcement and adhering to a company policy which is both more detailed and more prescriptive. Adherence to and application of policies will be a requirement of an employee's contract of employment. Accordingly it must be sufficiently specific and precise to enable departures to be identified and dealt with by some disciplinary measure if appropriate. Thus, for example, in the field of personnel or human resources, it would be reasonable to look to a policy on, say, equal opportunity to prescribe in some detail the company's requirements on how this is to be identified and applied.

The next two levels of the pyramid are clear in describing in even greater detail how the company is to put into practice the policies it has formulated. As with the higher levels, we are ensuring in more detail that each area of company activity is managed in such a way that there is consistency and integrity throughout.

Underpinning everything, of course, is monitoring, auditing and control. We all know that procedures, no matter how good they are or how carefully they are written, may be misunderstood or ignored. It is the role of audit and control to ensure that where this happens, it will be brought to light so that corrective steps can be taken.

The pyramid that we have described is not revolutionary. We all know that companies are run like that. It is one way of describing a corporate culture, because from the level of policy downwards, we are looking at elements which are peculiar to the individual company. To go back to the earlier definition of corporate culture, these features are what characterise and differentiate it from another company.

The pyramid illustrates the maxims that business ethics must be bloodstream and must be managed like other aspects of the business. It is significant that the three top levels of the pyramid are all described in terms that are integral to a company's ethical position: mission, principles, codes. These are the very words used in the vocabulary of ethical discussion. However the mission, principles and codes of a company will be initially the responsibility of its senior management – which, as we have seen, is consistent with the assignment of primary responsibility for the development of a company's code of ethics.

There is a strong case to be made that the company code of ethics should, in fact, be a company policy and accordingly it will be sustained by standards, procedures and programmes which in turn will be monitored and audited. Just as a policy on personnel or on safety will remain ineffective without the bases of the pyramid at the levels below policies, so a business ethics policy must be sustained by the same levels, that is by standards, by procedures and by controls and audits.

Many of the points thrown up by the surveys and the implementation steps identified by IBE will fit into one of the three bottom levels of the pyramid. A typical standard might be that of accuracy and completeness in financial records. A procedure for sustaining the ethics policy might be regular workplace discussion of ethical issues: a programme of ethics awareness modules in company training would again be a standard management discipline. In many companies where the code of ethics is well-integrated it is standard practice to consider the code of conduct as part of the regular appraisal of individual employee performance. This provides the opportunity for issues to be raised. A number of companies, such as Esso and Hewlett Packard, incorporate into procedures a formal written confirmation that the ethics policy has been seen, understood and discussed.

The bottom layer of monitoring, control and audit merits a word of elaboration. The question of ethical audits perplexes many but it should be an essential commitment. The auditing, monitoring function can be carried out in many ways. It can, of course, be located in the normal audit function (particularly internal audit) and scrutiny of company behaviour against its own policies is quite as appropriate in the field of ethics as in other parts of the business. Another dimension is to ensure – through management discipline – that ethical considerations are part and parcel of the review process. Let me give an example.

In a company for which I worked, the commitment to health, safety and the environment was accorded high priority as a fundamental principle. A statement in the documentation on company principles stated that whilst profitable performance was a high priority, it must never be at the expense of health, safety and the environment. During the development stage of a new plant an environmental/safety issue arose: if an unusual surge of gases occurred should they be vented to air or flared? The technical considerations were complex and the appropriate solution was not immediately evident – but time was short and the pressure for a decision was on. The director concerned pointed out the hierarchy of priorities within the ethics policy which established that environmental/safety considerations had higher priority than profit and a speedy decision. This was an example of the ethics policy as part of the decision-making process, that is, bloodstream.

But it was also a control mechanism and the board minute was an auditable record of why some delay was appropriate. The ethical consideration has become an integral part of the business decision and can be monitored as such.

Another form of ethical audit is a survey – of employees, customers or suppliers – to establish whether ethical policies are being observed or broken – or whether any near misses have occurred.

In considering how the ethical consideration is made part of the management process, it should be recognised that there are procedures and processes that can be adopted which help to institutionalise ethical considerations. The Institute for Global Ethics,[2] although it is not concerned solely with business ethics, looks at tools and guidelines for addressing the ethical dimension. It does this in small 'Ethical Fitness Seminars' which seek to cultivate awareness that sound ethics is essential for societies and by offering some practical tools to be used in dealing with dilemmas.

Steps identified by the Institute for Global Ethics in considering how an ethical issue may be approached are as follows:

- Be aware that an ethical issue exists
- Establish whose dilemma it is, that is, who has responsibility
- Develop a group assessment of the facts and apply some straightforward tests – the legal test, the 'stench' test, the 'front page of the papers' test, the 'could I tell my mother?' test
- If it is a 'right versus right' dilemma, what are the principles involved?
- Screen the dilemma through three principles: utilitarianism, the categorical imperative, the Golden Rule
- Look for the third way – turn the dilemma into a 'trilemma'
- Formulate a decision
- Reflect and consider.

It is important to have this identification of the steps that are involved in tackling an ethical issue or dilemma; it forms the basis for a clear management discipline.

There is one step in this procedure which merits some further explanation, because it addresses the matter of relativism that can so often bedevil the discussion of ethical issues.

If we follow the sequence identified by the Institute for Global Ethics and an ethical dilemma is identified, let us say that it is flagged by the 'front page of the papers' test. In other words we are looking at a decision or a problem which has the potential for public embarrassment. Most of us know in our daily lives that when an ethical dilemma occurs it is rarely straightforward or a clear decision between right and wrong, good or bad. More usually we are faced with two conflicting principles which are both desirable; it is right versus right. A couple of simple examples may illustrate the right versus right dilemma. A doctor is asked by a patient with a terminal illness whether he is going to die. The doctor has to choose between two rights: telling the truth or protecting a dying man from a distressing shock that may exacerbate the condition. In business, an industrial accident like a fire or an escape of chemicals may present a choice between human safety and environmental protection – both of which are 'right' but in a particular situation they may be in conflict. A choice must, nevertheless, be made.

In resolving dilemmas of this nature, the Institute suggests that three principles will help the process. These principles are:

* The utilitarian principle, which is ends-based and which can be expressed as 'the greatest good for the greatest number'.
* The categorical imperative, which is rule-based. Kant expressed this principle as based upon universal law: 'I ought never to act except in such a way that I can also will that my maxim should become a universal law.'
* The Golden Rule, which is care-based and expressed as 'Do to others as you would have them do to you.'

In a world where the universality or absolute nature of ethical principles is a contested proposition we cannot put forward any of these principles as an absolute (although it is very hard to find anyone who rejects the validity of the Golden Rule). However, if we test our behaviour against all three principles, we should improve our chances of emerging from our dilemma having stuck to our ethical guidelines.

Let me illustrate by a real-life example. A company where I was a director manufactured a product, the properties of which are quite harmless to human beings. It is extensively used as a carrying agent in medicines, as a food ingredient, and in cosmetics, for example. To meet safety and health standards it is manufactured to an exacting US pharmaceutical specification which allows for only less than 0.5 per cent impurity, that is, the product must be at least 99.5 per cent pure.

As manufacturers of this product we sold it on through distributors who in turn sold it to pharmaceutical, cosmetics, food companies and so on. A dilemma arose when a customer returned a batch of the product having identified an unusual smell. The product was analysed and found to be within specification. The smell was caused, however, by a significant concentration within the product of a chemical substance, the properties of which had not been tested in the context of use for human ingestion.

This situation posed a number of dilemmas of a legal, commercial, operational and ethical nature. Put simply, one aspect of the ethical dilemma was this. Should a wider public be warned that some of them might have used a product containing this unknown impurity? Against this we had to set the possibility of unnecessarily alarming people, most of whom would not be affected, since the degree to which the impurity had occurred was not known. There were, needless to say, many other considerations but for the purposes of illustration, let us consider this dilemma in its simplified form against our three principles.

From a utilitarian standpoint, we had to look at protecting the health and well-being of the greatest number of people, that is to say, everyone who might use the product that could contain the impurity. Likewise, any likelihood of a similar situation elsewhere had to be considered.

The rule-based imperative was that of transparency. This was a principle which meant that there should be no concealment and that full disclosures of relevant facts should be made to everyone who needed to know.

The Golden Rule imperative was that the risk to innocent and unknowing people should be established and minimised. In practice this meant constantly asking the question: 'Has the necessary action been taken as quickly and as comprehensively as possible to establish all the facts and to act upon them?'

The screening of decisions and actions in this way constitutes an ethical framework within which the management decisions can be taken. In other terms, the ethical considerations have become bloodstream and subject to the norms of good management practice. Without articulating the three principles in the way that the Institute for Global Ethics suggests, we did, in fact, apply them – because our code of ethics was institutionalised, understood by the management which had to deal with the problem, sufficiently comprehensive to provide guidelines and priorities and because, from the outset, the ethical dilemma was recognised.

The course of action adopted by the company was to initiate several steps. All batches of the product were withdrawn, all distributors and end-use customers were notified, a crash programme to analyse and test the impurity was put in place and a comprehensive risk assessment was made looking at every relevant factor, in order to identify any further hazard and to quantify the risks to those who might have been exposed to the impurity. All competitors and others who might be affected were notified and they were kept informed as the reasons for the impurity and its properties became known. The impurity turned out to be harmless. As a follow-up, major procedural changes in storage of the product were introduced, since it was shown that storage conditions had produced the unusual concentration of the impurity in question. Other competitors and manufacturers were told what had occurred, as a further follow-up action, so that they, too, could take appropriate precautions.

CONCLUSION

As we all know, ethical dilemmas are usually much less potentially dramatic than the example I have just quoted. But the same principles apply: ethics in the bloodstream and ethics treated as a management discipline. From this it will follow that the ethical dimension will become part of the corporate culture and will surely influence it.

One final point may be worth making in the context of bringing business ethics into the corporate culture. We all know that in today's world of intensive and ubiquitous media, the behaviour of companies is scrutinised as never before and that lapses will be severely punished in terms of reputation and public standing. Therefore the process by which ethical considerations are brought into the business has become of great importance. It would be unwise, of course, to see this process as a total safeguard. The process of bringing ethics into the bloodstream of the company may be the best insurance that we have against ethically unacceptable outcomes – but it is not a guarantee.

The standards which the corporation identifies and sets for itself are themselves the justification for the process. The utilitarian consideration alone is not sufficient. The development of a corporate ethical culture itself can be evaluated against the principles of utilitarianism, of the categorical imperative and of the Golden Rule.

Notes

1. Cooper, N. (1989) and Webley, S. (1988, 1992, 1993, 1995), Institute of Business Ethics, 12 Palace Street, London SW1E 5JA.
2. The Institute for Global Ethics, PO Box 563, Camden, Maine 04843, USA and 11 Northwick Close, London NW8 8JG.

References

Brigley, S. (1994) *Walking the Tightrope: A Survey of Ethics in Management* (London: Institute of Management).
Cooper, N. (1989) *What's all this about Business Ethics?* (London: Institute of Business Ethics).
Ethics Resource Centre (1994) *Ethics in American Business: Policies, Programme and Perceptions* (Washington, DC: Ethics Resource Center).

Industrial Society (1996) *Managing Ethics* (Managing Best Practice No. 26) (London: The Industrial Society).

Institute of Internal Auditors (1995) *Chief Executive, Internal Controls and Ethical Business Standards* (London: Institute of Internal Auditors).

Novak, M. (1996) *Business as a Calling: Work and the Examined Life* (New York: Free Press).

Pastin, M. (1987) 'Ethics and Excellence', *New Management*, 4 (4), pp. 40–3.

Sternberg, E. (1994) *Just Business* (London: Warner Books).

Webley, S. (1988) *Company Philosophies and Codes of Business Ethics* (London: Institute of Business Ethics).

Webley, S. (1992) *Business Ethics and Company Codes* (London: Institute of Business Ethics).

Webley, S. (1993) *Codes of Business Ethics – a Checklist and Illustrative Code* (London: Institute of Business Ethics).

Webley, S. (1995) *Applying Codes of Business Ethics* (London: Institute of Business Ethics).

Wilson, A. and Drummond, J. (1993) *The Importance of Being Ethical* (Ashridge: Ashridge Management College).

10 Business Ethics and Transnational Companies

Neil Hood

INTRODUCTION

Foreign direct investment (FDI) has been growing rapidly in the recent past. Indeed it has been growing faster than international trade, which has long been the principal mechanism linking national economies. In consequence the operations of transnational companies (TNCs) have a profound effect on most aspects of business life and on the prosperity of many nations. These investment flows are concentrated in a few countries, in that the ten largest host countries received two-thirds of the total inflows of $315 billion in 1995, while the smallest one hundred received only 1 per cent. Foreign direct investment is a major force shaping globalisation. The outward FDI stock which the 39 000 parent firms had invested in their 270 000 foreign affiliates reached $2.7 trillion in 1995. Moreover, FDI flows doubled between 1980 and 1994 relative to both global gross fixed capital formation and world gross national product. The value added of all foreign affiliates accounted for 6 per cent of world gross domestic product in 1991, compared to 2 per cent in 1982 (UNCTAD, *World Investment Report*, 1996).

To set some of this data into context, Table 10.1 shows some of the broad indicators of the growth of FDI outward stock by region and major country over the past thirty years. The flows remain highly concentrated but, in the context of this chapter, one point of particular interest concerns the growth of FDI in developing countries. Equally important has been the rapid growth of cross-border mergers and acquisitions and the extensive use by TNCs of alliances and other non-equity forms of business relationship. As the phenomenon of FDI has developed, so too has the volume of academic literature on the subject (Dunning, 1993). This chapter only touches on one small part of that galaxy.

Ethical aspects of international business have attracted increasing attention in recent years. However, within the academic literature, the focus has often been more on the conceptual than the empirical. Thus among the questions of importance considered have been those of cultural relativism (Freeman and Gilbert, 1988), global ethical systems (Buller, Kohls and Anderson, 1991) and the obligations of TNCs operating in other countries (Donaldson, 1989). The cross-national empirical research base is much less developed, although the need for it is widely acknowledged. Practitioners managing TNCs do not therefore have a large research database on which to draw from within the international business literature. There have been several recent attempts to address this situation, as evidenced by studies of corporate ethics in European TNCs (Langlois and Schlegelmilch, 1990), of the ethical perceptions of industrial sales staff in the USA, Japan and South Korea (Dubinsky *et al.*, 1991), and of the influence of country and industry on the ethical perceptions of senior TNC executives in the USA and Europe (Schlegelmilch and Robertson, 1995). Some aspects of these and other studies are considered later in the chapter.

Table 10.1   FDI outward stock by region and major country for selected years (percentage share of US$ totals)

Region	1967[a] %	1980 %	1985 %	1990 %	1995[b] %
North America	57.3	47.3	42.6	30.3	29.9
Canada	3.5	9.3	6.0	4.5	4.1
USA	53.8	38.0	36.6	25.8	25.8
European Union	n.a.	41.5	41.8	46.1	44.3
France	5.7	4.6	5.4	6.5	7.3
Germany	2.8	8.4	8.7	9.0	8.6
UK	16.6	15.7	14.6	13.7	11.7
Other Western Europe	n.a.	4.6	3.8	4.6	4.5
Switzerland	4.8	4.2	3.1	3.9	4.0
Other developed countries	n.a.	5.5	8.7	14.6	13.4
Australia	n.a.	0.4	1.0	1.8	1.5
Japan	1.4	3.7	6.4	12.2	11.2
Developing and newly industrialised countries	n.a.	1.2	3.1	4.1	7.9
China	n.a.	*	*	0.1	0.6
Hong Kong	n.a.	*	0.3	0.8	3.1
Singapore	n.a.	0.1	0.2	0.3	0.5
Taiwan	n.a.	*	*	0.8	0.9
Total(%)	100.0	100.0	100.0	100.0	100.0
Total (US$bn)	105.3	513.7	685.3	1685.1	2730.1

Notes: [a] The 1967 data was not directly comparable with later years. They have been included to provide an indication of the FDI position in the earlier postwar years. The figures relate to the outward FDI stock of developed market economies.
[b] Preliminary.
* means less than 0.1%.

Source: UN Economic and Social Council (1978) Table III-32 (for 1967); UNCTAD, *World Investment Report* (1996) Annex Table 4.

At one level large international companies as a group are no more than a special case of the wider study of business ethics. Their claim to distinctiveness may be regarded as residing in a number of particular areas of challenge, only some of which are considered here. First, TNCs need to practise business ethics in a cross-cultural context and as such face many different perspectives. One area where this is readily illustrated concerns the types of work practices employed by their suppliers. Second, there is the dilemma as to how TNCs handle environments where the ethical practices are lax by most recognised standards. Closely linked to this is the question of what might be expected of a TNC in such a context, for example, where sub-standard products are sold into an environment which has less stringent health and safety regulations (than the home country) in order to extend a product life cycle. While it might be accepted that the TNC should not act in any way which would harm consumers, there is the broader question of whether in such areas TNCs should be expected to show ethical leadership even if it is not in the immediate interests of their shareholders so to do. Third, there is the important issue of how TNCs deal with alliances, joint ventures and the increasingly complex set of network agreements which are often critical to their global and company-specific competitiveness. These arrangements represent a daily interaction of many executives with very different ethical standards and few may have traditional relationships of executive control and reporting as their basis. Fourth, there are the respective roles of self-regulation, legal regimes and codes of conduct in the many specialist operational areas which make up a TNC and the question of how these drivers impact on its behaviour.

From all of the above it will be evident that it is unlikely that any simple rules or algorithms can determine acceptable ethical behaviour across different cultures. This chapter does not attempt to do so and has much more modest objectives. It sets out to explore some of the ethical issues associated with operating TNCs and to examine a number of conceptual frameworks which might enable these to be better understood. Much of what it contains is exploratory and partial and it offers few solutions to this complex and controversial area of business practice.

DEFINITIONAL TERMS

This chapter uses the terms set out in Figure 10.1 as its working definitions. Ethics is viewed as, to some extent at least, culture-bound. Some would question whether different cultures really have different value systems and query whether international variations among managers are any more di-

196 *Business Ethics and Transnational Companies*

verse than the differences between managers in the same country or continent. Such a universalist value would claim that there is only one fundamental world management culture with minor variations in attitudes and values among different managers. The alternative view is that, while there is a degree of convergence in management practice, there remain differences in attitudes and values and these can be attributed to social, political and economic differences between countries. However, there are several studies to suggest that neither of these explanations fully account for the variations in values which are found on an international level, one of the earliest of which was Haire, Ghiselli and Porter (1966). They identified five broad clusters of world management styles (Nordic-European, Latin-European, Anglo-American, developing countries and Japan) and indicated that the differences were not related to the economic and political systems of the countries in which they worked. Similarly, England (1975) examined personal values in five countries and found significant differences between the five cultures – with some surprising similarities between Japan and Korea, and also between the USA and Australia.

- **DEFINITION:**   • ethics is an expression of values, norms, accepted standards, rules of conduct and moral judgements (about 'right' or 'wrong'), using recognised social principles in a particular societal context.
- **EXPLANATION:** • a set of accepted values, norms, standards
  • guided by normative social principles
  • in a particular societal context
  • with focus on individual behaviour and actions.
- **IMPLICATION:** • ethics viewed as 'culture-bound'
  • grounded in some concepts of morality and/or the socialisation of rules through the legislative/judicial system
  • potential divergence of legal/judicial and ethical/moral standards
  • variances in societal interests exacerbated differences in political/judicial processes, levels of economic development, and individual perceptions.

Figure 10.1   Issues in international business ethics
Source: Schollhammer (1996).

Many ethical issues do, however, transcend national barriers. For example, Langlois and Schlegelmilch (1990) showed in their study on corporate ethics and national character that fairness and honesty in a company's relations with the public are concepts found in corporate codes on business ethics in both the USA and Europe. They did, however, also show that in areas such as political affairs and employee relations the treatment of these issues in the codes was country-specific.

From the above, it is evident that many aspects of Figure 10.1 could be subject to debate. However, for the purposes of this exercise, it provides a useful point of departure. It recognises that in the international business arena the underlying purpose and rules of business are not always clear. In consequence, ethics cannot readily be viewed in terms of either a static code or a set of principles which are understood and subscribed to by all concerned. This situation is addressed by dynamic definitions such as that by Powers and Vogel (1980) that, in essence, ethics is concerned with clarifying what constitutes human rights and the kind of conduct necessary to promote it. Rather unsatisfactorily, this approach leans much on moral relativism since concepts such as 'human welfare' are perceived of in very different terms in different country environments and it would not in itself readily shape decision-making in the many ethical dilemmas which face the TNC. The prevailing norms to which it might conform in some countries might leave it with many discontented stakeholders in both home and host nations.

What is perhaps evident for a TNC is that some of the classical ethical concepts and concerns such as those set out below take on added dimensions. They do so not only because of the presence of their operations in different environments, but also because of their scale, relative power and the influence which they exert both on world trade and at a country level. As major global conduits of the flow of capital, technology and management skills, they also have a role in terms of setting the 'norms' within their many operational environments, although few TNCs would overtly seek such a role. All these are factors which give added weight to their practice in areas such as:

- *Ethical duality* – resulting from the divergence of legal and ethical standards. For the TNC this poses dilemmas such as what should guide an individual country manager's behaviour and action? Is legality in each country the minimalist resolution of ethical concerns? Is the exploitation of this duality an acceptable method of building competitive advantage on a global scale?
- *Ethical relativism* – ethical judgements perceived as being relative to a particular context and resolvable within that context alone. From this premise, does the TNC assume that if ethical norms are 'culture-bound', it is not possible to resolve ethical differences and conflicts of values between cultures? And how does the truly international executive team

comprising many cultures behave? Are TNCs required to recognise that country differences in approaches to ethical issues does not mean that there should be country differences in ethical principles? Do all TNCs require a corporate norm and can that be effectively captured in a single corporate code?

- *Ethical universalism* – here the focus would be placed on the identification of some universal societal values. The Kantian dictum is often cited as a potential guiding principle whereby an action is morally right only if the person performing it is motivated by goodwill and morally wrong if it is not. The concept of a 'kingdom of ends' and the need for these to be reconciled in order to balance the interests of all parties is a powerful, but not always a simple, one. For example, the TNC pursuing its ends can to some degree select the countries in which the conditions for pursuing these ends are maximised. In doing so it may also maximise the ends of the host government. But this apparent accommodation of interests may or may not have been achieved in a manner which will be perceived to be motivated by 'goodwill' by all parties. So in this area the dilemma for the TNC is whether it is possible to agree on universal moral norms or agree about norms which cover the 'universe' of their particular interests at any one time. Thus what began as 'universal' may become 'relative'.

IMPLEMENTATION

It is often argued in the business literature that 'good ethics is good business' and hence that ethical issues have to be constantly recognised, reassessed and resolved. However, where the approach to this has been through corporate codes of conduct, doubt has been cast in some quarters on whether some of these in practice were little more than window dressing. For example, Schollhammer (1996) matched 200 of the companies on the SEC list of 'questionable payments' and found that 75 per cent of them had codes of conduct specifically barring such payments. Clearly this type of evidence does not nullify the relevance of codes of conduct, but it reminds all concerned about the practicalities of adhering to them, not least in the multicultural environment of the TNC. In any event, and especially in Europe, many TNCs have only adopted such codes in recent years. It is also evident (Langlois and Schlegelmilch, 1990) that codes and national character are related. This study showed that European companies tended to emphasise employee responsiveness to company activities, while US TNCs stressed company responsiveness to employee requirements of fairness and equity. There is also some evidence to suggest that Europeans are generally less optimistic about the effectiveness of corporate codes of ethics than are Americans (Van Luijk, 1990; Becker and Fritszehe, 1987). Another primary concern for some people is whether it can be shown to be commercially advantageous for a corporation to apply consistently high ethical standards. For obvious reasons this question has proved difficult to answer at any level and the more so in the TNC context. Some are sceptical about the notion that ethics and profitability are compatible (Vogel, 1992) and the general evidence is mixed, although most findings seem positive to some degree. For example, Aupperle *et al.* (1985) reviewed past studies on the relationship between corporate responsibility and profitability and found a majority of positive findings, even though their own study was neutral. It is accepted that many such studies do not readily capture the full benefits of ethical behaviour in areas such as customer esteem, employee loyalty, the trust of other businesses and so on. All of these can be assets to be set against the liabilities of actively unethical behaviour by a firm. In some contexts, it has been suggested that ethical behaviour is connected with risk avoidance (McGuire *et al.*, 1988). The approach in this chapter resonates with that of Clive Wright in the preceding chapter. He observes that business ethics and a company code will only be effective if they are part of the bloodstream of the company.

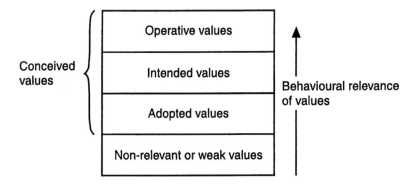

Figure 10.2   Value framework
Source: England (1978).

In order to take these issues further and explore some of the problems of business ethics in the international context, Figures 10.2 and 10.3 are useful. The core assumption is that personal value systems are an important (if not the principal) driver of corporate behaviour. Moreover, such a system is likely to be a relatively permanent perceptual framework which shapes and influences the general nature of the individual's behaviour. It can be thought of as an integrated group of attributes and beliefs which results from the interaction of the individual with his or her environment. The value framework in Figure 10.2, derived from England (1978), suggests several major classes of overlapping values. All possible values which could be held by an individual or a group might be described as the potential values and they fall into two types. The first are non-relevant or weak values, which have little or no impact on behaviour; the second are a series of conceived values, which may be translated from intention into behaviour. The latter (Figure 10.2) are of three different types: operative values (where there is a high probability they will be reflected in behaviour), intended values (important, but with a moderate probability of translation into behaviour because of situational factors) and adopted values (those which are less a part of the personality of the individual and affect behaviour largely because of situational factors).

England's basic framework can be usefully extended to highlight some important issues, as in Figure 10.3. As the figure suggests, there are a range of potential values in a TNC, and it is possible that these would be categorised in quite different ways at the individual, divisional, corporate or country levels. For example, an individual executive working within a TNC with high market shares in a given country might find herself rapidly adopting the values and behaviour which are those of the dominant market leader. These might be quite different from those which were her operative values when previously employed by a smaller competitor in the same industry and indeed be far from her intended values when she joined the TNC. The pressures of expectations regarding divisional and corporate performance might result in predatory pricing and other unfair (or illegal) competitive practices being an implicit element of the value system of this company and one which was not apparent even to an informed outsider.

Clearly in the interests of order, efficiency and control, these potential values are invariably subject to some shaping through corporate value statements, codes of conduct and so on. There is ample evidence from some of the more visible cases of corporate scandal that this can be an area of personal tension. For example, Gellerman (1986) drew attention to some of the commonly held rationalisations that led to misconduct. They stemmed from rather different views of the potential value systems and included the individual's belief that the questionable activity undertaken was within reasonable ethical and legal limits, that it was in the company's best interests, and that the company would even condone it.

Figure 10.3 indicates the major ways in which values can influence behaviour in this model, namely through a combination of behaviour-

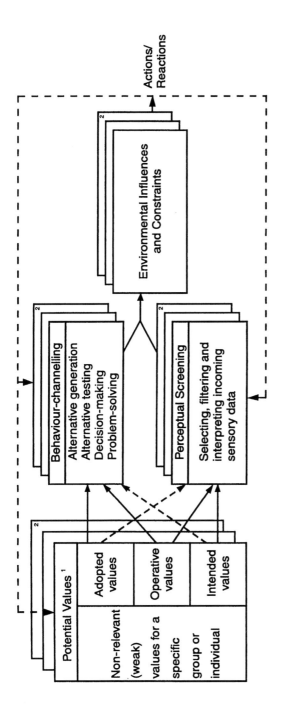

Figure 10.3   Relating values to behaviour in a TNC context

Notes: [1] There are several sets of potential values within a TNC. For example, those of the individual, the corporation, the division and the country. Equally, the TNC may or may not attempt to 'standardise' these and this might challenge the notion that personal value systems are relatively permanent.
[2] Different country and cultural contexts.

Source: Adapted from England (1978).

channelling and perceptual screening. At the simplest level, the behaviour of a manager will be channelled by the type of values held. Where a high premium is placed on the operative values of honesty and integrity, behaviour would be channelled away from questionable business propositions. Indeed it could be argued that such values would be essential to enable a balanced view to be taken on each of the elements of behaviour-channelling. For example, it is often in the heat of problem-solving and urgent decision-making that individual, and thus corporate, values are placed under considerable scrutiny and tested for their robustness. One example in a TNC context might be in the question of competitive sourcing of materials from a low-wage supplier in a developing country. Operative values of honesty and integrity are required to survive through rigorous price negotiations where many competitive suppliers are available and where the intention is to build on a longer-term partnership between buyer and supplier. It is interesting to note in the Langlois and Schlegelmilch (1990) study of codes of conduct that suppliers and contractors featured less frequently in European codes than they did in US codes, although the themes tended to be about partnership in both instances. In the terms of Figure 10.3, this operative value derived at corporate level might be expected to dominate in the example cited above.

The international business literature on business ethics provides some interesting examples of behaviour which can be interpreted within the framework of Figure 10.3. For example, on questions of cross-national selling ethics, Donaldson (1985) highlights potential conflicts between the sets of beliefs of home and host country managers, where host country standards appear inferior but to implement home country standards might seem to show a lack of respect for the cultural diversity and national integrity of the host country. In this instance the behaviour-channelling is subject to the added dimension of different country standards as well as environmental constraints. Some study results (Dubinsky *et al.*, 1991) suggest that when companies move into foreign markets and employ host country nationals as sales personnel, management needs to assess the ethical issues confronting the host country market. They show that neither transferring domestic company policies to foreign markets nor automatically adapting to local customs produces appropriate solutions for most TNCs.

As the figure suggests, perceptual screening also has a role to play, but a more indirect one where the power of personal values acts to select, filter and influence data from the environment. It will be evident that the TNC will be populated by managers who relate values to behaviour according to different patterns and who have personal value systems of many types. Not only that, however; as Figure 10.3 suggests, there is also the possibility that the many environments and business circumstances confronted directly influence both behaviour-channelling and perceptual screening. In other words, depending on the strength of personal values, the same manager might behave differently when operating in different parts of the corporation. This is possible, for example, where decisions are based mainly on pragmatism and guided by success/failure considerations. In effect, this may override (or be pressurised to override) an ethical–moral framework which would be inclined towards actions which were judged to be 'right' and away from those considered to be 'wrong'.

Within the complexity of a TNC network, Figure 10.3 suggests a series of feedback loops in response to actions/reactions on the part of the manager. This implies a form of environmental testing or experimentation in the relationship between values and behaviour at a corporate level. There is little doubt that this occurs daily in both minor and major issues, as the corporate antennae assess the implications of many types of behaviour. While Figure 10.3 implies a highly dynamic system, it also points to the importance of the corporate position taken within the potential values space. It is in this context that the use of, and necessity for, corporate codes can be readily illustrated in a TNC. The complex situations posited in Figure 10.3, whereby behaviour-channelling, perceptual screening and environmental dimensions are all multidimensional, are such that the individual executive could face a bewildering series of choices. In the absence of guidelines, the feedback loops could readily lead to changes in the potential values brought to bear on executive behaviour. This could apply to many problematic areas including employee conduct (gifts and entertainment, bribery, abuse of expense accounts, misuse of company assets), use of information (misuse of proprietary information, conflicts of interest, methods of gathering competitors' information), improper relationships with government representatives, and so on.

It is perhaps here that the importance of the positioning of a TNC in ethical space is best tackled. The working assumption in this chapter is that the TNC has to set operating standards by one means or another, in recognition of both the demands of corporate responsibility and the diversity of its environment and workforce. However, this is a highly dynamic situation and there is a constant need to review the corporate decision process to test its ethical standing. One interesting and useful approach to this is shown in Figure 10.4. In a TNC, decisions are positioned between two or more legal/ethical systems and therefore subject to scrutiny by a number of publics in areas such as product safety, patent infringement, pollution, payments and so on. These bodies may have widely differing views on issues such as the use of market power, resources, productivity and so on. In Figure 10.4, the inner circle represents the undisclosed corporate decisions, which are subsequently made public and can thereafter become the subject of public debate. The outer circle captures the outcome of such debate in which the society concerned determines the legal and ethical status of each decision. The TNC decision-making process has to take a view regarding the quadrant into which an issue with ethical implications is likely to fall. Even if the objective is for all of these to be in Q2, it is probable that, when codified, some will fall into other quadrants. To some degree, the ethical dimensions of a given situation will be linked not just to the decision itself but to the goals, methods, motives and consequences related to it. By linking Figures 10.4 and 10.3, this approach gives one generic illustration of the ways in which the feedback loops work in Figure 10.3 within many TNCs. The situations are often made more complex by the nature of the boundary lines between the legal and the ethical.

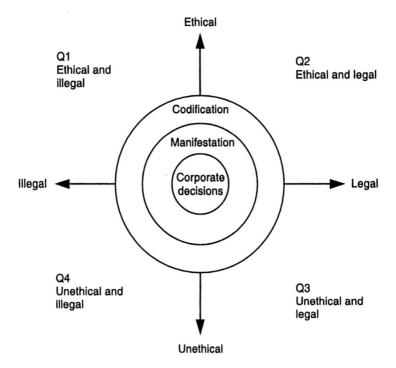

Figure 10.4   Classification of corporation decisions

Note: The process shown implies that in the inner circle decisions are made internally, then in the middle circle are revealed to public scrutiny. Arising from the ensuing debate, the decisions are codified in a process in which society determines the legal and ethical status of each decision.

Source: Adapted from Henderson (1982).

It will be evident in developing the ideas behind Figure 10.3 that there is an explicit acceptance that TNCs have to accept a level of social responsibility. This rejects the classic Friedman (1970) view that the drive for profit is the sole social responsibility of the corporation and is positioned closer to the stakeholder theory of the firm. Birsch (1990) and others have challenged the former position regarding corporate agency and the spirit of the age on corporate moral responsibility has changed markedly over the past thirty years.

In consequence of this position, and in pursuance of the question of potential (personal and corporate) values in Figure 10.3, there is ample evidence of variations in the types of ethical concerns between managers in TNCs. For example, Schlegelmilch and Robertson (1995), examining comparative ethical perceptions, found that US managers were much more likely than those from the UK, Germany or Austria to perceive personnel issues as ethical issues and to perceive that employee use of information constituted an ethical issue. In contrast, German and Austrian managers were more likely to consider political and local involvement an ethical issue of concern.

Among recent evidence Schollhammer (1996) found significant differences in the way TNCs approach, focus on and deal with ethical issues. In a study of US, Japanese and European-based TNCs, he found a high degree of unanimity about the importance and universality of a diverse set of ethical values and standards. However, significantly different weights were placed on specific ethical standards. For example, US TNCs gave more weight to organisational standards (explicit codes of ethics or corporate codes of conduct), Japanese TNCs emphasised interpersonal standards (such as those laid down by corporate ethics committees), while the European companies (who were mainly German) stressed personal ethical norms. He also found clear differences in the way TNCs approached ethical issues. For Japanese firms, the dominant method was to focus on compliance with legal or regulatory norms, for US firms a situational ethics approach (this involves a flexible application of rules of conduct according to individual circumstances) was dominant, while European TNCs apparently used a more uniform (universalist) approach to the resolution of ethical issues. While careful not to read too much into this type of evidence, it is interesting that it broadly relates to the types of managerial-style organisational classifications which are well-established for TNCs from these particular home regions.

In order to examine further some of the implications of Figure 10.3 at a more manageable level, the next few paragraphs consider the relationship between a TNC and a single subsidiary. Figure 10.5 sets out a model which was constructed for a rather different purpose (Birkinshaw and Hood, 1996), namely, to test the processes by which subsidiaries develop within a corporate network. It suggests that subsidiary development is a function of

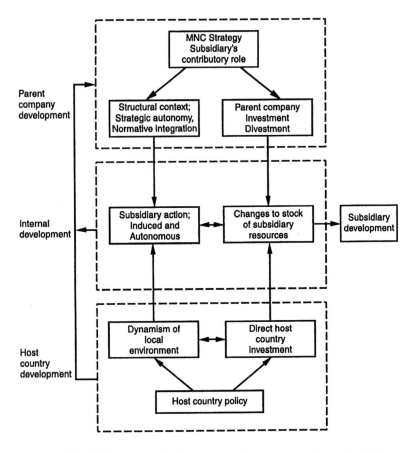

Figure 10.5   TNC parent–subsidiary relationships in the development context
Source: Birkinshaw and Hood (1996).

three groups of drivers: internal, parent company and host country. As initially conceived it made no assumptions about the ethical dimensions of any of the relationships implied within it – a common position for much business research. Its fundamental premise is that the nature of the change in the accumulation of subsidiary resources is at the root of its development, resources being defined in this context as specialised and durable, tangible and intangible assets. These subsidiary resources are regarded as being a fundamental contributor to competitive advantage at the TNC corporate level. Applying an ethical dimension to Figure 10.5, it is clear that there are many points at which operative values will have an important impact on behaviour in the terms set out in Figure 10.3. For example, the TNC strategy will determine the subsidiary's role and set the structural context in which it is required to operate. As part of that package, the TNC will negotiate with host governments and may explicitly seek a special accommodation with the government regarding the terms of market access, employment, local value added, support for infrastructure, taxation regimes, and so on. It will be clear that there are many stakeholders within Figure 10.5, and hence the TNC's management of the development of its subsidiary requires a balanced accommodation of stakeholder interests. To take one specific issue in this figure, the question of divestment and downsizing can raise important questions about the implied social contact with a labour force versus the rights of stockholders to have their assets efficiently managed. Equally, in another direction, the TNC may have a very different view from that of the host government as to how much competition should be allowed in a given market.

This section concerning the implementation of ethical dimensions within TNCs has been largely based on the model in Figure 10.3. It is founded on the view that corporations, including TNCs, do have to have a 'conscience' and rejects views to the contrary. One influential philosopher sharply expressed the opposite view in the following terms:

> It is improper to expect organisational conduct to conform to the ordinary principles of morality. We cannot and must not expect formal organisations, or their representatives acting in their official capacities, to be honest, courageous, considerate, sympathetic, or to have any kind of moral integrity. Such concepts are not in the vocabulary, so to speak, of the organisational language game. (John Ladd, quoted in Goodpaster and Matthews, 1982)

The role of moral projection on the part of the corporation is rejected in some quarters on the grounds that moral direction can only come through the 'system' of government (laws, regulations and so on) and in consequence it is argued that management has little role in influencing the thought processes of the organisation itself. The extreme end of this spectrum might be inclined to claim that corporate morality is best kept to glossy annual reports where it is safely insulated from policy and performance. These perspectives can scarcely be regarded as either tenable or credible in the environment facing TNCs at the end of the twentieth century.

COMING TO TERMS WITH THE NEW ENVIRONMENT

TNCs have perhaps always faced a highly diverse range of areas of potential conflict (Vernon, 1971; Gladwin and Walter, 1980). However, it is evident that international business is increasingly being confronted by ethical arguments. While consumers remain concerned about price and quality, how the product is manufactured and what values the manufacture represents exert an increasing influence on the consumer's choice. The European boycott on French products due to its nuclear testing programme and the pressure on Shell arising from its planned dumping of the Brent Spar are two recent examples of this. In many companies the reaction to this environment over the past decade and more has been the introduction of ethical rules or codes, appropriate training and monitoring committees. Such an approach may have sufficed in a stable environment and in hierarchical organisational forms where job descriptions and responsibilities were carefully defined. In such contexts, ethical dilemmas are relatively predictable. The late 1990s environment, and particularly that of the TNC, is very dynamic and within it the rule-based approach to business ethics may not be sufficient for an information-based society. For many TNCs, this has led to a growing focus on values rather than exact rules, providing they can establish a sound and coherent ethical platform. Clearly the TNC does not have *carte blanche* to establish an ethical platform since it has to build on the fundamental values which are common in the countries in which it operates. This is not an easy task as has been demonstrated above. Moreover, it implies establishing values and building a set of business ethics upon these, thus lifting the topic to a strategic rather than a tactical level. It suggests that these values are fundamental to the corporate strategic direction and not merely an indication of the quality of corporate manners – whether good or bad. The challenge in a TNC of being able to communicate these values to all the stakeholders is a large one.

There are a number of factors operating within the international environment which would call for a reappraisal of the role of values in TNCs. Among these is the fact that foreign direct investment has significantly increased the economic interdependence of nations, placing greater emphasis on the role of created assets and rather less on the natural endowments of countries. This in turn has resulted in the growing interdependence between TNCs and governments (Stopford, 1994) and raises the question of the role of TNCs in 'diplomacy' between nations. In reality the spectrum of TNC–government relations is a wide one, although there has been a tendency to greater convergence in governmental attitudes towards competing for the attraction of foreign direct investment. This in itself is another dimension in which there is scope for a reappraisal of the values adopted by TNCs.

There is another, even larger, issue. TNCs are the main agents of the transformation of the world economy. With the declining role of the nation state, they play an increasingly crucial role in the functioning of the world economy. Modern concepts of governance (Dunning, 1992) effectively

Neil Hood 209

require governments to respond to, and attempt to satisfy, TNC demands for trained human resources, good infrastructure, transparent and stable laws and regulations, and so on. As will be evident, such an enabling environment is not value-free and considerable obligations are implicitly placed on major TNCs in particular to exercise some measure of leadership in business ethics. This is not a mantle which some TNCs comfortably wear, for understandable reasons. There has been renewed debate in recent years about the appropriate regulatory environment for TNCs, recognising that they operate in environments populated by both 'hard' (binding) laws and regulations, and a variety of 'soft' (non-binding) standards (Kline, 1993). While there may be a case for a framework of global principles to guide investment relationships and TNC activities into the twenty-first century (Brewer and Young, 1995), most informed commentators would stop short of suggesting that these could be expected to determine ethical behaviour. On the other hand, they might help further to inform and shape that behaviour and that in itself could be a desirable outcome.

References

Aupperle, K.E. Carronn, A.B. and Hatfield, T.D. (1985) 'An Empirical Examination of the Relationship between Corporate Social Responsibility and Profitability', *Academy of Management Journal*, 28 (2), pp. 446–63.
Becker, H. and Fritzche, H. (1987) 'A Comparison of the Ethical Behaviour of American, French and German Managers', *Columbia Journal of World Business*, 22 (4), pp. 87–95.
Birkinshaw, J. and Hood, N. (1996) 'Development Processes in Multinational Subsidiaries', Working Paper 96/3, Institute of International Business, Stockholm School of Economics.
Birsch, D. (1990) 'The Failure of Friedman's Agency Argument', in J.R. DesJardine and J.J. McCall (eds) *Contemporary Issues in Business Ethics* (Belmont, Calif.; Wadsworth).
Brewer, T.L. and Young, S. (1995) 'Towards a Multilateral Framework for Foreign Direct Investment: Issues and Scenarios', *Transnational Corporations*, 4 (1), pp. 69–83.
Buller, P.F., Kohls, J.J. and Anderson, K.S. (1991) 'The Challenge of Global Ethics', *Journal of Business Ethics*, 10 (10), pp. 767–76.
Donaldson, T. (1985) 'Multinational Decision-Making: Reconciling International Norms', *Journal of Business Ethics*, 4, pp. 357–66.
Donaldson, T. (1989) *The Ethics of International Business* (Oxford: Oxford University Press).
Dubinsky, A.J., Jolson, M.A., Kotabe, M. and Lim, C.U. (1991) 'A Cross-national Investigation of Industrial Sales Peoples' Ethical Perceptions', *Journal of International Business Studies*, 22 (4), pp. 651–70.

Dunning, J.H. (1992) 'The Global Economy, Domestic Governance, Strategies and Transnational Corporations: Interactions and Policy Implications', *Transnational Corporations*, 2 (1), pp. 7–45.

Dunning, J.H. (1993) *Multinational Enterprises and the Global Economy* (New York: Addison-Wesley).

England, G.W. (1975) *The Manager and His Values* (Cambridge, Mass.: Ballinger).

England, G.W. (1978) 'Managers and Their Value Systems: a Five country comparative Study', *Columbia Journal of World Business*, 13 (2), p. 35–44.

Freeman, R.E. and Gilbert, D.R. (1988) *Corporate Strategy and the Search for Ethics* (Englewood Cliffs, NJ: Prentice-Hall).

Friedman, M. (1970) 'The Social Responsibility of Business is to Increase its Profits', *New York Times Magazine*, 13 September.

Gellerman, S.W. (1986) 'Why Good Managers Make Bad Ethical Choices', *Harvard Business Review*, July–August. 86 (4), pp. 85–90.

Gladwin, T.N. and Walter, I. (1980) *Multinationals Under Fire, Lessons in the Management of Conflict* (New York: Wiley).

Goodpaster, K.E. and Matthews, J.B. (1982) *Can a Corporation have a Conscience?* (Cambridge, Mass.: Harvard Business School).

Haire, M., Ghiselli, E.C. and Porter, L.S. (1966) *Management Thinking: An International Study* (New York: Wiley).

Henderson, V.E. (1982) 'The Ethical Side of Enterprise', *Sloan Management Review*, 23, pp. 37–47.

Kline, J.M. (1993) 'International Regulation of Transnational Business: Providing the Missing Leg of Global Investment Standards', *Transnational Corporations*, 2 (1), pp. 153–64.

Langlois, C.C. and Schlegelmilch, B.B. (1990) 'Do Corporate Codes of Ethics Reflect National Character? Evidence from Europe and the United States', *Journal of International Business Studies*, 18 (2), pp. 17–31.

McGuire, J.B. Sundgren, A. and Schneeweis, T. (1988) 'Corporate Social Responsibility and Firm Financial Performance', *Academy of Management Journal*, 31 (4), pp. 854–72.

Powers, C. and Vogel, D. (1980) *Ethics in the Education of Business Managers* (Hastington-Hudson: Institute of Society, Ethics and the Life Sciences, The Hastings Institute).

Schlegelmilch, B.B. and Robertson, D.C. (1995) 'The Influence of Country and Industry on Ethical Perceptions of Senior Executives in the US and Europe', *Journal of International Business Studies*, 26 (4), pp. 859–82.

Schollhammer, H. (1996) 'Key Issues in International Business Ethics: The Ethical Concerns of US, Japanese and European Multinational Firms', paper presented to AIB Annual Conference, Banff, September.

Stopford, J. (1994) 'The Growing Interdependence between Transnational Corporations and Government', *Transnational Corporations*, 3 (1), pp. 53–76.

UNCTAD (1996) *World Investment Report, Investment, Trade and International Policy Arrangements* (New York and Geneva: UN).

Van Luijk, H.J.L. (1990) 'Recent Developments in European Business Ethics', *Journal of Business Ethics*, 9 (7), pp. 537–44.

Vernon, R. (1971) *Sovereignty at Bay* (New York: Basic Books).

Vogel, D. (1992) 'The Globalization of Business Ethics: Why America Remains Distinctive', *California Management Review*, 35 (1), pp. 30–49.

11 Conclusion

Ian Jones and Michael Pollitt

THE ROLE OF BUSINESS ETHICS IN ECONOMIC PERFORMANCE

The broad premise of this book has been that 'good' business ethics is an important determinant of economic performance. The authors have examined a wide range of ways in which the transmission mechanism from business ethics to economic performance is working and should work in a typical Anglo-American economy such as that of the UK.

The theory and evidence which they present suggests that enlightened self-interest provides many good arguments for improving business ethics at the level they are formulated. While all of the contributors broadly agree on the importance of business ethics, Sparkes most clearly links business ethics and economic performance via his evidence on the correlation between superior share price performance and superior business ethics. His discussion emphasises the nature of the links between long-run financial success and socially responsible behaviour on the part of businesses.

While the authors agree on the importance of business ethics they present a variety of views on the subject, to some extent reflecting different political views on the determinants of economic performance. On the one hand, Deakin and Wilkinson argue for an extension of the law of contract to protect smaller supplier companies and to raise 'average' performance, while recognising that the best firms within the Anglo-American economies are among the most successful in the world, while on the other hand Barry argues in favour of a reduction in the current extent of the law. Deakin and Wilkinson present the 'Cambridge view' ('left-wing') that the relatively poor postwar performance of the UK economy suggests that it can learn from German and Italian experience. Barry (adopting a more conservative approach) rejects such a position in favour of the emerging view that Anglo-American capitalism is triumphing over its German (continental European) and Japanese (East Asian) variants as these economies are forced to go through painful industrial restructuring. As Deakin and Wilkinson's conclusion suggests, which view you favour depends on your interpretation of the relative economic performance of the German and UK economies and on your concern for the associated distributional (rather than efficiency) consequences of each variant of capitalism.

211

In between the opposing views of Barry and Deakin and Wilkinson on the degree of reliance which economies should place on their law in setting standards of conduct lie the other authors. Cadbury is hopeful that industry can regulate its own affairs without further legal changes. Wright agrees, stressing that good business ethics is good management. Hood is sceptical that legal or regulatory sanctions can be set to discipline the actions of multinationals. Sparkes directly counters Milton Friedman's view that, beyond the generic moral code, business ethics is 'pure and unadulterated socialism', in sharp contrast to Barry's robust advocacy of such *laissez-faire* capitalism. Sparkes points out that businesses which plan to be around for the long term must be socially responsible if only to anticipate future moral or environmental repugnance which might lead to legal action or financial problems.

While divisions along distributional and macroeconomic (and hence political) lines have emerged between the authors, this merely serves to illustrate that the study of business ethics raises political questions and is not simply a matter of identifying best practice and *suggesting* it be applied widely. Study of business ethics requires a recognition of the complexity of the links between business ethics and economic performance, links which have uncertain consequences and give rise to a range of distributional outcomes.

In the rest of this short conclusion we do two things: first, we draw together some of the main themes from the authors' work; and second, we highlight some of the questions raised by the authors.

THEMES

By way of briefly summarising the authors' contributions it is possible to identify a number of themes developed by one or more of the authors. These themes highlight the ways in which the ethical transmission mechanism works and how it might be made to function more effectively.

Cohen, in particular, suggests the importance of a *long-run perspective* for firms if they are to be successful in the current business environment. He argues that, as advanced capitalist nations get richer, individuals within them are expressing preferences for environmental quality which have forced firms and governments to act to reduce pollution and have forced firms to develop new 'environmentally friendly' products. Both Sparkes and Wright note the significance of recent environmental concern and its rapid effect on company behaviour, especially with respect to company reporting and advertising. All these authors suggest that companies will

Barry, and Wilkinson and Deakin, are arguing about the boun
w in setting ethical standards. However, it is clear that, wherev
dary is set, some aspects of decisions with an ethical dimension a
likely to be matters of individual judgement (e.g. the amount o
tion between manager and secretary) and still others matters o
y policy (e.g. expected mobility of managers between divisions)
and Wilkinson, in their discussion of the current state of the eco-
analysis of law, point to major simplifications and misunderstand-
hich economists working in this area are apt to make; joint work
n lawyers and economists would seem to be the obvious way for-
With respect to such progress, ongoing developments in the UK and
mpetition law very much reflect new information on best practice
her jurisdictions and from advances in economic theory and evid-
Further work needs to be done on the possible role for multilateral
nd regulatory arrangements especially with respect to TNCs.
bury and Wright raise the issue of the significance of codes of con-
corporate and industry-wide) in setting ethics. While these codes
o be increasingly popular among public companies they do raise a
er of questions as to their efficacy. Why are so many companies so
o adopt codes of ethics? Is it because many codes are mere window
ng and lacking in substance? Wright clearly argues for making ethics
f the decision-making process rather than for codes of ethics *per se*.
y empirical evidence is needed on whether codes of ethics do have a
icant effect on economic performance and on the determinants of the
of adoption of a code and of its detailed contents. Industry codes of
s, as discussed by Cadbury, might be important in forestalling legisla-
National and international comparisons (e.g. along the lines of
in and Wilkinson) of the performance of industries regulated by spe-
legislation, voluntary codes or general company law would enlighten
iscussion of the efficacy of industry codes. More transparency in de-
n-making, which codes often imply, may give rise to problems for the
ation of the incentive mechanism within the market system; by mak-
t less profitable to digress from stated ethical principles it may also be
profitable to make decisions which may raise ethical issues. This may
pen if for no other reason than that transparency involves revelation of
rmation about the internal workings of the organisation. As such, it is a
ter of debate as to which pieces of information should be revealed ei-
r by rule of law, industry regulation, industry code or company code.
Cohen's work suggests that the environment in which firms are operat-
will increasingly favour firms which recognise the change to post-
terialist values in advanced countries. If we accept this analysis of

have to change markedly if movements towards voluntary simplicity (vol-untary reductions in consumption) or towards greater concern for corpor-ate social responsibility continue to grow. Sparkes further suggests that where companies are unwilling to change spontaneously or through collect-ive industry action new laws and regulations may force them to. Long-run forces and interdependencies always exist within the economic system. What we authors do is highlight why firms should acknowledge them and take account of them in their decision-making.

It is something of a cliché for academics (and belatedly politicians) to argue for the importance of *education* as an answer to economic problems. While the authors collectively reflect the importance of education by pre-senting arguments for the efficacy of particular business ethics, Eatwell and Casson make the point most forcibly. Both authors place similar reli-ance on Adam Smith's concept of sympathy to argue that education plays two key roles in the ethical transmission mechanism: first, it gives indi-viduals the ability to make moral choices in their best interest (enlightened self-interest requires 'enlightenment'); second, education gives others the ability to judge the ethical validity of the actions of particular individuals.

Eatwell emphasises the key role of *transparency* (or openness) in de-cision-making in order to allow the self-disciplining mechanism of sym-pathy to work through public approval for individual actions. Casson further suggests that credibility for leaders comes from the consistency of mes-sages and actions. Thus, argues Casson, effective leaders will be those who are seen to do what they say; in such circumstances transparency allows leaders to build the credibility they need for effective leadership. At the level of corporate decision-making Cadbury and Wright both emphasise the need for transparency in their discussions of best practice management and recent company and industry codes of ethics.

Casson argues for the importance of the *role of leaders* (spiritual, corpor-ate, political, etc.) in communicating and demonstrating ethical principles to followers. Casson suggests that a decline of respect for leadership, a re-duction in its quality or an increase in the plurality of moral leaders poses functional problems for Western economies. The other authors provide examples of leadership within the field of ethics in the sense that successful economic units are demonstrating to follower units how to behave: Cohen cites examples of countries providing environmental leadership; Deakin and Wilkinson suggest the leadership of German contract law within the EU; Sparkes, Cadbury and Hood argue for the importance of leading corporations in the development of ethical investment and codes of ethics; and Wright suggests the crucial importance of leaders within the corpora-tion.

The chapters by Deakin and Wilkinson and Barry bring out some of the issues surrounding the *role of law* in setting business ethics. Both sets of authors argue the case for and against the extension of the law in certain areas in order to improve the functioning of the economy. Barry worries about the economic effects of what he sees as a tendency in recent years to 'criminalise' certain well-established business practices (such as insider dealing). By sharp contrast Deakin and Wilkinson argue for the extension of the law of contract in the UK because they believe that current law inhibits the emergence of a high-trust contract culture. As we noted above, Cadbury, Wright and Hood all question the efficacy of further legal requirements on business.

Several of the authors draw attention to the *cultural complexity* of economic decision-making in an economic environment characterised by large cultural differences between and within nations. Cohen highlights differing approaches to environmental issues among 'rational' and 'romantic' advanced nations. Wright suggests that company codes will have to be adapted to cope with differing surrounding cultures. Hood notes the particular problems of transnationals, trying to transmit core ethical values to foreign affiliates. Both Casson and Wright highlight the problem posed by moral pluralism within Anglo-American economies; they argue that the spread of a common set of best-practice ethics will always involve a certain amount of culture shock (Casson) and perceived moral imperialism (Wright).

SOME QUESTIONS RAISED BY THE AUTHORS' WORK

In this section we raise some of the questions and issues for further investigation suggested by the authors and some of the questions which their own work raises. We merely seek to comment on the authors' work, not on other literature.

Eatwell provides the basis of business ethics in the sense that it is discussed in this volume. In common with most of the other authors the motivation for ethical behaviour that is appealed to is one of enlightened self-interest. This clearly begs the question of whether there can or should be any other basis for arguments for business ethics? Many would answer that their ethics can and do exist independently of their anticipated effects, e.g. if ethics stem from religious beliefs. The difficulty for public companies is that appeals to other ethical bases for decision-making may lead to a conflict with the corporation's key objective: the maximisation of shareholder returns. Enlightened self-interest can easily be aligned with the

maximisation of shareholder value. Any othe
raises the question of who decides on the choice
vidual shareholders may not accept? In the pas
business and society may have partly defined
preserving full employment in postwar Japan), t
such social contracts may not be enforceable v
even international agreement.

Casson provides a theoretical analysis of the
economic performance. He suggests several way
leaders may be failing in Western economies. W
tention to provide an empirical analysis his wor
tions. Is it the case that the quality of leadershi
Casson suggests key roles for teachers and politi
leadership. Historical analysis of bribes, scandals
attitudes might provide some evidence on wheth
problem, while comparing the characteristics of l
population might demonstrate the extent to which l
or worse the characteristics of the general populatic
and economic literature has tended to emphasise t
countries, institutions and corporations in raising a
Casson further suggests that particular attention ne
content of moral teaching within the school curricu
the effectiveness of particular modes of teaching mor
possible along the lines of the attention being giver
ment in different countries in key subjects such as
asserts that 'no Western political leader has made a s
out workable rules for the conduct of moral debate in
communication' (p. 42). If we accept this claim son
'workable rules' is clearly desirable.

Deakin and Wilkinson, and Barry, raise the issue of
tween ethics and the law. Does ethics involve going b
observance of the law sufficient for one's behaviou
ethical? One extreme view might be that a minimalis
with individuals being left free to set their own star
(minimalist) law. Another extreme view might be that
the highest standard and seek to raise all those under it to
first view, reflected by Barry, might fail to provide prot
who take the law at face value (e.g. by offering basic e
and conditions) while the second view, reflected by Deaki
may impose unreasonably high standards (e.g. for small f
ive markets) or stifle innovation in standard setting by th

social trends, two major sets of questions arise in response to it. First, does globalisation and economic development in non-Western countries reduce the pressure on Western firms to behave ethically? International competition from developing countries who are prepared to accept lower standards of conduct may pose a severe threat to some Western firms. Second, to what extent do Prisoners' Dilemma problems (individual incentives to behave unethically, in the face of incentives for firms to be collectively ethical) conflict with any tendency towards a greater interest in the environment or business ethics? As Cohen also observes, scientific analysis is now crucial to the debate over long-run latent environmental forces. The ongoing debate into the actual consequences of environmental pollution and materialism will continue and tough ethical choices will need to be made (such as about the promotion of the motor car via continued road building). Response to such changes will not just be on the basis of future predictions but also of accumulating knowledge about current changes and the use of new measures of GNP and economic output and indicators of quality of life. Thus research into what is actually happening already and how we should value it is very important (such as into the question of whether it is better to throw away packaging or recycle it when looking at the lifetime environmental impact).

Sparkes argues 'that ethical investors are playing the unexpected role of pioneers who look at business in new ways' (p. 168). He provides some empirical evidence on the success of ethical investment. This clearly needs to be substantiated by further work. At the moment ethical investment represents a small fraction of total funds under management. It is not clear that it is easy to separate out the many different factors which determine fund performance and measure the ethical dimension. It also remains a moot point as to whether ethical investors actually have any effect on firm behaviour and how to measure that effect. Case study analysis of investor pressure and the decision-making mechanism by which firms gave in to such pressure would be very informative (e.g. W.H. Smith's decision to withdraw some top shelf magazines). Does the mechanism involve some financial penalty (lower sales or share price) or do non-financial factors (such as the non-financial 'quality' of the philosophical argument) play a role?

Hood raises some of the problems that TNCs have in ethical decision-making in a number of different cultures. He argues that there is a conflict between maintaining values which are part of a company's managerial competitive advantage and being sensitive to the local culture in which a foreign affiliate operates. Questions arise in trying to identify common values which would be acceptable across the world and in identifying the boundary between ethical decisions which can/should be handled by reference only to these common values and those which can be devolved to the local level. Work on identifying universal ethical principles may be helpful here such as that already embodied in *The Code of Ethics on International Business for Christians, Muslims and Jews – The Interfaith Declaration* (noted by Cadbury). However it may be that such written statements of common principles are themselves an ethical tool itself reflective of Western culture. An ongoing problem for transnationals may be that decisions which may be acceptable in one subsidiary may come under scrutiny from the public in another culture (e.g. bribes paid by a TNC in the developing world may come under scrutiny from its customers in the UK).

In conclusion we note three things. Firstly, the scientific investigation using modern research methodologies of the links between ethics and economic performance is in its infancy. Secondly, the public debate raised by these issues is necessary and important if socially acceptable decisions are to be taken on how to realise the parallel goals of raising ethical standards and raising economic performance. Thirdly, implicit in many of the authors' chapters is the point that business ethics and personal morality cannot be separated (a point recognised by Casson, Cadbury and Sparkes). Therefore in a democratic society individuals (rather than organisations *per se*) need to be convinced of the value of business ethics: 'business morality is personal morality writ large' (Cadbury, p. 83).

POSTSCRIPT

This book has not been about ethics *per se*: it has been an attempt to promote a greater awareness of the general issue of how enlightened self-interest works to encourage the widespread use of good business ethics. For those with strong ethical beliefs this is an encouragement; for those without them it is a spur to consider such beliefs more rationally. Thus we leave the reader, recognising that any analysis of the ethical transmission mechanism leaves largely unresolved the question of: what basic values should we accept?

Index

financial markets, 88, 99–104
see also City of London
Financial Reporting Council, 72
financial success, new measures
of, 159–62
Finlay Moses, 20
firms, *see* corporations and firms
fiscal stakeholders, 116–21
Fisons, 149
foreign direct investment (FDI), 193,
208
Fortune 500 companies, 121
France, 208
Freedom of Information Act, 4
Freeman, E., 98, 99
Friedman, M., 108n8, 121, 152–3,
205
Friends Provident, 147, 148, 150,
166
Fukuyama, F., 5, 10, 95

Galbraith, J.K., 93
game theory, 39, 56
Gellerman, S.W., 200
General Electric, 79
General Motors, 142
Germany
contractual practice in, 59–63
cooperative productive systems
in, 49
environmentalism in, 127, 132
social market economy in, 91–2,
100, 106
transnational companies (TNCs),
205
see also European companies
Ghiselli, E.C., 196
global warming, 113–14
CFC emissions, 4, 136n1
globalisation of trade
effect on business ethics, 1, 69,
176–7, 193–4
internationalisation of financial
services, 71
'good faith', contractual, 58, 59–60
governments
and the corporation, 15, 93, 95–6
and environmental dilemmas, 96,
111, 123–4

open government, 4
role in moral environment of
business, 28–9, 85, 87, 88–90,
100, 102–3, 107
and transnational companies
(TNCs), 207, 208–9
'green' consumerism, 3–4, 122
Green political parties, decline
of, 124
Greenbury Report, 3
Greenpeace, 135
groups, moral authorities and, 35,
40–2
Guinness company, 106
Gulliver, James, 106

Haire, M., 196
Hamilton, Alexander, 29n1
Hammond, Peter, 29
Handy, Charles, 159, 160, 161
Hawley, J.P., 117
Hayek, F.A. von, 45, 49, 57–8,
63–4, 85
Heinz, 137n6
Hewlett Packard, 187
high-trust productive systems,
49–56, 64–5
Hiorns, Brennan, 161
Hirschman, A.O., 20, 117
honesty, 31
Hutton, W., 108n1

'impartial spectator', 26–9, 34
industrial accidents, 114
Industrial Society, 180–1
industry committees on corporate
behaviour, 3
information technology, effect on
business ethics debate of, 1
Inglehart, Ronald, 125–30
insider dealing, 15, 70, 71, 99–104
Institute of Business Ethics, 4, 80,
173–4, 182–3
survey by, 180
Institute for Consumer Responsibility
(USA), 122
Institute for Global Ethics, 188–9
Institute of Internal Auditors, 180
Institute of Management, 180